Decolonizing the Undead

Decolonizing the Undead

Rethinking Zombies in World-Literature, Film, and Media

Edited by
Giulia Champion, Roxanne Douglas, and
Stephen Shapiro

BLOOMSBURY ACADEMIC
LONDON • NEW YORK • OXFORD • NEW DELHI • SYDNEY

BLOOMSBURY ACADEMIC
Bloomsbury Publishing Plc
50 Bedford Square, London, WC1B 3DP, UK
1385 Broadway, New York, NY 10018, USA
29 Earlsfort Terrace, Dublin 2, Ireland

BLOOMSBURY, BLOOMSBURY ACADEMIC and the Diana logo are trademarks of
Bloomsbury Publishing Plc

First published in Great Britain 2023
Paperback edition published 2024

Copyright © Giulia Champion, Roxanne Douglas, Stephen Shapiro and Contributors, 2023

Roxanne Douglas, Giulia Champion, Stephen Shapiro and Contributors have
asserted their right under the Copyright, Designs and Patents Act, 1988,
to be identified as Authors of this work.

Cover design: Rebecca Heselton
Cover image © YAY Media AS/ Alamy Stock Vector

All rights reserved. No part of this publication may be reproduced or transmitted
in any form or by any means, electronic or mechanical, including photocopying,
recording, or any information storage or retrieval system, without prior
permission in writing from the publishers.

Bloomsbury Publishing Plc does not have any control over, or responsibility for,
any third-party websites referred to or in this book. All internet addresses given
in this book were correct at the time of going to press. The author and publisher
regret any inconvenience caused if addresses have changed or sites have
ceased to exist, but can accept no responsibility for any such changes.

A catalogue record for this book is available from the British Library.

A catalog record for this book is available from the Library of Congress.

Library of Congress Cataloging-in-Publication Data

Names: Shapiro, Stephen, 1964- editor. | Champion, Giulia, editor. |
Douglas, Roxanne, editor.
Title: Decolonizing the undead: rethinking zombies in world-literature,
film, and media / edited by Roxanne Douglas, Giulia Champion, Stephen Shapiro.
Description: London; New York: Bloomsbury Academic, 2023. | Includes index.
Identifiers: LCCN 2022010092 | ISBN 9781350271128 (hardback) |
ISBN 9781350271166 (paperback) | ISBN 9781350271135 (ebook) |
ISBN 9781350271142 (epub) | ISBN 9781350271159
Subjects: LCSH: Zombies in literature. | Zombies in motion pictures. |
Zombies in mass media. | Zombies in popular culture. |
LCGFT: Literary criticism. | Film criticism.
Classification: LCC PN56.Z66 D43 2023 | DDC 809/.93375–dc23/eng/20220831
LC record available at https://lccn.loc.gov/2022010092

ISBN: HB: 978-1-3502-7112-8
PB: 978-1-3502-7116-6
ePDF: 978-1-3502-7113-5
eBook: 978-1-3502-7114-2

Typeset by Integra Software Services Pvt. Ltd.

To find out more about our authors and books visit www.bloomsbury.com
and sign up for our newsletters.

Contents

Acknowledgments	vii
Introduction: Decolonizing the Zombie *Roxanne Douglas and Giulia Champion*	1

Part One   Thinking Zombies

1	"Il y a des zombies dans ceci…": Dessalines, Disembodiment, and Early Haitian Literature *Elizabeth Kelly*	15
2	White and Black Zombies: How Race Rewrites the Zombie Narrative *Cécile Accilien*	30
3	Decolonizing the Zombie: *I Walked with a Zombie*'s Critique of Centrist Liberalism *Stephen Shapiro*	40

Part Two   Zombie World-System

4	Samurai Zombies: Japan's Undead Past *Frank Jacob*	61
5	Crude Monsters in the "Extractive Zone": The Creaturely and Ecological Zombie *Josephine Taylor*	74
6	Undead, Undeader, Undeadest: Narrating the Unevenness of Ecological Crisis in Nana Nkweti's "It Just Kills You Inside" *Fiona Farnsworth*	89
7	Zombie Proletkino: Labor, Race, and Genre in Pedro Costa's *Casa de Lava* *Thomas Waller*	106
8	"It Feels Like I'm Giving My Body Something It Needs in an Intense and Powerful Way": Netflix, *Santa Clarita Diet*, and the Neoliberal Feminist Encounter with Pleasure Politics *Roxanne Douglas*	121

Part Three Zombie Decolonial

9   De/Zombification as Decolonial Critique: Beyond Man, Nature, and the Posthuman in Folklore and Fiction from South Africa *Rebecca Duncan* 141
10 Zombies, Placelessness, and Transcultural Entanglement: Ahmed Saadawi's *Frankenstein in Baghdad* *Netty Mattar* 159
11 "First They Bring the HIV, then the Zombie": Portrayal of the West in Contemporary Indian Zombie Literature and Cinema *Abhirup Mascharak* 176
12 From the Mountain to the Shore: Migration, Water Crisis, and Revolutionary Zombies from Haiti to Peru *Giulia Champion* 191

Decolonizing Zombie Cultural Practice: An Afterword *Stephen Shapiro* 209

Notes on Contributors 215
Index 218

Acknowledgments

The editors of this book would like to thank all the contributors of this collection for sharing their stimulating and outstanding research. It has been a pleasure to work with a group of such exceptional scholars. We are also thankful to the Bloomsbury Editorial Team for their precious and generous assistance.

Introduction: Decolonizing the Zombie

Roxanne Douglas and Giulia Champion

This collection addresses the need to decolonize the zombie as a figure of (popular) culture. Hence, one might wonder why a zombie is not on the cover of this book. First, it is because images of zombies are often embedded within the same ethos this collection aims to challenge. Indeed, the zombie is not merely a blood-thirsty and blood-stained ghoul or a highly racist and racialized representation of formerly colonized or exploited communities. The zombie is so much more, as all the chapters in this collection evidence. The zombie can also be a metaphor for the demonization of different forms of "otherness," a conceptualization that is itself highly problematic. Indeed, in colonial and neo-imperial cultural productions and consciousness, exoticizing difference often means making it monstrous. It is often what the zombie has represented in Haiti's history of exploitation, and while chapters in this collection challenge the fact that the zombie merely represents slavery and exploitation, we would be remiss not to acknowledge this reality. As Joan Dayan notes, the zombie is a multifaceted term: "An especially important definition is that of Moreau de Saint-Méry, who presents for the first time in writing the night world of what he names *revenans* (spirits), *loupgaroux* (vampires), and *zombis*, which he defines as a 'Creole word that means spirit, revenant.'"[1] The zombie's status between life and death points to another demonized "in-betweenness," the racialized one of hybridity and miscegenation, another anxiety haunting Western consciousness and cultural productions strongly present in the Americanization (read the United States) of the Haitian zombie, explored in Cécile Accilien's and Giulia Champion's chapters. Hence, the zombie has a complex and importantly colonial history, and as a "revenant" it thus has a haunting presence like a spectral figure, often returning to the physical realm because of unfinished business; and what business is left more unfinished than the (de)colonial project?

This collection identifies different cultural productions and contexts that need decolonization and reconsideration, and the image on the cover embodies this need: the skulls and scythe echo representations of the grim reaper that are often present over October and November as Europe and the United States take over and capitalize on two celebrations that have been colonized and distorted by these spaces: Hallowe'en and el Día de los Muertos. The Celtic and the Mexican holiday, the latter also celebrated in different form across different countries in the Hispanophone Caribbean and Latin America, have been taken over to sell, as much as the zombie sells in popular culture. This phenomenon of cultural holiday appropriation in the context of the Día de los Muertos is incisively and beautifully explained by the Puerto Rican-American author Aya de León in "Dear White People/Querido Gringos":

> You arrived at El Día De Los Muertos like a Pilgrim, starving, unequal to survival in the land of grief, and the indigenous ceremonies fed you and took you in and revived you and made a place for you at the table. And what have you done? Like the Pilgrims, you have begun to take over, to gentrify and colonize this holiday for yourselves. I was shocked this year to find Day of the Dead events in my native Oakland Bay Area not only that were not organized by Chican@s or Mexican@s or Latin@s, but events with zero Latin@ artists participating, involved, consulted, paid, recognized, acknowledged, prayed with.[2]

El Día de los Muertos is a time in which one celebrates a state of communion with one's lost loved ones, a state that exists outside of this specific date and day and is a continued practice. A practice that in the necropolitics of today is further crucial as noted by Shiv R. Desai in a recent study wherein he investigates how the honoring and mourning of lost loved ones becomes further crucial when marginalized communities' lives continue to not be seen and treated as important. Shiv R. Desai's publication considers how, "through a Youth Participatory Action Research (YPAR) project," using a Día de los Muertos float can create a space for the mourning of extrajudicial death to achieve critical hope and radical healing.[3] This study, which is focused on the Black Lives Matter (BLM) movement, also intersects with Christina Sharpe's important work *In the Wake: On Blackness and Being* (2016). Sharpe elaborates a complex theorization of "living in the wake," a phrase to which she attributes multiple facets and meanings. Crucially, she explains that one of its elements is the idea of living in "a past that is not the past":

> The work we do requires new modes and methods of research and teaching; new ways of entering and leaving the archives of slavery, of undoing the

"racial calculus and... political arithmetic that were entrenched centuries ago" (Hartman 2008, 6) and that live into the present.... With this as the ground, I've been trying to articulate a method of encountering *a past that is not past*. A method along the lines of a sitting with, a gathering, and a tracking of phenomena that disproportionately and devastatingly affect Black peoples any and everywhere we are.[4]

Can academic discourse create a space that mourns as well as memorializes inequalities? All the while recognizing our own limitations, some of which are crucial for the authors of this introduction who recognize their own intellectual colonization as white European women. What are the different meanings of colonization when it is practiced by white "Western" academics? We hope that this collection, which is an international collaboration and therefore attempts to open a space to different voices, though still one that is privileged given the realities of contemporary academia, can begin to address some of these questions. And this is also what the cover represents: returning, or revenant, images of colonized cultural productions and practices coming back, or haunting, our contemporary epistemologies demanding to be returned to their initial cultures and respected for what they are. They demand that we learn from them rather than try to constantly define them from our own point of view. So, what can we learn from zombie tropes across the world?

Decolonial Zombie Scholarship: Katherine Dunham

Katherine Dunham is dressed in a striped black-and-white creole gown; the beat of the drum remains quick and steady as she holds her body taught, closes her eyes, and tilts her head to one side. Her body jolts with the rhythm as she removes the outer layer of her dress to reveal her white, linen underdress; her arms and shoulders, like her feet, are bare. She shakes her head with a pained expression and removes her headdress that matched her beautiful, ruffled gown, now spirited away by someone in the dance company. Her body remains compelled by the rhythm of drums as she is drawn closer and closer to her vodou master. Dunham is dancing the part of Louloise, who, in this "zombie scene" of the *L' Ag' Ya* (1938), also known as "Ballet Creole,"[5] has been bewitched by a vodou master and has become a *zombi* of Haitian folklore. According to Dunham herself, "legends of zombies—the dead come to life or the living so anesthetized by drugs as to appear dead."[6] Louloise's lover steps between the two figures and pushes her and the zombie master apart, breaking his captivating spell, and commencing the *ag'ya*, the fighting dance of Martinique. Dunham is not only a dancer, she is a scholar who practices dance.

This representation of the *zombi* might be a far cry from the image of the "halloweenified" zombie that many reading this volume may be familiar with—in Dunham's ballet, there is no hand being thrust out of the earth next to a gravestone, no eerily quiet shopping mall, and certainly no brain-hungry hoard. Zombies as we know them today are, as Giulia Champion notes in her chapter in this volume, monsters made by capitalism, for capitalism. In the contemporary Western popular imagination, the zombie shuffles around shopping malls as per the now ubiquitous George Romero tropes. However, the story of capitalism cannot be disentangled from that of colonialism, and neither can that of the zombie. According to Sarah Lauro, precisely due to its history, the zombie makes for "a convenient bogeyman in times of economic crisis, such as the great, global recession that marred the first decade of the new millennium."[7] Colonialism is the extraction of value from lands and peoples by a colonizer who does not belong to that land through violent means, while also dispossessing previous, native, inhabitants of that land. Nick Couldry and Ulises Mejias point out that when we discuss European colonialism as exceptional, and often that is what we mean when we talk about "colonialism" in general, it is because of "the scale of empire not just geographically but in having imposed a single universalizing narrative of values, beliefs, and politics, ushering in the beginning of modern globalization."[8] European colonialism not only changed the geopolitical landscape but also, through violent means, formulated the modern ways in which we think of race, nation, value, and our own position(s) in the world. Part of this colonizing project was the transatlantic trade of enslaved West African people. Similarly, colonialism has given popular culture just one version of the zombie, when it is a figure much more multifaceted and complex, as the different chapters of this collection demonstrate.

Decolonialization in the academy is about more than de-centering white Western voices; it is about the very question of how we generate knowledge, as Eve Tuck and K. Wayne Yang argue.[9] It is about the repatriation of knowledge, and perhaps even stories. Dunham was a dancer and anthropologist; she understood that the body itself can express knowledge. We draw attention to her work in this volume about decolonizing the zombie for a number of reasons: first, her scholarship did not align with European, colonial ontologies, or ways of making knowledge. Her methods of movement and expression, now known as the Dunham dance technique, "continue to define the style" of American concert dance, yet "most young dancers do not know about her contributions."[10] This perhaps makes Dunham, or at least her contributions to knowledge and art, somewhat zombified: her "Africanized principles of movement" such as "a flexible torso and spine, swiveling pelvis, odd isolations of arms and legs, the polyrhythmic and syncopated playfulness of the body" live on, animated, without much acknowledgment of where they came from.[11]

Dunham was an African American woman, born in Chicago in 1909, and so it is unlikely that she would have known about her precise ethnic origins if her family were in the United States due to the kidnap and enslavement of Black African people. Her research trip to Haiti in 1935 which inspired *L' Ag' Ya* was perhaps in itself a repatriation: while there were plantations which relied on the labor of enslaved people on the US mainland, Haiti is the only site where revolts successfully overthrew slavers and established a sovereign state. One wonders if Dunham's interest in Haiti was what we would now call decolonial, Sally Sommer writes that Dunham "was never fully accepted by the American anthropology community… because she was not an 'objective' observer. Dunham got down and danced with the people."[12] Objectivity, logic, and emotive detachment are mainstays of Enlightenment European knowledge production, whereas Dunham was perhaps embodying a generational knowledge and culture that was otherwise denied to her due to the enslavement of her own ancestors. She therefore devised dances that were "composites of actual dance rituals and on the other fictitious treatments often based on a story, Dunham made no claim to be totally ethnographic. In the concert halls and theatres, she expected her audiences to be enlightened and entertained by art, not anthropology."[13] Dunham represents a figure at the nexus of art and knowledge, of embodied practice and academic rigor, and perhaps offers a road map as to how to consolidate the realities of European encroachment and violence with indigenous cultural histories. Vèvè A. Clark points out that "the form of the ballet is creole in every sense of the term; that is, it is born of the American sensibility and mixes African and European elements."[14] The zombie as we know it today is perhaps in the spirit of Dunham's creolization of dance: it is a composite of Haitian folklore, and US-centric fears, primarily about the economy.

It has been recorded by a number of scholars that the zombie emerges as a symbol of the anxieties of enslaved Black people in Haiti, who themselves were extracted and taken to the land which had been violently seized from the indigenous Taíno populations.[15] Lauro details how "the zombie is an 'American' monster only in the sense that it comes directly out of a history of colonialism, enslavement, exploitation, and appropriation. The zombie's lineage can be traced to African soul capture myths that were carried to the New World aboard slave ships bound for the colonial Caribbean."[16] In this folklore, a *zombi* is controlled by a master, left "perpetually in a semiconscious state in between living and dead… In its earliest iteration, the *zombi* was read as symbolic of the Caribbean country's past as a plantation economy built on slave labor: drained of its own resources and existing only for the benefit of others."[17] The zombie as we know it today, titillating in its apocalyptic possibility, and sometimes ridiculous in iterations such as *Shaun of the Dead* and *The Dead Don't Die*, emerges from the fears of being controlled and dehumanized that were felt by enslaved people. The zombie, we argue in this edited collection, can and should be decolonized: this collection asks, how might our readings of the zombie, now a global figure, change or renew if we were more attentive to its roots? How does the colonial history of the *zombi* reanimate what the zombie might really be a tool to think about? What is at stake in the metaphor of the undead?

This Collection

Decolonizing the Undead: Rethinking Zombies in World-Literature, Film, and Media takes a new perspective on the rich allegory of the zombie using decolonial and non-Western approaches. With a diverse set of contributors, this edited collection reconsiders the zombie, as well as exemplifying such decolonizing practices for the contemporary Western university. The collection contains essays that consider the zombie in the postcolonial imaginary, including questions around hegemonic categories such as race, gender, and nation. The essays in the collection range from considering the significance of the zombie from Latin America, to Japan, to India, to the presence of the zombie on Netflix. Through a transdisciplinary and transcultural dialogue, and a diverse range of approaches and materials in the collection, *Decolonizing the Undead* complicates and challenges Western-based cultural understandings of the zombie's allegorical weight and value.

The zombie has captured the imagination of the West, particularly the United States, since 1932, when *White Zombie*, a film directed by Victor Halperin, burst onto screens. Hailed as the first zombie flick, the film follows a young white couple, Madeline and Neil, who come to Haiti for their honeymoon. Madeline is set upon by a white "voodoo" master, Murder Legendre, played by Bela Lugosi, and becomes the titular white zombie. The film was based on William B. Seabrook's

The Magic Island (1929), a travelogue which imported the zombie to the American popular imagination. Lauro points out that

> the zombie's uptake in U.S. popular culture was given life by an initial interest in the folkloric Vodou zombie, but the first films exoticized the Caribbean and eroticized racial difference in ways that were deeply problematic. The popularity of the monster, along with the fact that, as a creature derived from folklore, there was no estate to whom one had to pay copyright... ensured the reproduction and revision of the zombie's narrative.[18]

In other words, the zombie of US popular culture is a figure appropriated precisely because it could not be repatriated under copyright laws that prioritize individual ownership of knowledge, art, and stories. Lauro goes on to note that "this whitewashing of the zombie... represents a cultural appropriation of a myth that, ironically or aptly, was itself about appropriation—specifically, the appropriation of labor and life under colonial slavery."[19] Therefore, the figure of the zombie as Anglophone audiences know it today emerges due to the value that could be extracted from it by Hollywood, aligning with its Haitian roots. What is missing from US-centric visions of the zombie, however, is its emancipatory possibilities and symbolism that its folkloric form took. A number of chapters engage with this premise. It is worth noting that we have elected to spell zombie as "zombie" in this volume (unless a quote spells it otherwise), over "zonbi," "*zombi*," or "*zombie*." This choice has been made to make the text discoverable in searches of the emergent field in library and bookseller databases and websites; the marketability of a volume like this, ironically, drives some editorial choices. It likewise does not escape us that scholars and students who will use this volume will selectively extract value from its pages, perhaps through a digitized search function. Likewise, we have chosen to avoid using the spelling "voodoo" (unless a quote spells it otherwise), to denote the vodou religion throughout the collection, as the former spelling was popularized as a way of othering and exoticizing the religion in Anglophone medias about zombies. In not using this spelling, our aim is to afford dignity and respect to the vodou religion and cultural artifacts such as the zombie which have been otherwise appropriated.

Chapter Summaries

This volume is structured into three parts. The first, "Thinking Zombies," considers the ways that the zombie performs as an ontological frame, that is to say, how the zombie allows us to think about ourselves and our places in the world. For instance, Elizabeth Kelly's chapter, "'Il y a des zombies dans ceci...': Dessalines, Disembodiment, and Early Haitian Literature," considers how the fractured body of Jean Jacques Dessalines, who declared Haitian independence, characterized Haitian nation-building during and after the revolution. This is followed by Cécile Accilien's chapter—"White and Black Zombies: How Race Rewrites the Zombie Narrative"—which traces the way in which the zombie has gone from a racialized figure in the 1920s and 1930s US imagination in writings such as Seabrook's *The Magic Island* and the 1943 film *I Walked with a Zombie*, and films such as *White Zombie*, to being incorporated into white, family-friendly medias and activities. This chapter is then followed by Stephen Shapiro's "Decolonizing the Zombie: *I Walked with a Zombie*'s Critique of Centrist Liberalism," which considers the process of decolonizing knowledge production, and how the zombie may offer a "sentinel" way out of the "past's rotting matter" by challenging liberal assumptions about race and postcolonial subjectivities. These chapters taken together provide a historicized frame to think through the process of thinking with the zombie as a decolonial figure to drive scholarship.

The second part, "Zombie World-System," examines how the zombie can be used to reflect and expand our understanding of world-systems of knowledge, goods and resources, culture, and informational systems. Frank Jacob's "Samurai Zombies: Japan's Undead Past" details how the enmeshment of the zombie and samurai in *Yoroi: Samurai Zombie* encapsulates a struggle between modernity as defined by Western-centric capitalism and Japan's own colonial past as a means of negotiating a shifting national identity in a globalized world. Then, Josephine Taylor's "Crude Monsters in the 'Extractive Zone': The Creaturely and Ecological Zombie" examines petrofiction's encounter with the undead, and oil and oil systems as manifestations of the undead in China Miéville's *Covehithe* and Reza Negarestani's *Cyclonopedia*. Taylor discusses how dehumanized, unethical labor and ecologically disastrous practices becomes unmeshed in industries that are crucial to maintaining Western standards of life. Following this, Fiona Farnsworth's chapter, "Undead, Undeader, Undeadest: Narrating the Unevenness of Ecological Crisis in Nana Nkweti's 'It Just Kills You Inside,'" investigates toxicity and environmental crisis in the Cameroonian short story. Farnsworth's chapter engages with questions of necropolitics and disaster control, which are imbricated by the form of "It Just Kills You Inside." Here she discusses "the groundwork for a zombie story which is less about zombies and more about stories: one which not only registers ecological crisis and its uneven impact throughout the world-system but which foregrounds questions around the formal and aesthetic capacity of narrative to represent or obscure crisis immediately and long-term." This leads to Thomas Waller's chapter, "Zombie Proletkino: Labor, Race and Genre in Pedro Costa's *Casa de Lava*," which discusses how the zombie genre itself persists and reappears in non-Western contexts over the *long durée* "as *constitutive* and *co-productive* moments in capitalist value production," using Pedro Costa's films, primarily *Casa de Lava*, as a case study. Lastly, Roxanne Douglas considers how the "cognizant zombie" in Netflix series *Santa Clarita Diet* sits at the nexus of neoliberal feminist ideologies, embodied pleasure and agency, and digital data collection and control in "'It Feels Like I'm Giving My Body Something It Needs in an Intense and Powerful Way': Netflix, *Santa Clarita Diet*, and the Neoliberal Feminist Encounter with Pleasure Politics." These chapters not only offer a theorization of the zombie as a figure of the market, as many scholars have discussed, but turn to world literary systems to look toward the zombie as a complex figure that is not only of production but a way to think about and beyond globalization.

The third and final part, "Zombie Decolonial," builds on the principles of the previous two parts to examine decolonial representations of the zombie. Read together, these chapters offer a cross-section of how the zombie has manifested in postcolonial artistic production. The part opens with Rebecca Duncan's chapter that examines the slippage between formal decolonization in South Africa and how cultural values and production have remained colonized in "'De/Zombification as Decolonial Critique: Beyond Man, Nature, and the Posthuman in Folklore and Fiction from South Africa." In this chapter, Duncan uses Masande Ntshanga's *The Reactive* as a case study to examine how "existing occult narratives of zombification, proliferating across the sub-Saharan region, register the social and ecological effects of the human as a colonial institution, and how such discourses also potentiate a decolonial critique." This chapter is followed by "Zombies, Placelessness, and Transcultural Entanglement: Ahmed Saadawi's *Frankenstein in Baghdad*," by Netty Mattar. Going beyond typical readings of Whatsitsname's body as the fragmentation of Iraq or the wider Middle East, Mattar reads Whatsitsname and the zombie as comparable "radical figures of unbelonging, their attachments to place severed, and yet they are bound to the lands they are no longer a part of." Subsequently, Abhirup Mascharak's chapter, "'First They Bring the HIV, then the Zombie': Portrayal of the West in Contemporary Indian Zombie Literature and Cinema," explores how the US-centric zombie is remade and reimagined in Raj Nidimoru and Krishna D. K.'s *Go Goa Gone* to reflect contemporary anxieties over Westernization through sexualization. This chapter usefully details the recent history of Indian zombie cinema, analyzing the adoption of the US-style zombie to ultimately conservative ends.

This part concludes with Giulia Champion's chapter, titled "From the Mountain to the Shore: Migration, Water Crisis, and Revolutionary Zombies from Haiti to Peru," which investigates Julio Ortega's novel *Adiós, Ayacucho* (1986). This chapter first proposes to decolonize the Haitian zombie by excavating its emancipatory potential in relation to the Haitian Revolution and to then use this decolonized and emancipatory figure to read the Peruvian novel's undead protagonist, therefore, considering why both nations and the figure of the zombie need new, decolonized, narratives. The collection then concludes with an afterword by Stephen Shapiro, "Decolonizing Zombie Cultural Practice: An Afterword," which reminds us to "double-tap" on our way out of the collection: this chapter explores the politics of reading the zombie figure through the decolonial lens.

Conclusion

The idea and preparations for this collection preceded the Covid-19 pandemic, but, like many projects, has seen lockdown orders come and go and has faced disruption due to this. The Covid-19 pandemic saw many people return with morbid fascination to virus-disaster medias, such as mobile game "Plague inc.," and films such as *28 Days Later* and *Contagion* (*Contagion* briefly was one of the UK's top 10 films on Netflix in the early days of lockdown and supposedly inspired the Secretary of State for Health and Social Care in the United Kingdom during the pandemic, Matt Hancock's vaccine rollout),[20] zombie films and stories being among them. However, a real worldwide disaster did not deliver the individualist survival fantasy that was promised by zombie flicks. What did become obvious quite quickly was, for good or bad, globalization means that the health of one is the health of all. We are already in the hoard.

Furlough schemes and global supply chains likewise showed that the wealth of one was the wealth of all: Covid-19 laid bare the ways in which we are connected psychically, epidemiologically, environmentally, and economically on a global scale. This is not to say that this is an even experience: indeed, the pandemic only further emphasized existing global inequalities, which perdure in vaccine distribution today. At a smaller scale, many of us were separated from our own hoards, but, unlike the unruly glee offered by zombie cinema (after all, we watch to ask, "What would I do? How would my life be without rent, social niceties, taxes, social media, etcetera?"), many of us found ourselves alone, but with the baggage of rent, social niceties, taxes, social media, etc., very much intact. The zombie feels like a pressing image in the current moment, many experiencing burnout and emotional exhaustion while the pressures of capitalism continue to demand productive engagement with work. The figure on the cover of this collection looks back at us: some may read this as confrontational, or strong, while others may see the gape of the eye sockets as a blankness, a vacancy. In either case, the appropriated figure of the undead regards us, too, reflecting how we have internalized values that frame the cultural artifacts of colonized cultures, such as the *zombi*. Drawing inspiration from Dunham's enmeshment of the emotive and ontological, this volume is an attempt to challenge colonial ways of making knowledge by revisiting a revenant figure which lives on in Anglophone cultures by asking, How do we decolonize how and why we know things through the undead? The zombie is a metaphor, a tool to think with. Could we restore the rebellious unruliness of the zombie, rising against the master and establishing a new way of thinking about ourselves and our place in the world?

Notes

1   Dayan, *Haiti, History, and the Gods*, 37.
2   de León, "Dear White People/Queridos Gringos."
3   Desai, "Remembering and Honoring the Dead," 768.
4   Sharpe, *In the Wake*, 13, my emphasis.
5   Dunham, *Katherine Dunham Performing Ballet Creole (1952) | British Pathé*.
6   Dunham, *Island Possessed*, 179.
7   Lauro, "Introduction," x.
8   Couldry and Mejias, *The Costs of Connection*, 69.
9   Tuck and Wayne Yang, "Decolonization Is Not a Metaphor."
10 Sommer, "Katherine Dunham."
11 Sommer, "Katherine Dunham."
12 Sommer, "Katherine Dunham."
13 Clark, "Katherine Dunham's Tropical Revue," 148.
14 Clark, "Katherine Dunham's Tropical Revue," 149.
15 Cohen, "Undead (A Zombie Oriented Ontology)"; Lauro, "Introduction"; Dunham, *Island Possessed*.
16 Lauro, "Introduction," x, xi.
17 Lauro, "Introduction," x, xi.
18 Lauro, "Introduction," x.

19 Lauro, "Introduction," x.
20 Heritage, "Matt Hancock's Vaccine Rollout Was Inspired by Contagion. Here's What He Should Watch Next."

Works Cited

Clark, Vèvè A. "Katherine Dunham's Tropical Revue." *Black American Literature Forum* 16, no. 4 (Winter 1982): 147–52.

Cohen, Jeffrey Jerome. "Undead (A Zombie Oriented Ontology)." *Journal of the Fantastic in the Arts* 23, no. 3 (86) (2012): 397–412.

Couldry, Nick, and Ulises Ali Mejias. *The Costs of Connection: How Data Is Colonizing Human Life and Appropriating It for Capitalism*. (Culture and Economic Life). Stanford: Stanford University Press, 2019.

Dayan, Colin. *Haiti, History, and the Gods*. Berkeley: University of California Press, 1995.

Desai, Shiv R. "Remembering and Honoring the Dead: Dia de Los Muertos, Black Lives Matter and Radical Healing." *Race Ethnicity and Education* 23, no. 6 (November 1, 2020): 767–83.

Dunham, Katherine. *Island Possessed*. Garden City, NY: Doubleday, 1969.

Dunham, Katherine. *Katherine Dunham Performing Ballet Creole (1952)* | British Pathé. London: British Pathé. https://www.youtube.com/watch?v=iSTuO5E9_1g&ab_channel=BritishPath%C3%A9. Accessed August 7, 2021.

Heritage, Stuart. "Matt Hancock's Vaccine Rollout Was Inspired by Contagion. Here's What He Should Watch Next." *The Guardian*, February 4, 2021. https://www.theguardian.com/film/filmblog/2021/feb/04/contagion-film-matt-hancock-covid-vaccine-policy-hollywood. Accessed September 22, 2021.

Lauro, Sarah Juliet. "Introduction: Wander and Wonder in Zombieland." In *Zombie Theory: A Reader*, edited by Sarah Juliet Lauro, vii–xxvi. Minneapolis: University of Minnesota Press, 2017.

León, Aya de. "Dear White People/Queridos Gringos: You Want Our Culture but You Don't Want Us—Stop Colonizing the Day of the Dead." Blog. *Aya de León* (blog), October 31, 2014. https://ayadeleon.wordpress.com/2014/10/31/dear-white-peoplequeridos-gringos-you-want-our-culture-but-you-dont-want-us-stop-colonizing-the-day-of-the-dead/. Accessed September 22, 2021.

Sharpe, Christina. *In the Wake: On Blackness and Being*. Durham: Duke University Press, 2016.

Sommer, Sally. "Katherine Dunham: African-American Dancer, Choreographer, Anthropologist, Writer, Activist and Voodoo Priestess." *The Guardian*, May 23, 2006. https://www.theguardian.com/news/2006/may/23/guardianobituaries.booksobituaries. Accessed August 7, 2021.

Tuck, Eve, and K. Wayne Yang. "Decolonization Is Not a Metaphor." *Decolonization: Indigeneity, Education & Society* 1, no. 1 (2012): 1–40.

Part One

Thinking Zombies

1

"Il y a des zombies dans ceci...": Dessalines, Disembodiment, and Early Haitian Literature

Elizabeth Kelly

Revolutionary Saint Domingue has been codified in a number of striking narratives that are consistently focused on tortured bodies—the ravaged bodies of the enslaved populations, the women raped, the men, women, and children tortured, and the victims of mass execution. While contemporary histories move toward considering the ideological motivations for the series of conflicts and revolts that comprise what we now call the Haitian Revolution, representations of these events by late eighteenth- and early nineteenth-century eyewitnesses, biographers, and historians outside of Haiti instigated particular narratives of violence and suffering that persist today. Interestingly, the revolutionaries themselves and the growing Haitian literary communities of the early nineteenth century also developed a competing discourse surrounding the body and the spirit that laid a fertile groundwork for considering the zombie in nineteenth-century Haitian contexts.

For Jean-Jacques Dessalines, famous for declaring Haitian independence in 1804 and for his military and political exploits, Haitian identity was embodied in his person, both unrestrained by enslavement and Western morality and powerfully weaponized against the French. He stages his own body as representing a triumphant figure in which various seen and unseen forces might be unified as a nation, and reads the remains of the French dead as testifying to that power. Nineteenth-century Haitian historians painstakingly detailed the events surrounding Dessalines' death and dismemberment, paying close attention to how his parts were sold and then recollected. They created a narrative that reinscribed the power of Dessalines' body, and Joan Dayan argues that Massillon Coicou's 1906 play, *L'Empereur Dessalines* (The Emperor Dessalines), reinvigorated these narratives by announcing Dessalines' ascension into the Vodou Cosmology as Ogou Desalin, a *lwa*, or spirit intermediary linked to war, attachment to land, and sovereign power. Coicou's preface argues that the act of reassembling Dessalines' body signals the embodiment of the new nation, placing both these values and Dessalines' body as central to Haitian identity.[1]

Nearly seventy years before Coicou's play, Ignace Nau, an already prominent literary figure in Haiti and France, serially published *Isalina, ou, Une scène créole* (Isalina, or, a Creole Scene) in *La Revue des Colonies* (1836–7). This text is commonly considered the first piece of Haitian prose fiction.[2] The tale centers on a love triangle and highlights a seemingly picturesque rural Haitian existence until, upon hearing that the eponymous character has been attacked, the village elders remark, "*Il y a des zombies dans ceci…*" (there are zombies involved in this…). The text presents the zombie as a form of disembodiment empowered to resist the confines of rural Haitian culture. The zombies haunting Nau's text can be profitably read as an extension of Dessalines' modes of thinking about the relationship between the body and the spirit, situating the disembodied figure as central to Haitian life in the new nation. The Haitian zombie arose within a set of existing popular narratives surrounding embodiment and disembodiment long before the twentieth century, presenting a resistant figure not only limited to resisting colonial power but also extended into the nation of Haiti.

Toussaint Louverture, Kinship, and the Suffering Body

Although the disembodiment of Dessalines has been widely studied and his understanding of the relationship between the body, the disembodied spirit, and the new nation is much more radical and pronounced than his revolutionary predecessor's, Haitian sensibilities surrounding that relationship arise from Toussaint Louverture's treatments of the body and the body politic. Nineteenth-century historians and biographers of Toussaint Louverture tended toward formulaic characterizations that very much fed into existing discourses casting slaves and former slaves as heroic Africans, natural healers, and saviors of white bodies. Louverture himself carefully negotiated his world of letters, and well understood the effects of recording his own interpretations and motivations in the massive volume of proclamations, letters, and journals he continued to write until his death. Throughout his writings, Louverture consistently relied upon a well-defined set of bodily metaphors to negotiate his complex relationships to French colonial officials, Haitian colonial subjects, and eventually the Haitian people. Louverture stages French officials as father figures and the French in general as his brothers. As conflicts rise, he begins to refer to what would become the Haitian people as "brothers," and eventually positions himself as the "true father of all blacks," as opposed to the French, who have become "idolatrous fathers." Eventually, he stages both French and revolutionary betrayals as wounding his body. Louverture's radical repositioning of black embodiment began a mode of thinking that evolved through Dessalines' proclamations and eventually through the disembodied spirits (or *zombis*) of early Haitian literature. The clear shift in bodily metaphors between Louverture's and Dessalines' writings is not unlike the dual readings of the zombie figure, who has been read as "not merely an allegory for slavery, but... also a representative of resistance."[3]

Well aware of the Eurocentric perceptions of the colony and the precariousness of his alliances with the French, Louverture figured his identification with French Republicanism as a bodily experience, describing his reactions to mistreatment of French prisoners and the fate of his country in bodily terms. In a letter dated May 18, 1794, Louverture wrote, "My heart bled and I shed tears over the unfortunate fate of my country... My heart is broken to contemplate the event that occurred against a few unfortunate whites who were victims in this affair. I am utterly unlike many others who witness scenes of horror in cold blood."[4] He again calls attention to his French heart and its accompanying humanity, noting that on entering Petite Rivière in February 1796, the pleas of the women and children of color "created in me so much emotion that I could only listen in this moment to my French and humane heart; I gave them their lives, the women and all the men."[5] Louverture appears to be defending his decision to spare the population, particularly the men who may well have participated in fighting for the enemy. In this way, he skillfully avoids any critique of his decision. In both instances, Louverture inscribes his sympathies and his alliances on his body, and by extension on the body politic of the country.

Louverture also tended to refer to his relationships with the French in general, particular French leaders, and, later, the Haitian population, in familial terms that extend his metaphors of bodily relation. The most striking and well-preserved examples of this are found in his correspondence with General Étienne Laveaux, the interim governor-general of Saint Domingue from 1793 to 1796. Throughout their correspondence, Louverture repeatedly and warmly addresses Laveaux as *mon père* (my father); his understanding of the paternal relationship as a corporeal bond reaches its apex in February 1796. Laveaux faced growing unrest in the Northern Department, which eventually led to Laveaux's capture, Louverture's rescue, and the latter's appointment as governor-general of the colony. Well aware of Laveaux's perilous situation and his own potential to rise to power, Louverture pledged his loyalty to Laveaux, writing:

> general, Toussaint is your son, he cherishes you; and your grave will be his, and he will support you at the peril of his life; his arm and head are always at your disposal and if he has to succumb, he will carry with him the sweet consolation of having defended a father, a virtuous friend, and the cause of liberty.[6]

Here Louverture stages his own feelings for Laveaux as instigating physical reactions ("tears of tenderness") and establishes a linkage between the lives of these men that reaches beyond a metaphorically filial relationship. In positioning himself as a loyal son, Louverture creates a bodily metaphor that preempts his succession to power. Louverture's loyalty is also coded as a commitment of his body (arm and head) and even his death to Laveaux's cause, a connection that would be echoed and reinterpreted by Dessalines.

While the intense, personal loyalty Louverture's writings depict toward Laveaux was certainly more steadfast than his loyalties to the French in general, metaphors of kinship were rampant throughout his writings. The tumultuous relationship between Louverture's armies and the French is coded as one of broken familial bonds, with Louverture writing to Laveaux on May 18, 1794, "I was abandoned by the French, my brothers. But my late experience has opened my eyes to these treacherous protectors."[7] As loyalties shifted throughout the year, and his own reconciliation with the French seemed more possible, on March 22, 1795, Louverture juxtaposed the French, whom he coded as kin, with the Spanish, English, and royalists, to whom he assigned a cannibalistic (and extra-familial role), stating that "the French are our brothers, the English, the Spanish, and the royalists are ferocious beasts who only caress to suck at their leisure, until they are satiated, the blood of their women and children."[8] The relationship between Louverture's enemies and the people he addresses is described as a potential corporeal nurturing, as a mother breastfeeding a child, that has been perverted into a very different formulation of bodily nourishment in cannibalizing women and children.

Louverture often relied upon familial relationships to code shifting loyalties, frequently positioning himself moving up on a patriarchal ladder. In May 1795, Louverture wrote to Laveaux about the rebellion of Thomas, in which the *cultivateurs* (in this context, agricultural laborers) "armed themselves against me and I received for my pains a bullet in the leg, from which I still feel sharp pain."[9] Here Louverture focuses on the physical reminder he carries of the rebellion, while aligning the injustice of their violence against him with physical pain.

Louverture later characterizes his suffering at the loss of his own sons to France as a bodily wound, having been quoted in Madiou's history and elsewhere as stating, "My children, if you leave me, you open a wound in my heart that will never be closed."[10] The metaphorical wound here is not inconsistent with his language of wounding involved in his separation from the French, as mentioned above. In a letter dated August 31, 1796, Louverture, a devout Catholic, exhorted Laveaux to remember, "We imitate Jesus Christ who died and suffered for us, to give us an example of a virtuous wise man is made to suffer, but, he who allows our suffering will also console us. We must put all our hope in him."[11] Louverture implies that both he and Laveaux must suffer in order to maintain virtue—a theme he returns to later in his own writings.

Deborah Jenson also argues that Louverture uses tropes of bodily suffering and healing in order to consider the psychological positioning of political participation in the colony, noting that "through figures of pain and healing, he conveys a vivid psychological and physical political subject."[12] Louverture's repeated references to the pain endured in what he saw as French colonial leaders' betrayal present political disenfranchisement as a direct form of physical suffering, and one which could be healed through an aggressive treatment, which he also describes in physical terms. In a letter dated only "*la 24 l'an sixième de la République*" (the 24th of the 6th year of the French Republic, which was 1798), Louverture references healing as follows:

> Palliative remedies only flatter the pathology, and one must get to the source to heal it. As you do not know the colony, I fear that you are being diverted from all your good intentions with regards to the well-being of the republic, and are encouraging your subordinates who will perish a thousand times for the colony and the execution of the orders of the Directory that will be transmitted to us by you.[13]

Jenson reads this letter as Louverture positioning himself as "not just the pained subject, but also the doctor threatening to excise the pathology at its source."[14] The role Louverture establishes for himself poses sovereign power as a means of resolving suffering and suggests that his own intervention may well be to heal the disruption and abuses of colonial power in the colony.

Louverture's writings also show that he was adept at understanding and manipulating the already-existing discourse of suffering bodies in Haiti that had previously been established in the first eyewitness accounts of the revolution. Louverture consistently used metaphors of the bodily relation to sort out his own complex ties to French colonial agents and positioned himself as a protector of white bodies when it best suited his goals. He expressed his filial loyalty and his status as a protector of bodies as an extension of French Republicanism. He was also adept at using metaphors of suffering and healing to consider the state of the colony and later the nation, understanding his own political power as being intimately connected to his written legacy, a disembodied form that did indeed supersede the limits of his body, which was buried in an unmarked grave.[15]

Dessalines the Disembodied

By contrast, Dessalines' proclamations reveal a very different set of bodily metaphors, although it is clear that some of the rupture Louverture coded through bodies was carried into Dessalines' writings as well. Dessalines highlighted an understanding of embodiment that Fishburn argues was "particular to African slaves, who crafted for themselves (and for us) a therapeutic anti-humanism (a destructive hermeneutics), one that redefines what it means to be human, one that is not based on the dualisms of mind and body, subject and object, self and other—but on their necessary intertwining."[16] Dessalines' own treatment of the body in oral and written proclamations, at least as they have been preserved by eyewitnesses and historians, presents a clear example of this. Like Louverture, he attempted to assert himself as a protector of white bodies, but as relations with French colonial powers became increasingly fraught, Dessalines began to establish radical understandings of the Black body as a source of power and of the new nation that included both the living and the dead. Dessalines' entry into the Vodou cosmology as a disembodied figure associated with a non-Western past and a unifying figure for the past and present nation of Haiti is also consistent with his own understandings of the roles of living and dead bodies in creating the new nation.

Dessalines understood his own body as both a source of power and a weapon in the fight for independence. He also expected his troops to consider the power they might derive from their own bodies. Madiou reports that at the 1803 Battle of Croix-des-Bouquets:

> Dessalines saw the soldiers of the 8th flinching and rushed into the midst of them, reviving their courage. At the same moment, two regiments of the four fired the deadliest barrage. The shaken *indigènes* again lost ground. "Forward! Forward" cried Dessalines, braving death with the front lines. The soldiers responded to his voice "General, we have no powder." Dessalines, boiling with anger: "Take them with your nails and teeth!"[17]

Dessalines' physical presence is figured as inciting courage in his soldiers, and his references to the body as a form of weaponry speak to an understanding of the body that is radically removed from the figure of the tortured Black body Louverture often called upon. The soldiers' bodies become a source of power that had hitherto been unrealized, particularly in terms of its potential to resist French control of the colony.

On the eve of independence, Dessalines also began to rely upon racial difference as a rallying point to unify the Black and colored populations against the French. After Louverture's arrest in 1802, Dessalines spoke to a crowd of African bands of rebels attempting to unify them on the basis of race and creole identity:

> No! No! We will never make peace with the whites! Look at my face!... Am I white? Do you not recognize the hero of Crête-a-Pierrot? Was I white at Petite-Rivière in Arbonite, when the expedition arrived? Ask these hills covered with French bones. Will they name Dessalines the hero of these trophies?[18]

Dessalines not only points to race as the unifying factor in rallying the armed forced in the final push for independence but also refers to the bodies of the French as his trophies, or corporeal proof of his victory. He stages a direct relationship between his own body as representing a triumphant modality in which various forces might be unified and the remains of the French as testifying to his power.

Dessalines also relies upon nineteenth-century understandings of racial difference in his most radical proclamations, using them as a basis for rejecting the ties of kinship and loyalty Louverture so carefully constructed in his letters. In one of the longest proclamations included in Madiou's history, Dessalines is reported to have asked his audience, "What do we have in common with these murderous people? Compare their cruelty to our patient moderation, their color to ours, the extent of sea that separates us, our savage climate, we say enough that they are not our brothers, that they will never become so."[19] Dessalines relies upon the material conditions commonly associated with race (including climate and geography) to construct the Haitian people as distinct from the French. In doing so, he argues for a radical break from not only the French government but also the assimilationist position Louverture often supported toward French culture.

Like Louverture, at least in his later writings, Dessalines also relied upon metaphors of kinship to unify the Black and colored populations in Haiti. Dessalines' understanding of kinship, however, extends beyond death in a way that is very much consistent with West African systems of belief and in some ways echoes Louverture's appeals to Laveaux. He begins by asking the audience to

> cast round your eyes on every part of this island; seek there your wives, your husbands, your brothers and your sisters—what did I say? Seek your children—your children at the breast, what has become of them? I shudder to tell it—*the prey of vultures*. Instead of these interesting victims, the affrighted eye sees only their assassins—tigers still covered with their blood, and whose terrifying presence reproaches you for your insensibility, and your guilty tardiness to avenge them—what do you wait for, to appease their manes? Remember that you have wished your remains to be laid by the side of your fathers When you have driven out tyranny, will you descend into their tombs, without having avenged them? No: their bones would repulse yours.[20]

Dessalines' own words speak to the connection between the independence of the nation of Haiti and the dead, who here present disembodied figures that have the power to accept or reject the living citizens of Haiti. The dead here are positioned as integral to citizenship in the nation of Haiti and belonging in a national, creole identity.

Positioned in the midst of a complex set of relations between Black bodies, resistant spirits, and Haitian identity is another figure whose presence and relation to the zombie cannot go unnoticed. Madiou's history references a rebel named Jean Zombi, a figure who is sometimes credited with an origin for the figure of the Haitian zombie. Much has been made of this figure, although there is no known historical record of him outside of Madiou's history. Madiou's Jean Zombi is wild-eyed, apparently of mixed race, and having a particularly brutal nature.[21] Joan Dayan has famously argued that Jean Zombi's presence here signals the entry of the zombie as a creole figure that stands in for a new and powerful identity, while others point out this figure as a means of "attribut[ing] exceptional cruelty only to some individual figures such as Zombi rather than the Haitian leaders and rank and file."[22] This reading is certainly consistent with Madiou's repeated emphases on Dessalines' generosity and mercy.

Rather than entering the critical discussion of the origin of the zombie in the figure of Jean Zombi, I argue that the surrounding embodiment and power in Haiti shifts a great deal between Louverture's and Dessalines' written works. Louverture carefully constructed a familial discourse that would empower him through consolidating ties to French leaders and attempted to establish a patriarchal relationship between the Haitian people and the French. As these relations dissolved, Louverture represented the betrayals of the French as an issue of familial relations gone wrong, and the break with French leadership as a bodily sickness. Dessalines' proclamations reveal an interesting genealogy of his own treatment of bodies that promotes the kinds of understandings of the relationship between the living and the dead that are central to West African and Haitian systems of belief. While earlier in the revolutionary struggles Dessalines struggled to fashion himself as particularly invested in showing mercy to the French, he later began to move toward a radical understanding of Haitian independence expressed through metaphors of the body and the spirit. First, he began to understand the Black body in itself as a source of resistance to colonial power. He consolidated this understanding in radically rethinking notions of nationhood in order to constitute an alternative understanding of the relationships between the bodies of the Haitian people and their conception of nationhood. Finally, he drew on alternate understandings of the relationship between living and dead bodies in demanding that the Haitian people answer to the bones of the ancestors. Here he sets the stage for the modes of disembodiment that would later appear as modes of resistance in Haitian culture and literature, including the zombie in early Haitian literature.

Isalina's Zombies

Joan Dayan proposes that Dessalines' entry into the spiritual world of the Haitian imaginary signals a genesis that began in the 1791 ceremony of Bois-Caïman and continues today. While Dayan traces the path of the disembodied Dessalines into modern oral cultures of Haiti, very little scholarship considers the role of disembodiment in early Haitian creative literature. Scholarship on Haitian literature tends to ignore Haitian prose contributions in the nineteenth century, generally focusing on the vast literary movement of the 1920s and 1930s, much of which attempted to reinvigorate Haitian culture as a response to the 1915 US occupation of Haiti. In the shadow of this wealth of poetry, plays, and novels are the works produced in Haiti before the US occupation, many of which creatively reimagine the complex relationships between the body, the disembodied subject, and liberty and sovereignty in the new nation of Haiti.

Among these works are Ignace Nau's *Isalina, ou, Une scène créole*, which appeared in the *Revue des Colonies* in serial form between 1836 and 1837, and is considered "the first known work of prose fiction in the Haitian literary tradition."[23] Very few critics have responded to *Isalina* despite the relative fame of the Nau brothers, at least in their time.[24] In the only substantial contemporary study of *Isalina*, Anna Brickhouse reads the novella's picturesque setting and emphases on clear markers of rural Haitian culture, including ritual practices, as answering the call for indigenous literatures in Haiti. Nau's identification of such rituals as central to rural life and Haitian identity also presents what Kate Ramsey reads as a critique of the Boyer regime's recent criminalization of non-Western ritual practices.[25] While Brickhouse argues that the role of ritual in *Isalina* is to restore the balance of social structure, the novella also presents forms of disembodiment as a powerful means of resisting the confines of that structure. The story itself contains the first known literary reference to the zombie, employing a means of disembodiment that, like Dessalines' lwa, contains the potential to resist political and social restrictions to liberty.

In short, *Isalina* is the story of a love triangle mediated by ritual practice. The eponymous character is caught between Paul, her intended, and his baptismal brother, Jean-Julien, who attacks her in a cemetery when she refuses his advances.[26] After the attack, the villagers suspect that Isalina has been bewitched. On the advice of his mother, Paul seeks out the help of Galba, an oungan, or ritual specialist, who determines that Isalina has been attacked by Jean-Julien and bewitched by Marie Robin, a local practitioner of *la science*, a term that carefully avoids the pejorative and illegal notion of *sortilège*, or malicious magic, with substantial powers. Galba prescribes a set of rituals aimed at freeing Isalina from the trance and eradicating Jean-Julien's love for her. The ritual works in curing Isalina, and the story ends with her formal betrothal to Paul.

At the height of the novella's conflict, Isalina is forced to choose between Paul and Jean-Julien, a choice that pits her physical safety against her social reputation. Choosing the latter, she is pushed into a gravestone and injured. The reader finds out that at some time after, she was "bewitched" by Marie Robin at Jean-Julien's request. Paul hears of the attack from some workers traveling through the area, who report that "the situation was mysterious, and all the old villagers believe there is witchcraft involved."[27] They give a scant description of what they know about the attack, to which there were no witnesses, and end their conversation with the question "*Il y a zombies dans ceci, n'est-pas?*" (There are zombies involved in this, don't you think?).[28] While a lack of evidence (here only the unconscious Isalina and an apparently unused knife) may indicate a mystery of sorts, Nau's readers may well have questioned why zombies might come into play at this point in the story.

Although there is no mention of these zombies throughout the remainder of the text, the reference stands in of the dual nature of the zombie in Haitian tradition, which can refer to "both spirit, and, more specifically, the animated dead, a body without mind."²⁹ Both meanings are reflected as the story unfolds. Isalina is repeatedly referred to as having been murdered ("*a été assassinée*") despite the text's insistence that she is very much alive, and the practitioner who eventually returns her spirit to her body recognizes that her inanimate body is under partial control by a competing ougan. There is also the possibility in the text that, due to a lack of evidence, the villagers suspect a disembodied spirit has, in fact, attacked Isalina. Here, Isalina's disembodiment arises, at least on a material level, out of her unwillingness to speak against her betrothed and defy social constraints on her choice in lovers, and her body becomes what Dayan calls "mindless" not only because of the ritual but because she becomes an object over which the men battle through the ougans they employ.

Interestingly, Isalina's condition can be registered on multiple levels within the text. First, as the other characters' treatment of her implies, she has been rendered a zombie by an outside power. Second, as Brickhouse argues, "the narrator suggests in the first section of the story that Isalina's delirium and her rejection of Paul have an empirical source, one that readers see firsthand in her fall and the injury to her head."³⁰ Finally, the text lends itself to the implication that her illness reflects her inability to pursue her own romantic choices. This final possibility considers her ultimate powerlessness within the context of the story; she can neither voice her choice in lovers nor protect herself from the very real physical and social dangers she faces. The resolution, however, implies that the first of these options is the most convincing. Considering Isalina bewitched, Paul seeks out the help of Galba in freeing her.

Before accepting Paul's request for his services, Galba asks a number of questions that betray an awareness of several possible causes of Isalina's illness, the most telling of which is when he asks Paul how Isalina reacts to Jean-Julien. Here, Galba's investigation asserts the possibility that Isalina's conduct may be caused by unfaithfulness rather than being bewitched but goes on to perform an investigatory ritual that involves several layers of disembodiment. Galba begins the ritual alone and in silence, until Paul hears "voiceless moans and convulsive sighs."³¹ Galba returns from his trance "with a singular expression of knowing" and asks Paul to gaze into a series of cards he has placed on a board. The cards reveal the figures of Jean-Julien and Marie Robin through a means that implies that their disembodied spirits appear there. The narrator writes "a shadow passed over the card and settled there for a moment. The features were the facsimile of a real person" that Paul recognizes as Jean-Julien.³² Galba then asks Paul to gaze into a basin of water, which reveals the image of Isalina, kissing Jean-Julien's hand. The enraged Paul moves to shatter the basin, and Galba reminds him that what he sees are "only images." Despite the immateriality of the vision, Galba sprinkles powder into the basin and assures Paul that "Isalina is saved" by his actions, asserting that he has been able to affect her bodily illness and the discomfort of her mind through the images themselves.[33]

Brickhouse reads Galba's intervention as resolving the central crisis of the story—Isalina's rejection of Paul. Brickhouse argues that "the end of the tale established a new genealogy—and effectively restores what is salvageable from the old, disrupted one—through the paternal figure of the *papa-loi*, to whom Paul ultimately offers himself as his son."[34] Galba's role here as a practitioner is entirely consistent with conceptions of Vodou practice, which Kate Ramsey notes are frequently thought of as "the entire range of spiritual and healing practices undertaken within extended families and through relationships with male and female religious leaders, called, respectively, *ougan* and *manbo*."[35] Nau's reluctance to specify such rituals as part of what many of his contemporaries outside of Haiti would term "Vodou" can be read as portraying a more nuanced and particularly Haitian understanding of the term that Nau did not assume his readers would share.

Despite the patriarchal tone of the story, the character who suggests the greatest potential for resisting the strict social structure is Marie Robin, a practitioner who never actually appears in the story. Paul recognizes Marie Robin in the Queen of Spades card Galba uses in the ritual, and his startled reaction "What! Marie Robin! Eh! My God! I am so lost" implies a profound respect for her power within the community.[36] Marie Robin is herself entirely absent from the story, but her disembodied intervention in the plot contains a great deal of power to threaten the established social order.

Brickhouse's reading centers on Nau's story as answering a call for indigenist literature in Haiti's newly accessible public sphere and begins to address the complex layers of patriarchal power at stake in such a tale. I would argue here that Isalina's disembodiment exposes her subjugated position in the face of particularly gendered systems of power presented through the villagers, the institution of marriage, and the men who use her body and her spirit as sites of masculine struggle. Her disembodiment at the hands of Marie Robin allows for an even more complex reading of the text; despite Marie Robin's role as a hired intermediary, the power to disrupt the genealogy Brickhouse identifies here does provide a force of disruption within the text that is enacted and recognized through Marie Robin's disembodiment. While nineteenth-century creative Haitian works were rarely widely disseminated, *Isalina*, often cited as the first piece of Haitian prose fiction, was both published in a forum that facilitated a relatively large reading audience and was thought of, at least by its author, as presenting a uniquely Haitian text. Certainly its focus on disembodiment as a means of both exerting and subverting social power establishes in a literary context the importance of the relationship between the body and the spirit in disrupting power dynamics in the early nineteenth century.

When we consider the rise of the zombie in nineteenth-century Haitian contexts, it is fundamental to think about the ways in which a literary sphere born in the midst of the Haitian revolution thought about power, bodies, and the spirit. Louverture's careful entry into a fraught discourse surrounding Black bodies began as a means of writing back against narratives that both helped and hindered Louverture's causes. Deborah Jenson has noted that "Where his successor Dessalines is today the popular hero of Haitian political consciousness… it was Toussaint who forged a dialogue of tenuous peer relationship with metropolitan and colonial leadership, and out of it an enduring foothold for critique and mobility," and that he did this through the world of letters.[37] Much of this critique was staged through repositioning kinship and bodily relations, and despite the profound differences between Louverture and Dessalines' literary tactics, this critique carried forward as the new nation formed. Juxtaposing the kinds of disembodiment both championed and posthumously attributed to Dessalines to the literary treatment of disembodiment in a text like *Isalina* creates an interesting arc of development for bodies and the disembodied in Haitian contexts. The zombie, the apex of the disembodied figure moves beyond an anticolonial figure, instead becomes a figure of unlimited potential to critique, reimagine, and disrupt the exercise of power over bodies, no matter the source of that power.

Notes

1 Dayan, *Haiti, History, and the Gods*, 31.
2 It should be noted that "Le Mulâtre," published in *La Revue des Colonies* in 1837 by Victor Séjour, the son of Haitian immigrants living in New Orleans, is now also hailed as the first work of African American fiction.
3 Lauro, *The Transatlantic Zombie*, 31.
4 Nesbitt, *Jean-Bertrand Aristide Presents Toussaint Louverture and the Haitian Revolution*, 9–10.
5 Laurent, *Toussaint Louverture*, 342–3. All translations of Laurent's edition are mine.
6 Laurent, *Toussaint Louverture*, 347–8.

7 Laurent, *Toussaint Louverture*, 104.
8 Louverture, *The Haitian Revolution*, 14.
9 Laurent, *Toussaint Louverture*, 185.
10 Madiou, *Histoire D'Haiti*, Vol. II, 208. All translations of Madiou are mine.
11 Laurent, *Toussaint Louverture*, 428.
12 Jenson, *Beyond the Slave Narrative*, 60.
13 Jenson, *Beyond the Slave Narrative*, 60.
14 Jenson, *Beyond the Slave Narrative*, 60.
15 It is not without irony that Louverture's prison notebooks are still held in the Archives Nationales de France at Pierrefitte-sur-Seine, still marked by his blood, and buried in the Marine Committee files. They are rapidly decaying and are protected only by a thin folio of paper at the bottom of a box containing miscellaneous correspondence.
16 Fishburn, *The Problem of Embodiment in Early African American Narrative*, 44.
17 Madiou, *Histoire D'Haiti*, Vol. 3, 87.
18 Madiou, *Histoire D'Haiti*, Vol. 2, 441.
19 Madiou, *Histoire D'Haiti*, Vol. 2, 147.
20 Rainsford, *An Historical Account of the Black Empire of Hayti*, 263.
21 Hoermann, "Figures of Terror," 159.
22 Hoermann, "Figures of Terror," 159.
23 Brickhouse, *Transamerican Literary Relations and the Nineteenth-Century Public Sphere*, 116.
24 Underwood, *The Poets of Haiti*, n.p. Ignace and Émile Nau were well known in Haiti in the 1830s for their publication of *Republicain*, a literary magazine that was censored by the Haitian government; Daut, "The 'Alpha and Omega' of Haitian Literature," 1.
25 Ramsey, *The Spirits and the Law*, 58–62.
26 The term *frère de baptême* (baptismal brother) in the most literal sense indicates children baptized together, but in Haitian traditions, the term also implies extended kinship ties.
27 Nau, *Isalina*, 41. All translations of Nau are mine.
28 Nau, *Isalina*, 42.
29 Dayan, *Haiti, History, and the Gods*, 37.
30 Brickhouse, *Transamerican Literary Relations*, 116.
31 Nau, *Isalina*, 53.
32 Nau, *Isalina*, 55.
33 Nau, *Isalina*, 56.
34 Brickhouse, *Transamerican Literary Relations*, 116–17.
35 Ramsey, *The Spirits and the Law*, 7.
36 Nau, *Isalina*, 54.
37 Jenson, *Beyond the Slave Narrative*, 47.

Works Cited

Brickhouse, Anna. *Transamerican Literary Relations and the Nineteenth-Century Public Sphere*. Cambridge: Cambridge University Press, 2004.

Daut, Marlene L. "The 'Alpha and Omega' of Haitian Literature: Baron de Vastey and the U.S. Audience of Haitian Political Writing." *Comparative Literature* 64, no. 1 (2012): 49–72.

Dayan, Joan. *Haiti, History, and the Gods*. Berkeley: University of California Press, 1995.

Fishburn, Katherine. *The Problem of Embodiment in Early African American Narrative*. Westport: Greenwood Press, 1997.

Hoermann, Raphael, "Figures of Terror: The 'Zombie' and the Haitian Revolution." *Atlantic Studies: Global Currents* 14, no. 2 (2016): 152–73.

Jenson, Deborah. *Beyond the Slave Narrative: Politics, Sex, and Manuscripts in the Haitian Revolution*. Liverpool: Liverpool University Press, 2011.

Laurent, Gerard M. *Toussaint Louverture, à travers sa correspondence 1794–1798*. Madrid: Industrias Graficas España, 1953.

Lauro, Sarah Juliet. *The Transatlantic Zombie: Slavery, Rebellion, and Living*. New Brunswick: Rutgers University Press, 2015.

Madiou, Thomas. *Histoire d'Haiti*. Vols. 1, 2, & 3. Edited by Gérard M. Laurent. Port-au-Prince: Editions Henri Deschamps, 1989.

Nau, Ignace. *Isalina, ou, une scène créole*. Port au Prince: Coucoune, 2000.

Nesbitt, Nick. *Jean-Bertrand Aristide Presents Toussaint Louverture and the Haitian Revolution*. Edited by Nick Nesbitt, Introduction by Jean-Bertrand Aristide. London: Verso, 2008.

Popkin, Jeremy. *Facing Racial Revolution: Eyewitness Accounts of the Haitian Insurrection*. Edited and Translated by Jeremy Popkin. Chicago: University of Chicago Press, 1997.

Rainsford, Marcus. *An Historical Account of the Black Empire of Hayti*. Edited and Introduction by Paul Youngquist and Grégory Pierrot. Durham: Duke University Press, 2013.

Ramsey, Kate. *The Spirits and the Law: Vodou and Power in Haiti*. Chicago: University of Chicago Press, 2011.

Underwood, Edna Worthley. *The Poets of Haiti, 1782–1934*. Translated by Edna Worthley Underwood, woodcuts by Pétion Savain, glossary by Charles F. Pressoir. Portland, ME: The Mosher Press, 1934.

2

White and Black Zombies: How Race Rewrites the Zombie Narrative

Cécile Accilien

Images of zombies in the United States are believed to have their origins in encounters that soldiers had with Haitian Vodou during the US Occupation of Haiti, which lasted from 1915 to 1934. Since then, the fascination with zombies as a concept and a cultural phenomenon has become a staple of US popular culture. The zombie figure—a corpse that is under the control of a living human being—has appeared in Michael Jackson's 1983 music video "Thriller," in which he dances with a group of zombies, as well as in anime and manga comics, art, and video games. Zombies are now so engrained in the US imaginary that in 2011, for example, the Centers for Disease Control and Prevention called its emergency preparedness plan the "Zombie Preparedness Campaign" to teach the public about being prepared for various emergencies, including floods, tornadoes, hurricanes, and earthquakes.[1] The plan contains the following slogan: "Get a Kit/Make a Plan/Be Prepared." Similarly, a nonprofit community service and disaster preparedness organization based in St. Louis, Missouri, is known as the Zombie Squad. After watching the British horror movie *28 Days Later*, a group of friends decided that zombies could be used as a metaphor to help people think about how to be prepared for any type of real-life emergency. The organization has a large online presence.[2] The CDC and the Zombie Squad appear to be taking advantage of the fact that, given the resurgence of zombies in popular culture, the image of a zombie apocalypse will make people take disaster preparedness more seriously.

Meanwhile, in Haiti, a Black and economically disadvantaged country in the Global South that has been forced to bear the moniker "the poorest country in the Western hemisphere," the figure of the zombie continues to be frightening, a symbol that references the ongoing power of histories of colonialism, slavery, and imperialism. Haiti gained its independence from the French in 1804 after a twelve-year revolt, yet the US government did not recognize the new nation for over fifty years because acknowledging a Black country's independence would have forced it to deal with the presence of slavery in the United States. Slavery was not only a very profitable business, it was also at the foundations of the nation's economy. Yet slavery was in part justified by white colonizers who cast Blacks as savages who needed to be saved. Zombies are often conflated with "voodoo," a term that represents a biased misrepresentation of the Haitian Vodou religion. The Vodou religion was brought to the so-called "New" World by people ripped from the African continent starting in the seventeenth century, but into the present day, the Vodou religion has been demonized by both Americans and Europeans, and has served as propaganda for evangelists under the guise of saving souls. "Voodoo" and, by extension, zombies have long been used to vilify Haiti and to present Haitians as a people unable to govern themselves.

William Seabrook popularized the concept of the zombie for US audiences in his sensationalist book *The Magic Island*,[3] drawn from his experiences of living in Haiti for two years during the 1920s.[4] This account was the basis of the film *White Zombie* (1932), directed by Edward Halperin, which originated the genre.[5] The film is a simple tale of a white couple who goes to Haiti to get married. A plantation owner falls for the woman and, with the help of a "voodoo" master, transforms her into a zombie. Some Haitians are represented as evil beings who participate in the zombification of others. As Zachary Crockett and Javier Zarracina note, "*White Zombie* explicitly stoked America's worst fears of voodooism and turned the spiritual belief system into a horror motif. Haiti is presented as a primitive, orderless place where witchcraft and zombies run rampant."[6] The title of the film expresses the operative assumption that zombies are Black unless otherwise noted. Here, the zombie's whiteness makes her more terrifying in the context of the white popular culture of this era, with its fears of miscegenation, because a white person becomes "Black."

Toni Pressley-Sanon asserts that films such as *White Zombie* (1932) and *I Walked with a Zombie* (1943) result from "the foreign white male imagination [and] acted as cathartic expressions... of their fear of a black nation."[7] She further notes that these films represent "white male imperialist longing for a return to the colonial period."[8] But these films demonstrate, I think, something more complex than simply colonialist nostalgia. Rather, they suggest that within these longings for simplified power is hidden a sense of the deep wrongness of the basis of that power. This is the continuation of the narrative of Haiti being a frightening and unruly place—a narrative that began toward the end of the eighteenth century, with the beginning of the Haitian Revolution, as enslaved African and African-descended people in Haiti rose up against the colonizers/enslavers. Thus the power and fear of Haiti, in the way that it performs the ongoing raw wounds left by slavery and colonialism in the white imaginary, seemed to potentially inflame white guilt on a subconscious level, and was therefore relegated to the category of irredeemable "other."

The sequel to *White Zombie*, called *Revolt of the Zombies* (1936), along with films such as *I Walked with a Zombie* (1943), was instrumental to Haitian culture, and by extension Haiti itself, becoming synonymous with the zombie narrative in US popular imagination. And since the 1968 movie *Night of the Living Dead*, directed by George Romero, the concept of the zombie has been used to describe various ills in our contemporary culture, be they ecological disaster, racism, scientific excess, capitalism, or uncontrollable consumerism.[9]

In the United States, there was renewed interest in zombification from a sociological and medical perspective with the publication of Wade Davis' bestseller *The Serpent and the Rainbow: A Harvard's Scientist's Astonishing Journey into the Secret Societies of Haitian Voodoo, Zombies, and Magic* (1985), in which he investigated indigenous plants that are used to zombify people. In the book Davis explored the case of Clairvius Narcisse, who was zombified for a period of two years, and came to the conclusion that this zombification was probably due to the use of tetrodotoxin, a hallucinogenic plant known as datura, mixed with cultural beliefs. Davis' claims were challenged and criticized due to scientific inaccuracies, but the book nonetheless served as inspiration for Wes Craven and Bill Pullman's popular horror film *The Serpent and the Rainbow* (1988), which popularized zombie images and their connections to Haiti for a new generation. The harm done by such characterizations is that Haitian people and Haitian culture may be automatically linked to zombies. Zombies do not have human qualities; they are not able to think and they attack other human beings. Thus, in the US popular imaginary, Haitians themselves become zombie-like creatures, "voodoo" practitioners, and devil worshippers; simply by virtue of their place of birth, they have no morality, and they are represented as being rightly punished because of this.

Race is central to portrayals of zombies in the United States—because zombies have been incorporated into white forms of representation, they can appear at an event such as a family celebration in the white Midwest, and yet the frisson of fear they still generate in this context is owing to the obscured fact of long-term misunderstandings of and biases against Haitian culture. As a Haitian American who lived in Kansas from 2015 to 2020, I was fascinated by an annual local phenomenon known as the Lawrence Zombie Walk. When I attended my first Zombie Walk in October 2016, I was at once amazed, amused, and annoyed by the performance. In this exclusively white, Midwestern setting, the zombie figure had become the focal point of a celebration, fun for all ages. When I attended the event, some people danced to Michael Jackson's "Thriller," while others visited so-called zombification stations or took "blood baths," in which they had fake blood poured on them. There were also the usual festival staples, like face painting for adults and children and food trucks. Some zombies wandered the street aimlessly, while others interacted with the crowd. At the beginning of the walk, people generally gather in South Park at sundown and walk down Massachusetts Street, the main street in downtown Lawrence, where a large number of businesses are located, to watch the zombies. The colorful and disturbing scenes included people with ripped-off clothing and lots of blood. Some people pretending to be zombies spit blood at the crowd. There were also groups of people in South Park with toy guns shooting at the zombies. One local reporter described the scene:

> Fake blood drips down his suit as the zombie shuffles down Massachusetts Street. One arm clutches a brain and the other arm hangs by a thread and falls to the ground. The zombie turns to the man next to him. "Can you give me a hand?" he asks. Parade watchers laugh as the man picks it up and the two continue their walk down the street. Terry Taylor and his wife, Liz Taylor... have attended the Zombie Walk since the first one took place. They loved the event for the ability to bring people together in the name of spooky things... For the Taylors, it was especially important to make the Zombie Walk as friendly as possible. There's just a big, good community feeling of everyone coming together and enjoying this—and that's what it should be.[10]

All of this is staged and performed in the name of fun and service to the community. People bring items to donate to the local food and homeless shelters, as well as to the Lawrence Humane Society and ARC of Douglas County, an organization that provides services to individuals with intellectual and developmental disabilities. The Zombie Walk is a "family" event meant to entertain, ostensibly for a good cause. One Zombie Walk participant commented,

> I was talking to my friend about what if tourists were to come [to Lawrence] and not knowing what is going on, go downtown and see all these zombies. What would they do? I would freak out. I would be like, whoa, what is going on in this town? If you didn't know and you just kind of came by it would be really awkward.[11]

As the image of the zombie has fully entered the US mainstream, it has been largely stripped of its power to truly terrify (in the assessment of this participant, the scene is at most "awkward").

As I observed the spectacle, I considered this simultaneous mockery and adoption of the figure of the zombie. As performed by white residents of Lawrence, the zombie had become unmoored from its origins, "othered" in a way that seemed, erroneously, to have nothing to do with race whatsoever. Images of the zombie in US pop culture are connected to the history of Haiti, yet the reality of Haiti has often been erased from these images, creating a blank space where the dominant culture inscribes its own values and anxieties. People were apparently ignorant of the origins of the zombie trope and its connections to race and the history of slavery and colonialism, not thinking in the slightest about the history of what they were doing. They performed this identity freely, unconscious of being observed by someone from Haiti with a strong sense of what the zombie meant in other contexts. This is the performance of a power differential that functions when members of the dominant culture adopt signifiers from less dominant or actively oppressed cultures and not be held accountable for reproducing relations of dominance.[12]

It is critical to counterbalance such popular culture representations of zombies with portrayals of zombies by Haitian authors in order to avoid marginalizing the origins of the concept and thereby in a sense seeming to tacitly accept the way in which the dominant popular culture in the United States represents it. The differences between how the zombie figure appears in Haiti and in Kansas, for example, highlight the ongoing sociopolitical power of the United States, which includes its capacity to decide when it wants to either denigrate or embrace a particular "othered" cultural phenomenon. (To throw these dynamics into relief, it is instructive to consider what would happen if the people impersonating zombies in Lawrence, Kansas, were immigrants from Haiti or other islands in the Caribbean.)

In the Haitian context, the zombie is generally not viewed as a sensational (if tamed) image of otherness. In Haitian folklore, a zombie is a frightening figure. Everything that surrounds the zombie narrative is evil and devoid of hope.[13] The term refers to someone who died of unnatural causes, such as murder, and whose body lingered at the gravesite. If a witch doctor, or *bòkò*, found the corpse while it was lingering at the grave, he or she could revive it and use it as a slave. (A *bòkò* is generally defined as a magician who has the power to heal.) This creature that exists in a state between life and death is then referred to as a zombie. In the Haitian context, zombification is associated with enslavement, stolen labor, and the exploitation of the laboring class. It is also a crime. Article 246 of the Haitian Criminal Code states that it "[i]s considered attempt on life by poisoning the use made against a person of substances which, without giving death, will cause a more-or-less prolonged state of lethargy, regardless of the manner in which these substances were used and regardless of the consequences."[14] The existence of this law evidences the fact that in contemporary Haiti, zombification is not simply a myth, or even just a metaphor. It is a practice that the law sees fit to regulate.

Although zombies are not, in fact, central to the practice of Vodou, there are people who may call themselves *manbo* or *hougan* (Vodou priestess or priest) or *vodouyizan* who, in fact, practice zombification. The late Ati Max Beauvoir, considered to be one of the most respected hougan in Haiti and around the world, proposed the following link between vodou, social justice, and zombification. He noted instances when a vodouyizan may be zombified—for example, if someone has committed a crime against the community or other people, because it is believed that you should not kill people. According to Beauvoir, generally if the person is judged as a criminal, the *vodouyizan*, in accordance with others in the community, keeps the body but takes away the person's spirit, which makes them unable to function because they no longer have the willpower to act.[15] Thus, the zombification phenomenon may function as a way to gain justice—justice that in this case exists outside the formal bounds of "the law."

René Depestre points to the fact that many Haitian people believe in the real presence of zombies in his novel *Hadriana in All My Dreams* (1988), which is set in the southern Haitian town of Jacmel during the 1938 carnival. He writes:

> According to Uncle Ferdinand, a zombie—man, woman, or child—is a person whose metabolism has been slowed down under the effects of some organic toxin, to the point of giving all appearances of death: general muscular hypotonia, stiffened limbs, imperceptible pulse, absence of breath and ocular reflexes, lowered core temperature, paleness, and failure of the mirror test. But despite these outward signs of death, the zombie actually retains the use of his or her mental faculties. Clinically deceased, interred and buried publicly, he or she is raised from the grave by a witch doctor in the hours following the burial and made to labor in a field (a zombie garden) or in an urban workshop (a zombie factory). Whenever there are doubts as to whether or not someone has died of natural causes, steps are taken to avoid all risks of zombification.[16]

In Haiti, as we can see clearly here, the zombie is primarily associated with fear.

Depestre riffs on the plot of the film *White Zombie*; the title character, Hadriana, is a white French woman living in Haiti who, on the morning of her wedding to a young Haitian man from an elite family, is transformed into a zombie after she drinks a mysterious potion. She collapses at the altar, and thus her wedding becomes her funeral. The community is fascinated with Hadriana's race and complexion, so even though she is transformed into a zombie, their fear is surpassed by their fascination with her whiteness, in a reference to the plot of *White Zombie*. Through his conscious juxtaposition with an imperial narrative of Haiti, Depestre indicates the way in which zombies and zombification register very differently in the Haitian imaginary than they do in the US imaginary. For instance, the zombifier Lil' Joseph and his wife Faith zombify people in order to exploit them. They have no scruples or morals:

> Lil' Joseph and his wife Faith.. showed up at the HASCO sugar factory leading a party of ragged peasants, all of whom were raring to do some serious cutting on the plantations of the American company. As they were being hired, these men—their expressions dull and their eyes vacant—proved incapable of stating their names.... Witnesses to the scene realized that they were dealing with a zombified workforce—a bunch of poor wretches who had been taken one night from their "final" resting place and made to slave away in the service of a cruel master.[17]

It is no coincidence that the individuals who are zombified are working in an American sugar company. Sugar production is intrinsically connected to European colonialism and slavery in much of the Caribbean, and the Haitian zombie is synonymous with slavery and with other malevolent and destructive forces. Depestre writes, "The fate of the zombie might be compared to that of the colonial plantation slave of old Saint-Domingue. Its destiny corresponds, on the mystical plane, to that of the Africans deported to the Americas to replace the decimated Indian labor force in the colony's fields, mines, and factories." Indeed, he continues, the "zombie is in fact one of the traps of colonial history—something Haitians might have internalized and integrated into their own worldview. It could be a symbol of an imaginary world borne of tobacco, coffee, sugar, cotton, cacao, or spice—one of the many symbols of the ontological shipwreck of man on the American plantations."[18] Zombies in the Haitian context do not have agency and power—in fact, they are quintessentially *dis*-empowered beings. It is worth noting that in this sense they are the polar opposite of the zombie figures roaming around Lawrence, Kansas—individuals who have chosen to adopt the guise of the zombie, and who are not scary specifically by reason of their agency. In the Haitian context, by contrast, people do not choose to be zombies—they are *zombified*, a fate not to be wished upon anyone. In this rendering of a white zombie, Depestre calls attention to the fact that white colonialists have coopted the figure of the zombie—but in the process, they become zombified as well. Thus the process of systematized oppression may ultimately devour those with power as well as those without it.

The white American fascination with zombies promises to continue, as is evident from the movies and TV shows depicting zombies in various settings and the fact that the zombie culture is an integral part of many people's worlds—yet as the participants in the Lawrence Zombie Walk turn themselves into bloody and soulless entities, we see the meta-history of colonialism and imperial oppression inscribed on white bodies. And in Haiti, which continues to suffer the consequences of the transatlantic slave trade, colonization, neo-colonization, occupation, dictatorship, economic and political disempowerment, and environmental disasters such as earthquakes and hurricanes, the zombie remains a real and terrifying figure.

Notes

1 See https://www.cdc.gov/cpr/zombie/index.htm. See also Khan, "Preparedness 101."
2 See Westhoff, "Doomsday Disciples."
3 Seabrook, *The Magic Island.*
4 Two other films worth mentioning from that era are *Ouanga*, directed by George Terwilliger (1936), and *I Walked with a Zombie*, directed by Jacques Tourneur (1943).
5 Halperin, *White Zombie.*
6 Crockett and Zarracina, "How the Zombie Represents America's Deepest Fears."
7 Pressley-Sanon, *Zombifying a Nation*, 9.
8 Pressley-Sanon, *Zombifying a Nation*, 25.
9 Romero, *Night of the Living Dead.*
10 Counts, "How Local Business Brought Lawrence's Annual Zombie Walk Back from the Dead."
11 "Lawrence, Kansas, Zombie Walk."
12 We see this process unfolding as well, for example, in the musical *Zombies*, which premiered on the Disney Channel, whose target audience is primarily children aged six through sixteen. From the Atlanta Zombie Apocalypse to the Francisco Zombie Walk and the Chicago Zombie March, zombies are also becoming an integral part of tourism campaigns and local entertainment in the United States.
13 "Figure of exploitation *par excellence* and staple of the Vodou universe, the Haitian zombie is a being without essence—lobotomized, depersonalized, and reduced

through malevolent magic to a state of impotence. Without any recollection of its past or hope for the future, the zombie exists only in the present of its exploitation. It represents the lowest being on the social scale: a non-person that has not only lost its humanity, but that has accepted, without protest, the status of victim" in Glover, "Exploiting the Undead," 107–8.

14 Guha and Boring, "Does the Haitian Criminal Code Outlaw Making Zombies?"
15 Saint-Louis, "My Interview with Max Beauvoir Part #3."
16 Depestre, *Hadriana in All My Dreams*, 127–8.
17 Depestre, *Hadriana in All My Dreams*, 134–5.
18 Depestre, *Hadriana in All My Dreams*, 169.

Works Cited

Counts, Katie. "How Local Business Brought Lawrence's Annual Zombie Walk Back from the Dead." *The University Daily Kansan*, October 18, 2019. http://www.kansan.com/arts_and_culture/how-local-business-brought-lawrence-s-annual-zombie-walk-back/article_c9db301e-f1e3-11e9-8b5c-1bfd07fed771.html.

Crockett, Zachary, and Javier Zarracina. "How the Zombie Represents America's Deepest Fears: A Sociopolitical History of Zombies, from Haiti to the Walking Dead." *Vox*, October 31, 2016. https://www.vox.com/policy-and-politics/2016/10/31/13440402/zombie-political-history.

Davis, Wade. *The Serpent and the Rainbow: A Harvard's Scientist's Astonishing Journey into the Secret Societies of Haitian Voodoo, Zombies, and Magic*. New York: Simon & Schuster, 1985.

Depestre, René. *Hadriana in All My Dreams*. Translated by Kaiama L. Glover. Brooklyn, NY: Akashic Books, [1988] 2017.

Glover, Kaiama. "Exploiting the Undead: The Usefulness of the Zombie in Haitian Literature." *Journal of Haitian Studies* 11, no. 2 (Fall 2005): 105–21.

Guha, Anne, and Nicolas Boring. "Does the Haitian Criminal Code Outlaw Making Zombies?" *In Custodia Legis: Law Librarians of Congress*. Library of Congress, October 31, 2014. https://blogs.loc.gov/law/2014/10/does-the-haitian-criminal-code-outlaw-making-zombies/.

I Walked With a Zombie. [Film] Dir. Jacques Tourneur, Los Angeles: RKO Pictures, 1943.

Khan, Ali S. "Preparedness 101: Zombie Apocalypse." *Public Health Matters Blog*, May 16, 2011. https://blogs.cdc.gov/publichealthmatters/2011/05/preparedness-101-zombie-apocalypse/. Accessed May 28, 2020.

Lauro, Sara Juliet. *The Transatlantic Zombie: Slavery, Rebellion and Living Death*. New Brunswick, NJ: Rutgers University Press, 2015.

Lauro, Sara Juliet, ed. *Zombie Theory: A Reader*. Minneapolis: University of Minnesota Press, 2017.

LHS Budget. "Lawrence KS Zombie Walk," YouTube, October 31, 2012. 1m9seconds-1m27s. https://www.youtube.com/watch?v=LnAS8xp94Ew.

Martin, Kameela L. *Envisioning Black Feminist Voodoo Aesthetics: African Spirituality in American Cinema.* Lanham, MD: Lexington Books, 2016.

Night of the Living Dead. [Film] Dir. George Romero, Pittsburgh, PA: Image Ten, 1968.

Ouanga. [Film] Dir. George Terwilliger, New York: George Terwilliger Productions, 1936.

Pressley-Sanon, Toni. *Zombifying a Nation: Race, Gender and the Haitian Loas on Screen.* Jefferson, NC: McFarland Publishing, 2016.

Saint-Louis, Valerio. "My Interview with Max Beauvoir Part #3: Vodou, Sanpwel, Bizango, Zombification." September 18, 2015. https://www.youtube.com/watch?v=KY5NNfnk8OY.

Seabrook, William. *The Magic Island.* New York: Harcourt, Brace & Company, 1929.

The Serpent and the Rainbow. [Film] Dir. Wes Craven and Bill Pullman, Los Angeles: MCA/Universal Pictures, 1988.

Westhoff, Ben. "Doomsday Disciples." *St. Louis Riverfront Times*, February 7, 2007. https://www.riverfronttimes.com/stlouis/doomsday-disciples/Content?oid=2483838. For more information, see https://www.zombiehunters.org/forum/.

White Zombie. [Film] Dir. Victor Halperin, Hollywood: United Artists, 1932. https://www.youtube.com/watch?v=lQ0hL4EBC58.

3

Decolonizing the Zombie: *I Walked with a Zombie*'s Critique of Centrist Liberalism

Stephen Shapiro

What does it mean to decolonize the undead? If we seek to disinter the past in order to liberate ourselves from our own contemporary nightmare, then studies of Gothic, Horror, and the Weird must be central to any emancipatory endeavor. For narratives and figurations of the undead are rich with guiding spirits for the future. Could the zombie be a sentinel, rather than obstacle, for a way forward out of the past's rotting matter?

Yet removing the past's trauma of violence and social inequality is not simply an act of flipping the switch, of jolting peoples from conditions of coerced inertia into ones of liberated vitality. No substantive social change will occur unless it contains a thorough engagement with the structural conditions that created the catastrophe in the first place. Could a decolonial approach help us here, and how would that differ from other emancipatory intentions? Nick Couldry neatly summarizes the distance of a decolonial approach from prior endeavors. He argues that an earlier "postcolonial critique" responded to the conditions of historical colonialism by making a "counter-claim against capitalism, globalism, and neoliberalism in our times, as it seeks to make evident their colonial roots even if these roots are partially obscured by contemporary ideologies."[1] Here "postcolonial theories posit that the foundation of colonial modes of representation is *difference*" which is "not merely a passive description, but a form of systemic violence."[2] Tied to this critique is a suggestion that Enlightenment-era knowledge claims, especially those using "the language of modernity and universal knowledge, inscribed in historical discourses,"[3] were imperialist devices deploying civilizationist claims to ensure that colonial subjects emulated their colonizers.

Decoloniality, on the other hand, for Couldry, provides "strategies for surviving in a neo- or postcolonial context" by looking for "intellectual resources from beyond the Western canon," especially ones "inspired by movements from the Global South."[4] Additionally, while postcolonialism was perceived as sacrificing economic factors in favor of more cultural ones, decolonial theory understands "coloniality of power as both an ideological and material phenomenon."[5]

We might add to this criticism of postcolonial discourse theory the claim that it not only marginalized the role of capitalism as a primary driver of modernity but also that the keyword "Western" was used in as homogenizing fashion as was "Orientalism," as the former term both erased conflicts, counter-alliances, and political alterations *within* the so-called West and reinstated a mirror image of civilizationalist claims, wherein the ideal was now located in "the Rest," rather than "the West," as if non-Western nations are exempt from their own capitalist procedures and historical inequalities.[6]

Building on Couldry, I want to add a Warwick School perspective that uses a world-systems knowledge movement as a way of unthinking the categories of cultural analysis that obstruct a decolonial motivation. From world-systems analysis, we initially take the claim that a capitalist world-system emerges in the late fifteenth century and it is one that operates through the creation of social inequalities (rather than simply social differences) as a way to achieve its drive for endless accumulation for accumulation's sake. One feature that distinguishes a world-system from other materialist approaches on international divisions of labor is its insistence that capitalism must operate through labor relations that are weakly proletarianized, often involving poorly, precariously, or frankly unwaged and coerced labor. Recent arguments regarding racial capitalism and the persistence of bound labor and necropolitical mastery within capitalism are ones that fundamentally belong to and help differentiate world-systems perspectives from other "global" approaches.

For our purposes, it will not immediately be the elements of the world-system itself that can decolonize the zombie but their use within Immanuel Wallerstein's description of centrist liberalism's secular trend (or long duration). Wallerstein argued that the interlaced American, French, and Haitian Revolutions, along with rebellions in Ireland, Egypt, and among the indigenous peoples of South America, created two self-evident social truths.[7] The first was the inevitability of ongoing social transformation. No longer would it be possible to imagine eternal or unchanging societies. Tied to this realization was a second truth involving the shift of power away from the sovereignty of blood aristocracies and the Roman Catholic Church to forms of democratic or popular rule.[8]

Modernity of change and popular rule then gave rise to three metastrategies in response. Wallerstein calls these metastrategies, ideologies.[9] First to appear was conservatism, exemplified by the writing of Burke and de Maistre. Conservatism sought to slow down the trajectory of these truths by advancing the notion that small groups should continue to rule, and these would be the ones associated with pre-existing elites, like the gentry, according to ideals of family, community, tradition, established religion, and resistance to transformative legislation. The third ideology came later during the 1840s and is variously known as radicalism, socialism, communism, or Marxism. This perspective not only embraced the new truths but also sought to accelerate their arrival through sudden, mass discontinuity, that is, revolution.

In between conservatism and radicalism, both chronologically and positionally, is centrist liberalism. Liberalism accepts the inevitability of change and democracy, but it seeks to moderate their tempo and regulate their expansion in order to prevent explosive and disruptive social changes, especially those that might limit capitalist accumulation. Liberalism sought to ensure this control by a *gradual* expansion of voting suffrage, as the means for managing the extension of representative democracy beyond white, propertied men, and guarding access to (higher) education, as the apparatus that would credentialize the expertise of the technocratic and bureaucratic managers who sought to legitimize themselves as the best rulers of society, ones empowered ostensibly on merit, rather than blood lineage, cronyism, or popular authority.

While each ideology claimed to be against the post-sovereign state, each had their own strategy for using it to their own ends. Conservatives sought to legislate and criminalize threats to their authority. Radicals sought to organize political action as a way of occupying the state in order to re-engineer or dismantle it. Liberals *theorized*; they deployed a set of statist concepts, which they then gave themselves the task of administering, and they refashioned a set of institutions as their material barracks and proposed an intertwining set of binary oppositions as a means of canalizing and controlling popular rule.[10] Among these distinctions are the separation between the public and the private, normal and abnormal, and, above all, citizen subjectivity and those consigned to social death as exchangeable objects: women, non-whites, proletarians, and so on. Consequently, liberals' rhetoric of universalizing equality was a promise betrayed in practice by their introduction of a new set of social distinctions to replace older aristocratic and religious ones. As Wallerstein explains:

> When inequality was the norm, there was no need to make any further distinction than that between those of different rank—generically between

noble and commoner. But when equality became the official norm, then it was suddenly crucial to know who was in fact included in the "all" who have equal rights—that is, who are the "active" citizens. The more equality was proclaimed as a moral principle, the more obstacles—juridical, political, economic, and cultural—were instituted to prevent its realization. The concept, citizen, forced the crystallization and rigidification—both intellectual and legal—of a long list of binary distinctions that then came to form the cultural underpinnings of the capitalist world-economy in the nineteenth and twentieth centuries: bourgeois and proletarian, man and woman, adult and minor, breadwinner and housewife, majority and minority, White and Black, European and non-European, educated and ignorant, skilled and unskilled, specialist and amateur, scientist and layman, high culture and low culture, heterosexual and homosexual, normal and abnormal, able-bodied and disabled, and of course the ur-category which all of these others imply—civilized and barbarian.[11]

Centrist liberalism's theories were then institutionalized in two main ways. First, since formal education was made into a central mechanism for producing expertise, liberals spent a tremendous amount of effort toward reconstructing the university for their own ends. The older faculties of law, medicine, theology, and philosophy were transformed into contained disciplines that were given control over aspects now considered to be autonomous fields, each with their own particular methodologies, as a way of verifying truth claims made by trained experts. So, for instance, economics was given the marketplace; political science, the state; sociology, the study of the so-called advanced civil societies; anthropology, the study of "primitive" groups without a large textual record; and Orientalism, as the study of former world-empires, which did have textual archives but whose government had fallen into disrepair, such as China, India, and Egypt.[12]

One more academic field was constructed that has consequences for this study: Classics. In the early nineteenth century, spurred on by Romantic celebrations of Greek Independence efforts against Ottoman Turkey, ancient Greece and Rome were moved out of the disciplinary category of Orientalism as a way of creating a white, non-Muslim past that would be taken as the genetic foundation for Western European civilization's development into modernity.[13] This distinction was also a feature of competition within the core nation-states of the capitalist world-system since Germany and Britain devoted particular attention to the invention of a Greco-Roman classical tradition, as a means of differentiating themselves from Napoleonic France and its occupying links to Egypt.[14] Yet this tactical deployment involving the separation of "white" Greece and Rome from

"Black" Egypt was never a clean break or without a paradoxical self-awareness of its incoherence. The resulting strained awareness of the inconsistencies within this invented division was compensated by the creation of cultural productions that might mediate its tensions. One of these "odd" categories is that which we today call "Gothic" (and Horror and the Weird). It is not accidental that the two national cultures that largely produced Gothic narratives are the ones that sought to position themselves in opposition to Napoleonic France's reopening of the door to Africa and the Middle East through its invasion of Egypt accompanied with a host of academic observers. As Gothic-associated cultural productions are inescapably the terrible child of centrist liberalism's production of disciplinary subjects and its creation of modern mythologies about European genesis, they also became a lens through which we can see the machinery of the capitalist world-system and its historical conflicts and transformations.

For instance, liberalism's knowledge formations were aided by their incorporation of Baconian science and Newtonian concepts of uniform, linear time and the reproducibility of events, especially as the social sciences were tasked to produce quasi-empirical, normative "laws" that could simplify social complexity into knowable laws.[15] Claims for the correctness of developmental predictability seemed believable because centrist liberalism was lucky in its timing to appear during a long phase of global expansion. As liberalism's knowledge claims and theoretical prognostications seemed to be true, centrist liberalism became so dominant that it forced conservatives and radicals to accept and adopt many of its claims.[16]

Throughout the nineteenth century, liberalism managed to endure through various capitalist crises as it disarmed working-class rebellion through its skilled management of nationalism, reinforced through its educational structures, and controlled wealth redistribution through social welfare schemes. European welfare was largely financed through imperialist carving up the world in renewed instances of colonial brutality. Here liberalism's theoretical claims of knowable processes were turned into civilizational claims that embedded racism and the "white man's burden" of sociologizing the anthropological, of making the colonized mirror the colonizers, and looking to dictate the pace for their gradual incorporation toward citizenship. Yet when inter-imperialist tensions resulted in the First World War and ensuing demands for national self-determination, liberal planning was then turned into a model for the entire globe's development, a pathway that recently decolonized nations should follow.[17] When postwar liberalism began to fall into crisis by the 1960s, it had nowhere else to go and slowly began to recede before neoliberal tactics. It is this decline of liberalism's long secular trend, one going back to the late eighteenth century, which has created a space and context for decoloniality beyond postcoloniality.

In terms of the above, to decolonize does not mean simply insisting on anti-Eurocentrism. It is not "the West," or even European-oriented ideas, that ought to be the target of decolonial critiques. Instead, decolonial criticism should be directed against centrist liberalism and its deployment of developmental regulation, linear prediction, and the maintenance of the binary exclusions of citizen and social death in order to maintain capitalist profiteering. In this sense, the decolonial project differs from one version of the "postcolonial" one in that it sees the goal of gaining citizenship privilege by the recently emancipated as itself a limit. Hence, decolonization is not the pluralism of diversity; it is the detonation of the theoretical claims of liberalism, especially the ways in which the personnel of institutional knowledge formations (i.e., the assumed writers and readers of this collection) consider their evidentiary material as a means of legitimizing their own social authority, privilege, and status. If intellectual resources from the Global South are often invoked, this has more to do with their likelihood of having less liberal centrist content than from any difference within an itself essentialized notion of the West.

The mandate to decolonize the undead comes then as a means of dissecting Gothic narratives, broadly conceived, to show their anatomy as a product of the developmentalist and civilizational split that separated Greco-Roman "classics" from Afro-Egyptian orientalisms. As discussed below, the figuration of the zombie endorses centrist liberalism's conceptual divisions of citizen and subject of social death, often in ways that still bear the imprint of Anglo-German competition against France and its colonies. Thus, to decolonize the zombie means, first, going beyond simple emancipation or independence claims in order to challenge the method underpinning the citizen-state subjectivity/social death objectivity split and, second, highlighting the context of conflicts for hegemony within the capitalist world-system.

Decolonizing Literary and Cultural Studies

If decolonizing literary and cultural studies means unthinking liberalism's assumptions, some guidelines are consequential. We must look for regularities of appearance within a phase's curation of cultural expression, rather depend on fictions of transhistorical autonomous lineages. Here we must self-emancipate from a literary-studies Newtonianism that insists on seeing narrative generic figurations as a cultural "tradition" that has an untroubled, linear developmental passage. Instead, we need to see each cluster of figurations as a *curation*, a selection and arrangement of particular elements, some of which are familiar, albeit obsolete, while others are new due to the onset of emerging historical events and pressures. Each historical phase foregrounds and disregards specific figurative elements, often highlighting features that its immediate precursor moment disregarded. By insisting on a universal or "authentic" meaning of the zombie and its putative folklore as determining the present, we participate in centrist liberalism's recolonizing of cultural elements for its own purposes. Instead, we need to gain a better sense of why and how cultural figurations function within their own conjuncture.

For instance, while it has become common today to insist on the context of Atlantic slavery and rebellion in treatments of the zombie, this focus can often obscure the actual problem that sparks zombie figuration at different times.[18] As Kee says, "Because zombies become intertwined with the ways in which many people conceive of vodou and Haiti, the tendency to associate zombies with slavery (and nothing else) ties these three concepts (Haiti, vodou, zombie) together in a way that is indicative of an overall victimization."[19] Yet throughout the nineteenth century and well into the mid-twentieth, the primary and initiating reference for most treatments of the zombie was not slavery in itself, as a transhistorical feature, but the uncertain status of the Black Republic after the declaration of Haitian independence. If Atlantic slavery and resistance was, indeed, the unchanging primary coordinate for zombie curation, then we would expect these tales to have been simultaneously prevalent throughout continental North America during this time.

Instead, nearly all the zombie tales in this phase closely link accounts of rural events within commentary on the various ways in which Haitian self-governance was perceived to have failed. In reality, the Black Republic's establishment was frustrated, not least by the imposition of crushing debt payments by France as a prerequisite of international recognition of Haitian self-determination. The period's zombie curation by Euro-American commentators contemplates liberalism's failed mythologies and bad faith claims, by suggesting that zombification is an apt metaphor for Haiti itself, as no longer a colony, but not yet an inter-state equal. In these stories, it is the figures of the Black Republic, and not either colonial slavery or the Revolution, that stand as the narrative touchstones.

Examples of this emphasis include "Salt Is Not for Slaves," the 1931 story penned by Canadian Garnett Weston under the pseudonym before he wrote the script for *White Zombie* (1932), which is narrated by an old woman, herself a zombie, who tells a story of incomplete liberation specifically as a result of Christophe, "Emperor Henry of Haiti['s]" proximity to a plantation run by a zombie overseer in lieu of an absent planter.[20] Inez Wallace's short story, "I Walked with a Zombie," used as the initial impetus for the later film of that name, begins: "Haiti, the dark island of mystery, where such incredible figures as Christophe, the Black Napoleon, rose to world fame as the Negro emperor."[21] Judge Henry Austin's "The Worship of the Snake," a 1912 first-person reportage in *The New England Magazine*, which may well have been the inspiration for H. P. Lovecraft's description of a vodou-like ceremony in "The Call of Cthulhu," likewise begins his essay by directing the reader's imagination to "the pleasure palace of the mad negro Christophe."[22] A December 13, 1937, *Life* magazine article, "Black Haiti: Where Old Africa and the New World Meet," cited as a source in the shooting script for *I Walked with a Zombie*, balances a sensationalized reproduction of "the only zombie ever photographed," an image provided to them by Zora Neal Hurston, against a realist documentary photospread of a vodou ritual.[23] Yet it, too, begins by speaking of "Christophe, black king of Haiti," who "was born a slave and his driving fury in life was to make his people respected… Today, as in the day of Christophe, the Negros of Haiti have no love of superimposed Western grandeur. They prefer the intricate, if primitive, culture that is their own." That Christophe, rather than L'Ouverture or Dessalines, is the familiar touchstone suggests that nonfilmic Anglophone zombie figurations before the Second World War highlight the Haitian Republic's challenge to models of linear nation-state development, more than standing as a reminder of Atlantic slavery or the Revolution's rebellion.

Furthermore, the complicated tripartite grouping of white creoles, the Black enslaved, and the mixed-race "free people of color" confuse the binary logics of nineteenth-century racial categories. For example, Austin conveys that zombification is not emancipation, but a competitive ruse to gain coerced labor from white slavers. The "trance-producing poison" was a device to steal the enslaved "because slaves, as valuable chattel, were carefully enumerated and a search would be instituted by the masters if a negro disappeared."[24] Consequently, a poison simulating death allowed for the enslaved to be buried in order for later exhumation. But this rising up did not result in emancipation. Instead it simply transferred the subject from being in bondage to a white master to being in bondage to a non-white one. In this sense, zombie curation before the mid-twentieth century locates a crisis of frustrated liberation, a failure of state equality, and liberalism's broken promise about the gradual expansion of suffrage and education's conscious-raising.

The first cluster of Hollywood films, from *White Zombie* (1932) to *I Walked with a Zombie* (1943), is substantively different from prior curations as they clearly select and disregard earlier elements in immediately noticeable ways. First, the Hollywood films distance themselves entirely from any historical recollection of the Republic and are as much influenced by *Jane Eyre* and *Dracula* (and their own filmic adaptions) as they are by African-transplanted rituals. Even in pre-code Hollywood, and its greater comfort in displaying the outrageous, the films are silent on the topics that appear in nearly every prior Anglophone discussion of vodou: human sacrifice ("the goat without horns") and cannibalism. Moreover, the films even abjure any mention of animal sacrifice or the use of snakes as a fetish for the spirits.

Second, the Hollywood films entirely silence the role of Haiti's disempowerment within the capitalist world-system as these films exclude the prior accounts' standard element of narrating the white narrator's encounter with Haitian political and social elites. For Hollywood, Haiti and its imagined surrogates are places without any kind of national government. This amnesia is intentional, since even William Seabrook's *The Magic Island* (1929) continually embeds his sensationalism with accounts of American military-backed capitalist interests in occupied Haiti. Austin's preceding essay piece for *The New England Magazine* focuses on President François Antoine Simon's government and ends with Simon telling Austin, "My policy is to encourage American capital."[25]

Rather than approach zombies from the perspective of the de facto zombification of the Haitian State by imperial interests, the pre–Second World War American cinema often uses the zombie to stage performances of gendered sexual violence as a way of raising concerns about the period's nascent feminism that may disrupt codes of racial segregation. The traffic in zombified women encodes a concern about "passing" (in both directions) across the color line in ways that social authorities cannot control. The 1936 film *Ouanga* situates zombie making as the result of a light-skinned plantation owner's anger at being refused by a white plantation owner, Adam Maynard (Philip Brandon), as a suitable wife. On board a ship returning from New York, where Klili Gordon (Fredi Washington) has presumably been passing as white, she is told by Maynard that he cannot marry her, since "you belong with your kind." Back on the island, Maynard's Black overseer Lestrange then courts Klili, justifying this advance because he notes that Maynard's new wife is "white." Klili replies, "I'm white, too, as white as she is." After insistently showing her face, hands, and chest to Lestrange (and the viewer), she asks if they look Black. Lestrange replies, "Your white skin doesn't change what is inside you—you're Black. You belong to us. You belong to me." Lestrange, played by Jewish American Sheldon Leonard in a filmic act of passing, then forcefully grabs and kisses her. The ensuing plot involves Klili's response to her racial dismissal and gendered body's inequality by zombifying Maynard's wife in an act of revenge.

The context of American domestic racism sets the grounds for a counterpoint. In the same year as *Ouanga*, two Black American female anthropologists traveled to Haiti on fellowships to pursue ethnographic accounts of vodou, both of which include a discussion of zombies: Zora Neal Hurston, who would publish her accounts of oral folklore as *Tell My Horse* (1938), and Katherine Dunham, whose research would not find publication until her memoir, *Island Possessed* (1969). Both accounts break from Hollywood's concerns as they seek, to varying effect, to revalue the African cultural legacy without sublimating it to the normative embodied forms of white America.

While Hurston's now well-known writing has been criticized for insufficiently challenging her white readership, Dunham's work uses zombie citation as a means of foregrounding historical complexity and cultural variegation. Both a classically trained dancer and academic student of anthropologist Melville J. Herskovits, who provided Dunham with letters of introduction gained from his own field research that led to *Life in a Haitian Valley* (1937) and the two-volume *Dahomey: An Ancient West African Kingdom* (1938), Dunham would combine her awareness of dance and training in field-participant research to study African cultural pathways in the New World through kinetic performances.

Dunham's Haitian research would find its first public presentation, however, not in print form, but through the staging of African-influenced dance, in movies like *Stormy Weather* (1943) and Dunham's own choreographed theater pieces, like *L' Ag' Ya* (1938), a tale of a love triangle that includes a sequence involving a visit to the Zombie King. In this zombie curation, Dunham seeks to make a claim for American culture as noteworthy for its cultural heterogeneity, much as had Du Bois early in his career. The anthropological model that Dunham was trained within depended on a declension model of cultural transmission and loss, wherein African tribal practice becomes folklore in the ruralized Caribbean and then secularized in America, where urbanized Black populations maintain formal elements of movement, but have little sense of the initial spiritual context for African dance. In this, Dunham follows Herskovits' lifelong scholarly project that argued for continuities of African culture in the New World and against the notion that the enslaved were entirely voided of cultural memory by the Middle Passage and ensuing conditions of enslavement. In the larger context, the cultural pathways argument resists the mid-century's notion of pluralist consensus, which claimed the United States as a "melting pot," wherein all prior (European and African) ethnic allegiances would melt into a monoculture.

Dunham's and Herskovits' research is positioned against liberal developmentalism, especially as Dunham's choreography from the 1930s argues for the value of combined and unevenness within the United States. In an account of the politics driving these pieces, Dunham argues that Caribbean immigration to the United States "has given African tradition a place in a large cultural body which it enjoys nowhere else," even if the originating logic of the dances is weakly held. For while African culture changes more in the United States than elsewhere, these alterations are to be celebrated as creating a "sound functional relationship towards a culture which is contemporary... The curious fact is that it will be the American Negro, in his relatively strong position as part of American culture, who, in the final analysis, will most probably guarantee the persistence of African dance traditions."[26]

Yet Dunham's performances of vodou dance for white Northern audiences are less concerned with questions of authenticity, since the staging involves Broadway-stylization of different African and Caribbean eurythmics; passing, as the erasure of difference; or even "cultural appropriation," than as a gesture embracing the articulation of differences within a complex whole. In formal terms, this ideal was achieved through the "Dunham technique," wherein each body part moves simultaneously and independently of one another, while creating an overarching physical gestalt. Just as African dance flourishes in an otherwise white dominant America, Dunham's own dance zombie figurations are not bound to an idealized territorial origin or unchanging folklore. Instead, the zombie in Dunham's hands makes sense only within its own historical conjuncture and location within the American metropole where the zombie stands as an exemplary figure that is both-and-neither of white America and Black Africa. While contemporary zombie figurations often seem unaware of their predecessors within Haiti, for Dunham, this does little to diminish their value.

By the late 1960s writing of *Island Possessed*, Dunham's cultural viewpoints have aligned more with the period's rise of political negritude and Black Power. The title of *Island Possessed* conveys three of the book's main themes: the legacy of the recently ended military occupation of Haiti by the Americans; the vodou culture of loa or spirit-god possession that pervades Haiti, especially in its rural regions; and, finally, the absence of sexual violence for a young, single Black American female, often traveling alone for late-night rituals, as if to counter Hollywood's obsessions with the targeted female body. Dunham argues, perhaps overly idealistically, that while Haiti has a long history of revolutionary upheaval, it had little interpersonal violence or abuse of children before Pap Doc Duvalier and the rise of the Tonton Macoutes.

Dunham's dance anthropology inescapably led to her hearing accounts about zombies, about which she says there are two kinds. The first is of a "truly dead person who by the intervention of black magic has been brought back to life." To prevent this transformation, some family members keep watch over the recently deceased until the corpse disintegrates, while others "hammer a long iron nail into the forehead of a dead person so that all bodily functions are interrupted beyond revival," a feature that Romero seems to have recovered and reinserted into his own filmic curation of zombies.[27] The other kind of zombie is a person who is given a potion of herbs that simulates death in ways that allows them to be buried and later excavated, "not for evil deeds generally, but... serviceable work of tilling and cultivating fields." For the former, salt-eating results in disintegration, while for the latter, it acts as an antidote to the incapacitating poison.[28]

Hearing of a Bokor who makes zombies, mainly as a device to keep several women as compliant wives, Dunham travels to Leogane for a visit. In this account she presents a relatively different view of the cultural entanglements that have given rise to the island's zombielore. While Haiti is known for its nonbinary race-caste system involving the larger categories of whites, Blacks, and mulattos, Dunham suggests that even within the Black community there remain long-standing differences among those who are descended from Africans coming from Dahomey (present-day Benin), the Congo, and present-day Nigeria. While vodou rituals are ones from Dahomey and are associated with the Rada Iwa loa, the tales of zombification and cannibalism are features ascribed to Congo rituals involving the Petwo Iwa loa. Dunham's distinction may be supported by the common etymological citation of "zombie" as coming from *zumbi* and *nzambi* in Kikongo language, rather than the Fon spoken by those from Dahomey, and that a slave revolt in late seventeenth-century Brazil was led by Nganga Zumbi/ Ganga Zumba, who claimed Kongo descent.

Dunham's purpose in relating the encounter seems to speak to the larger project of the memoir, written after Dunham had moved to Senegal. For while African religion becomes synthetic in the New World, where Dahomey rituals and iconography have fused with Catholic ones, Dunham suggests that there is little intermixture between different African pantheons, either in Africa or in the New World. Hence the contact and tensions between Congo and Dahomey contingents over social hierarchy *within* the Black Haitian community may be generating the circulation of zombie tales. In her account of the visit to the Congo Bokor, Dunham unexpectedly flees the scene after being invited to participate in an initiation ritual. The reader is left to intuit that Dunham feared the onset of sexual violence that the memoir otherwise claims is absent in Haiti. In this sense, *Island Possessed* uses zombie curation less as a means of addressing white readers' fears or fantasies, or even to defend the contribution of Black Americans in the nation's patchwork, than to consider what might be the obstacles to a pan-Africanism conceptualized outside a narrowly defined national liberation movement. The zombie stands as an object question about what tensions exist that prevent the creation of a culture of the Global South and what pan-Africanism might look like outside the scarring legacy of the artificial national boundaries created by former imperial powers. It is within this space between Dunham's 1930s cultural front politics about American heterogeneity and a 1960s concern for a Black (BIPOC) International that one of Hollywood's most decolonial films appears, *I Walked with a Zombie* (1943).

Decolonizing the Cinema: I Walked with a Zombie

The RKO studio film, *I Walked with a Zombie* (1943), exemplifies one means of decolonizing the zombie by challenging liberal assumptions. This film belongs to a sequence of Val Lewton-produced and Jacques Tourneur-directed films, mainly shot either in the immediate months before the United States' formal entry into the Second World War or immediately afterward: *Cat People* (1942), *I Walked with a Zombie* (1943), and *The Leopard Man* (1943). These films share a similar structure as they present the encounter of three different knowledge formations: one by exotic/ethnic/indigenous peoples (Catholic Serbians/Caribbean Blacks/New Mexican Latinx and Native Americans); the viewpoint of the assumed viewer, a white, Protestant American; and the expertise of a seemingly liberal figure of academic or professional knowledge. Each film begins with a "regular" white American (Oliver Reed in *Cat People* calls himself a "[normal] good, plain Americano") who has a naïve or incredulous encounter with a subaltern or foreign figure marked by a traumatic history of grieving, domination, and continued exclusion or marginalization from contemporary society.

Presented with an inexplicable event of horror, the normative character (and viewer) looks to the superiority of white professional authorities for explanation and social repair. In each film, however, these figures of epistemological authority are revealed to be not only simply wrong but, moreover, the source of evil itself. In *Cat People*, the posh English-accented psychiatrist activates his Serbian patient's were-shifting with a lecherous kiss that is symbolically visualized as rape, as he had previously displayed the sword-cane used to stab and kill her by violently thrusting it in and out of its sheath. In *The Leopard Man*, the tweedy East Coast former professor and now ethnographic museum curator is revealed to be the serial murderer of ethnic women. In *I Walked with a Zombie*, the female physician, the widow of a missionary before her marriage to the plantation owner, claims that she alone is responsible for turning her adulterous daughter-in-law into a zombie. In all three films, the explanations by the exotics or subalterns who speak English with accents are revealed to be either true or more worthy of consideration than that of the morally depraved, but high status, white figure of knowledge and expertise.

The typical American's ultimate realization that they failed to protect others due to their own willingness to be led by familiar authorities also leaves them traumatized, based on a combination of the shattering of their faith in authority and recognition that this faith left them passive and thus also complicit in the enactment of evil. In each film, "horror" is used to disrupt the placid surface that disfigures unquestioned (racial) privilege. Taken as a unit, it is hard not to see these films by the Jewish Russian émigré Lewton and the French-born Tourneur as constituting a message to its audience, the "plain Americanos," that something quite bad is happening to exotic Europeans in the 1940s. While these foreigners seem odd, their (Jewish) suffering needs to be taken seriously, especially if domestic, liberal white elites do nothing.

While each of these films enacts the passage from incredulity to guilt, *I Walked with a Zombie* most thoroughly achieves its decolonial purpose of delegitimizing liberal knowledge, as it asks its audience not only to question white authority but to interrogate their own forms of cultural consumption and the ways in which the "zombie" of dulled sensation is not the Black Caribbean but themselves, the audience that may sit inert in the face of social catastrophe in the world beyond the cinema. The movie begins with a naïve Canadian nurse, Betsy, who is contracted to aide Jessica, an oddly affectless wife of a plantation owner on St. Sebastian, a fictional Caribbean island. While Betsy repeatedly fantasizes about the island, and its possibilities for her own romantic awakening with the plantation owner, she is repeatedly told, to no effect, about its foundation in slavery. The continuing presence of slavery's trauma is materially foregrounded, for instance, in the plantation owner's courtyard with a St. Sebastian-like statue that was the figurehead of the ship said to have brought over the initial slaves for the canefields. The lines between Betsy's erotic yearning and the Black community's burden of slavery's wake cross paths when she takes Jessica to the island's vodou *houmfort* (or temple) for help in her patient's recovery.

Told by Black female servants how to arrive and move beyond a guarding zombie, Carrefour (Darby Jones), by wearing a pass token, Betsy guides Jessica through the canebrake, losing the pinned token (albeit to no real effect), before coming to a stylized performance of a sabre dance in a vodou ritual. As people line up to speak to the presumed Houngan into a hole through the temple's closed door, Betsy joins the queue. When she speaks to the opening, the door unexpectedly opens, and Betsy is pulled inside. There she sees Mrs. Rand, the physician mother to the plantation owner, who explains that she has been ventriloquizing vodou rituals to more successfully dispense Western medical advice to the island's Black population. While Betsy is talking to Rand, the sabre dancer pierces Jessica and, after seeing no blood or pain reflex, exclaims, "zombie." Hearing the commotion, Rand tells Betsy to take Jessica quickly back to the plantation. When the local authorities later investigate the presence of a white zombie, Rand confesses that she believes she is responsible for zombifying Jessica to prevent her from leaving one of Rand's sons for the other. While the film shows the sabre dancer later using a doll to pull Jessica to the houmfort, aided by Carrefour, it ends with Jessica's white lover taking her into the sea for what appears to be a murder-suicide. Although the shooting script concludes with a final scene in Montreal with Betsy now married to the widowed planter, the actual film ends on a downbeat and depressed voiceover that offers no happy end for the viewers.[29]

The film's choreographed vodou ritual makes it appear exotic, but the scene is not sensationalized. Lewton and Tourney researched vodou seriously from the sources available to them (the shooting script begins with the claim that it is "based on scientific information from articles") and hired Leroy Antoine, an editor of Haitian and vodou songs, as an advisor due to his own awareness and publication about vodou practice and music.[30] Indeed, vodou and zombification is calmly acknowledged as an unexceptional part of the contemporary fabric of Caribbean society. When the Rada drumming is first heard, it is explained to Betsy as "Saint Sebastian's version of the factory whistle," a means of calling workers to the cane mill. When Betsy appears with Jessica at the houmfort, the ceremony's participants barely notice their presence and make no effort to prevent their viewing. The threat in the film is not ultimately Carrefour, whose role is to *protect* the houmfort, but that someone *else* has created the Jessica zombie, and for what ends? While the film evades the history of Haiti by setting its action on a fictitious island, where no record of past Black rebellion exists, it does elliptically implicate American militarized capitalism, as Mrs. Rand's name indicates the link between rule and knowledge. While the military-serving RAND corporation would not be created until after the Second World War, its abbreviation, "research and development," was already a prewar commonplace as the name for corporate scientific planning units.

I Walked with a Zombie's achievement lies not simply in its acknowledgment of African religion's dignity, the history of slavery, and the duplicity of white liberals but in its meta-reflexive intervention to its viewers about their own consumption. For the canebreak and houmfort sequence visualizes the act of going to a cinema itself, with Carrefour made to stand like a ticket-taker, Rand's dress suit (inappropriate for Caribbean heat) like that of a clichéd movie director, the door with a hole looks like a film apparatus with a director watching action through a seeing optic, and the sabre dancer literally ends the scene with a "cut" accompanied by a one-word exclamation.

Lewton uses horror not merely as a device to give visual recognition to the peoples who are often made to stand as mute icons of their own suffering but as a medium for the viewer to question their own mode of observation.[31] *I Walked with a Zombie* uses zombie curation both as a suggestive device about the looming Nazi threat and also as a way of encouraging the viewer to reflect on their own act of film-watching, especially the ethnographic newsreels that often prefaced the regular movie offering, and to decolonize their own minds by questioning the liberal expertise that they have taken for granted as commonsense. In this sense, a decolonial culture may free both the living and the undead from centrist liberalism's nightmare.

Notes

1 Couldry, *The Costs of Connection*, 76.
2 Couldry, *The Costs of Connection*, 76.
3 Couldry, *The Costs of Connection*, 78.
4 Couldry, *The Costs of Connection*, 80.
5 Couldry, *The Costs of Connection*, 81.
6 Lazarus, "The Fetish of 'the West' in Postcolonial Theory," 43–64.
7 Wallerstein, *After Liberalism*, 126–44. See also Wallerstein, *The Global Left* and *The Modern World-System IV*.
8 Wallerstein, *After Liberalism*, 130.
9 Wallerstein, *After Liberalism*, 72–93 and Wallerstein, *The Modern World-System IV*, 1–19.

10 Wallerstein, *The Modern World-System IV*, 15–16, 153, 168, 219–73.
11 Wallerstein, *The Modern World-System IV*, 146.
12 Wallerstein, *The Modern World-System IV*, 219–73.
13 Wallerstein, *The Modern World-System IV*, 55–6.
14 Wallerstein, *The Modern World-System IV*, 55–8, 267–9.
15 Wallerstein, *The Modern World-System IV*, 7.
16 Wallerstein, *After Liberalism*, 72–93.
17 Wallerstein, *The Modern World-System IV*, 252–71.
18 Lauro, *The Transatlantic Zombie*, 7, 50.
19 Kee, *Not Your Average Zombie*, 6.
20 Hutter, "Salt Is Not for Slaves," 14 (39–53).
21 Wallace, "I Walked with a Zombie," 95 (95–102).
22 Austin, "The Worship of the Snake," 170 (170–82).
23 Anon., "Black Haiti," 27 (27–31).
24 Austin, "Worship of the Snake," 174–5.
25 Austin, *The New England Magazine*, 5–6.
26 Dunham, "The Negro Dance," 225 (217–22).
27 Dunham, *Island Possessed*, 184.
28 Dunham, *Island Possessed*, 185.
29 Siodmak and Wray, *Shooting Script for I Walked with a Zombie*.
30 Siodmak and Wray, *Shooting Script for I Walked with a Zombie*; Bowman and Leroy, *The Voice of Haiti*.
31 Nemerov, *Icons of Grief*.

Work Cited

Austin, Henry. *The New England Magazine*, July–August (1911): 5–6.
Austin, Henry. "The Worship of the Snake." *The New England Magazine*, June (1912): 170–82.
"Black Haiti: Where Old Africa and the New World Meet." *Life* 3:24 (December 13, 1937): 27–31.
Bowman, Laura, and Antoine Leroy. *The Voice of Haiti: An Unusual Collection of Original Native Ceremonial Songs, Invocations, Voodoo Chants, Drum Beats and Rhythms, Stories of Traditions, etc., of the Haitian People*. New York: Clarence Williams Music Publishing, 1938.
Couldry, Nick, and Ulises A. Mejias. *The Costs of Connection: How Data Is Colonizing Human Life and Appropriating It for Capitalism*. Stanford: Stanford University Press, 2019.
Dunham, Katherine. *Island Possessed*. New York: Doubleday & Co, 1969.
Dunham, Katherine. "The Negro Dance" (excerpt). In *Kaiso!: Writings by and about Katherine Dunham*, edited by Verve A. Clark and Sara E. Johnson, 217–22. Madison: University of Wisconsin Press, 2006.

Haining, Peter. *Zombie! Stories of the Walking Dead*. London: W. H. Allen & Co, 1985.

Hutter, Garnett Weston. "Salt Is Not for Slaves." In *Zombie! Stories of the Walking Dead*, edited by Peter Haining, 39–53. London: W. H. Allen & Co, 1985.

Kee, Chera. *Not Your Average Zombie: Rehumanizing the Undead from Voodoo to Zombie Walks*. Austin: University of Texas Press, 2011.

Lauro, Sarah Juliet. *The Transatlantic Zombie: Slavery, Rebellion, and Living Death*. Camden: Rutgers University Press, 2015.

Lazarus, Neil. "The Fetish of 'the West' in Postcolonial Theory." In *Marxism, Modernity and Postcolonial Studies*, edited by Crystal Bartolovich and Neil Lazarus, 43–64. Cambridge: Cambridge University Press, 2002.

Nemerov, Alexander. *Icons of Grief: Val Lewton's Home Front Pictures*. Berkeley: University of California Press, 2005.

Siodmak, Curt, and Ardel Wray. *Shooting Script for I Walked with a Zombie*, 1943. https://www.dailyscript.com/scripts/i-walked_with_a_zombie.html.

Wallace, Inez. "I Walked with a Zombie." In *Zombie! Stories of the Walking Dead*, edited by Peter Haining, 95–102. London: W. H. Allen & Co, 1985.

Wallerstein, Immanuel. *After Liberalism*. Cambridge: Cambridge University Press, 1995.

Wallerstein, Immanuel. *The Global Left: Yesterday, Today, Tomorrow*. London: Routledge, 2022.

Wallerstein, Immanuel. *The Modern World-System IV: Centrist Liberalism Triumphant, 1789–1914*. Berkeley: University of California Press, 2011.

Part Two

Zombie World-System

4

Samurai Zombies: Japan's Undead Past

Frank Jacob

The *samurai* is probably one of the most well-known Japanese icons and a figure of self-identification for cinema audiences in the East Asian country.[1] Traditionally, Japanese films are divided into two genres: *jidaigeki*, epic films that deal with the past and especially the samurai,[2] and *gendaigeki*, films that deal with current events or questions related to identity or society.[3] Consequently, films about the warrior class of Japan's past have historically always had a prominent place on the screen. Nevertheless, other genres, including Japanese horror films, have also become quite popular in recent years and even inspired Western remakes like Gore Verbinski's *The Ring* (2002), similar to the classics by Kurosawa Akira[4] that inspired John Sturges' *The Magnificent Seven* (1960) and Sergio Leone's *A Fistful of Dollars* (1964).[5] In the booming zombie film genre in Japan,[6] elements like the samurai were blended in and thereby represent a symbiosis of historical and zombie identities. Such films could be again divided into zombie comedy, like *Samurai of the Dead* (*Shinsengumi obu za deddo*, 2015) or splatter films, although often also comic, like *Samurai Zombie: Headhunter From Hell* (*Yoroi: Samurai Zombie*, 2008).

After a section with an initial discussion of the samurai as a Japanese symbol that in itself seems to be immortal and the cultural context of the zombie in Japan, the present chapter will discuss how far *Yoroi: Samurai Zombie* is not just a Japanese zombie film but an exaggeration of an obsession with the past that is represented as something that haunts people even today and leads to some kind of deadly struggle. The zombie identity here would then be mixed with a historical samurai identity, and I would suggest that the symbiosis of samurai and zombie could be understood as emblematic of the struggle for Japan's identity, a country that is considered modern in a Western sense but often seems to be controlled, even haunted, by traditions that go way back in time. The samurai zombie would therefore be a semiotic construction for Japan's undead past.

Samurai, Zombies, and a Country between Tradition and Modernity

Considering how long the samurai ruled Japan as a warrior elite—from the twelfth to the nineteenth century, tightening their political rule even further after Tokugawa Ieyasu unified the country again after the Battle of Sekigahara in 1600 and a long period of internal wars—it is not surprising that many films dealing with Japan's history would focus on one or other aspect of this centuries-long history.[7] Ironically, the samurai and their warrior code (*bushidō*) became particularly famous when Nitobe Inazō (1862-1933) published his book about the "soul of Japan" in 1900.[8] At this point, the samurai as a ruling class had already vanished and the country had been forced through a modernization process—the Meiji Restoration[9]—due to which society had changed tremendously, while the Japanese leadership intended to combine Western knowledge with Japanese traditions (*wakon yōsai*).[10] Some intellectuals of this first modern period in Japan's history, the Meiji period (1868-1912), like Fukuzawa Yukichi (1835-1901), began to discuss the question of Japan's identity more intensively and whether it should be considered an Asian country at all.[11] The politicians were first and foremost interested in a strong nation-state that was economically and militarily strong (*fukoku kyōhei*) as they wanted to avoid becoming a colonial or semi-colonial country like China.[12]

Western imperialism was considered dangerous for the sovereignty of the Japanese state, yet nationalist elements in Japan also argued that modernization according to Western standards would sacrifice traditional values. These nationalists, often organized in small secret societies, depicted themselves as patriots (*shishi*) and the heirs of the samurai.[13] They tried to force the government into a more aggressive foreign policy to continue or fulfill Toyotomi Hideyoshi's (1537-98) dream of a Greater East Asian Empire under Japanese leadership.[14] The samurai spirit, so to speak, haunted Japan during its modern period as well, when national conservative forces regularly reminded the country of its past.[15] The samurai remained undead, and there were some spectacular suicides, like those of Nogi Maresuke, a famous general of the Russo-Japanese War who killed himself in 1912 after the death of the Meiji Emperor Mutsuhito (1852-1912),[16] and the famous author Mishima Yukio (1925-70), who protested against Japan's Westernization after a failed coup d'etat with his ritual suicide.[17] The samurai and their spirit consequently seemed to be "undead," reminding Japan of a past the country seemed to have left behind.

In particular, after 1945 and Japan's defeat in the Pacific War, the American occupation, and a forced process of democratization,[18] the samurai spirit was considered to have been responsible for the nation's expansive foreign policy and the destruction of large parts of Asia, as well as their final suffering from the atomic bombs. While avant-garde artists and filmmakers were pointing to this relationship between destruction and a form of authoritarianism,[19] often falsely simply referred to as Japanese fascism, the government of Japan and a majority of the population had no interest in remembering the past and rather turned to highlight its importance for the US security system in the early Cold War in Asia and began to rebuild the economy of the East Asian country, which would soon begin to play an economically leading role again. Yet the samurai seemed to have become immortal and remained not only a historical but often also a spiritual or cultural point of reference.

Although it took until the late 1970s for the first zombie films, like George A. Romero's *Dawn of the Dead* (1978), to reach Japanese shores,[20] there was already a visual culture in place that dealt with different kinds of horror stories, often about ghosts, a genre of stories already quite popular in the Edo period (1603–1868) and illustrated in many woodblock prints (*ukiyo-e*) of the time.[21] There were also *yōkai*, supernatural spirits or monsters, stories about which were an essential part of Japanese folklore.[22] It was therefore not surprising that zombie stories, be they shown on the big screen or told in probably the most popular media form in Japan, *manga*, became quite popular.[23] The zombie genre is broad in Japan, as there are low-budget productions that often gain cult status within the zombie-loving community, such as the latest low-budget hit *Kamera o Tomeru na!* (2017), a variety of zombie manga for all kinds of readers,[24] and foreign imports like the *Resident Evil* (2002–16) series starring Milla Jovovich and representing a kind of international zombie renaissance since the early 2000s.[25] It must be considered that the "first zombie film," *White Zombie* (1932),[26] had more to offer than just horror; according to Japanese scholar Fukuda Asako, in fact, it offered a deeper contextualization of its time, that is, Western societies in the 1930s, and contemporary problems.[27] The popularity of zombies in the late third of the twentieth century and the beginning of the twenty-first century must consequently be related to more than the effects of cheap splatter productions in which the "running zombie"[28] replaced older and visually less violent versions of the undead.

Zombies present an ambiguity.[29] They are human-like, as they were human in the past, but at the same time, they are undead, although no longer alive either.

And, of course, they pose a threat to human beings, who could turn into zombies easily. Considering the history of Japan, however, there is an ambivalent way to interpret the "undead" past. When we take a look at the historical roots of the zombie, namely slavery in the French colony of St. Domingue and their liberation during the Haitian Revolution,[30] the interrelationship between "zombieness" and space-time-continuum of their genesis becomes obvious. American scholar Sarah J. Lauro, in her book *The Transatlantic Zombie: Slavery, Rebellion, and Living Death* (2015), highlighted that "[i]n contemporary accounts of the Haitian Revolution, the ferocity of the rebels was denigrated: they were less than men; they were animals or machines run amok. This is the transformation by which the dehumanized slave becomes the inhuman rebel."[31]

Consequently, and in its Haitian context, "the zombie is not a figure of resurrection but only of living death, and insofar as the zombie metaphorizes both slavery and slave rebellion . . ., its ability to represent not merely enslavement, but liberation from that state, is tempered by its irresolvable dialecticality."[32] It is important, for the Japanese context, to understand this diversity of the zombie image. While in the Haitian context, as Lauro clearly explained and analyzed, "the figure of the zombie clearly represents one or the other: the history of a people's enslavement or that of their fierce resistance to oppression,"[33] there are multiple perspectives of the zombie image in Japan as well. On the one hand, it can represent an undead past of Japan's history, that is, the history of the samurai and their fall due to the social changes in accordance with Japan's modernization since the beginning of the Meiji Restoration (*Meiji ishin*) in 1868.[34] While the samurai class had been abolished, the samurai spirit, as expressed by Nitobe Inazō and others, continued to in a way haunt Japan and the extremist forces would gain more influence since the end of the Taishō period (1912–26) and lead the country toward an aggressive foreign policy. Regardless of the intent of many Japanese, to simply forget about these past events, the samurai, as a symbolic resemblance, dead and yet undead like a zombie, seems to remain an aspect of popular culture in particular.

There has, however, from a more global perspective, recently been a reverse with regard to the zombie image related to TV series like *iZombie* (2015–19),[35] but even if comedies seem to be particularly en vogue today, for example, *Zombieland* (2009) and *Zombieland: Double Tap* (2019), the threat of the zombie remains. Nevertheless, especially in Japan, the threatening zombie image appears to be more than imagined, considering the mass of the zombie-like workforce who are obliged to function according to social expectations. Sleeping salarymen and businesswomen,[36] without control over their human well-being, populate the subways of the Japanese metropolis as the "living dead" every day, exhausted, almost no longer conscient, zombie-like. Japan consequently provides multiple possibilities to understand the zombie: a long gone past that is nevertheless essential for the perception of Japan, and a present business model that demands dehumanization from its workforce and the negation of any kind of work-life balance.

At the same time, there is a strong interest in seeing zombies breaking down existent orders in splatter comedies when the zombie element becomes the one that rules and often simply destroys the daily routine by turning people who appear to be like zombies into real ones. It is not the intent of the present chapter to provide the ultimate answer to the question of why zombie stories are so popular in Japan, however, especially since it seems to be a mix of all these factors: visual and narrative traditions that reach back to the Edo period, a positive identification with a zombie apocalypse that destroys the exploitative work system of the world, or at least some traceability of a zombie identity in the personal lives of so many Japanese, forced into social conventions.[37] In the following discussion of *Yoroi: Samurai Zombie*, I will try to emphasize some of these aspects with regard to the film, which is one example of Japanese splatter films that deal with the zombie, but which also combines its story with the samurai, as it is a samurai zombie that returns from the dead to demand blood.

Yoroi: Samurai Zombie (2008)

The plot of the film, directed by Sakaguchi Tak and written by Kitamura Ryūhei,[38] which received relatively positive reactions from the critics after being shown at the Bucheon International Fantastic Film Festival in South Korea,[39] is relatively simple and easily explained. The film was advertised on film blogs as "providing fresh ground meat" for Japan's horror genre.[40] It is a true splatter highlight, although comic as well, in which a kidnapped family, two criminals, and a samurai zombie get to meet each other, an incident that would not remain bloodless. It is a "low-budget massacre," including flying body parts and liters of film blood. A family—Shigeo (Fukikoshi Mitsuru), Yasuko (Oginome Keiko), Asami (Nakajima Airi), and Ryota (Sakurazuka Yakkun)—is on their way to vacation but is taken hostage by two criminals, namely the couple Aihara (Ishida Issei) and Jirō (Ueda Hiromi), who force the family to drive them.

When the car has to stop because of a blown tire, Shigeo is sent away to get help. He wanders through the landscape until he reaches an old cemetery, where he starts to dig in the ground until he finds an old sword, with which he decapitates himself. Due to this act and the blood on the ground, which reaches an old tomb, the samurai zombie is awakened and begins to hunt the remaining family members as well as the two kidnappers. The final battle between the zombies, led by the undead samurai, and the humans begins in a ghost town. Rather than spoil the film for the reader too much at this point, I will discuss some of its elements here instead of shedding too much light on the plot.

The low-budget production provides colorful criminals who remind the audience of cosplayers rather than actual criminals, a trend that can be observed in other genres, where the bad guys are often presented as exaggerated caricatures as well. At the same time, elements related to traditional Japanese ghost stories can be identified, as Shigeo's suicide seems to act as a trigger for the arrival of the zombies. The death of a human being releases the undead. And these resemble both a past that has long gone and, at the same time, the struggle between modernity and tradition, between Japanese and Western values. This is comically represented by the battle between Aihara and the samurai zombie, one using a gun, the other a sword. This motif reminds the cineast of Kurosawa's *Yojimbo* (1961), where the bodyguard also has to face the bad guy in an unequal battle of sword against pistol in the end, or—on a broader scale—even of *The Last Samurai* (2003) and the heroic battle of the samurai against a modernized army, a romantic mise en scène that is historically inaccurate.

The samurai themselves seem to haunt the family and the two criminals for no specific reason, simply considering them to be intruders. Their anger consequently reflects Japanese anger against Western intrusion, a form of cultural colonialism, which the historical samurai must have felt between the opening of Japan in 1853 and the end of the rebellions against the new state in 1877, when the Satsuma Rebellion under the leadership of Saigō Takamori was violently suppressed by the new conscript army. In a way, one could argue that Japan is still struggling with regard to its identity. While politicians like Abe Shinzō, who recently resigned but has paved the way for a more nationalist tone of Japanese politics, support a more nationalist course, highlighting particularly Japanese values, others argue for a further and maybe second "opening" of the country due to its demographic problems. The idea that Japan is consequently haunted by its own past is something that seems to be an obvious aspect of the film. The fight between the humans and the zombies is consequently a resemblance of the conflict humans have to face with their past, their cultural identity, and the social expectations that determine their fate, at least to some extent, even in modern-day Japan. The zombie is therefore an essential part of the human, in this case the Japanese self, one that is often forgotten, but one that will also never be fully dead.

Besides this subconscious aspect, the "samurai headhunter" that is presented in *Yoroi: Samurai Zombie* is also a caricature of the Japanese samurai, a loyal subordinate whose life was and still seems to be determined by his identity. Just as the early modern warrior could not escape his life and even had to commit suicide to honor his superior, the zombie identity seems to be related to a curse: not being able to fully die. Considering the Buddhist ideas that were particularly strengthened during the Tokugawa period, the samurai could consequently not fulfill his legacy and pass on but remained dead, yet not dead enough. This aspect also points to the fact that while the samurai disappeared physically in late nineteenth-century Japan, their spirit with regard to honor and war still seems to haunt the island nation in the twenty-first century, when ultra-right-wing societies demand a national strength that would continue Hideyoshi's ambition for an Asian Empire.

That especially the experience of Japan's expansionist ambitions can lead to a different, as mentioned above, a second, interpretation of the image of the samurai in relation to Japan's aggressive foreign policy since the late sixteenth century can be observed in other Asian countries, where the historical victim experience of a colonial or later imperialist invasion created a different image of the zombie. Usually the colonizers "get marked as the first world"[41] and therefore intend to destroy the existent political and social order or at least change it to fit the needs of the imperial center. Such a historical experience, as it was, for example, created by Hideyoshi's expansion to Korea, and the latter's annexation by Japan in 1910, leading Japanese settler colonialism on the Korean Peninsula to its climax and final takeover,[42] until today influences the way zombies are depicted for the Korean screen, for example, in Netflix's first original Korean series, *Kingdom*, which tells the story of a political intrigue and the danger of a "zombie attack" that in a way resembles the invasion by Hideyoshi, which supposedly had happened three years before the actual plot's timeline. The story consequently stages an experience of "zombie colonialism," because, as Eve Tuck and K. Wayne Yung emphasized in their article "Decolonization Is Not a Metaphor" (2012), "[e]xternal colonialism often requires a subset of activities properly called military colonialism—the creation of war fronts/frontiers against enemies to be conquered, and the enlistment of foreign land, resources, and people into military operations."[43] The colonizer-colonized dichotomy[44] in *Kingdom* is consequently created by the struggle between the heroes, the Korean defenders of the Joseon dynasty (1392–1897), and the invading zombies, representing the Japanese forces that would not only threaten the historical dynasty in the late sixteenth but should also abolish it in the late nineteenth century.[45]

Conclusion

Regardless of these possible interpretations of *Yoroi: Samurai Zombie* that are related to reflections on Japan's history and the concept of *wakon yōsai*, the film is an example of Japan's zombie entertainment industry, which also amalgamates different interests for its audience. Nevertheless, it provides just one possible interpretation of the zombie image in relation to Japan's past, as the short reflection on that image in former colonized spaces, namely Korea after Hideyoshi's invasion or in the period of Japanese rule between 1910 and 1945, could hopefully show.

Considering the success story of *jidaigeki* in the past, it is, however, not surprising that *Yoroi: Samurai Zombie*, in contrast to productions related to former spaces and times of Japanese colonialism, like *Kingdom*, attempts to mix the historical genre with the very popular zombie genre as well and create some kind of hybrid of itself again that eventually must nevertheless remain one-sided. The Western zombie genre and the Japanese samurai genre are brought into coexistence in a single film, while focusing on the haunting aspect of Japan's own past. Since there are other examples of such a genre mix in the last decade, this is probably also related to commercial aspects, although, as it seems, the regional approach in East Asia to the zombie genre varies according to the historical experiences of colonizer or colonized. At the same time, as has been shown, this amalgamation of images, topics, and stories is, in a way, a continuation of the idea of *wakon yōsai*, albeit in the context of popular media. Hence the zombie genre might offer Japan a chance to further decolonize the depiction of its own past, if a true amalgamation and acceptance of the historical experiences of its former colonies would be included in future approaches by films in that genre.

One could consequently conclude here that samurai have survived in an only semi-memorized way for one and a half centuries and will probably continue to appear in different film genres whenever someone sees this historic element fit for the plot. That this happens at all is clear evidence that the samurai will never fully disappear. They remain, however, so to speak, only one-sided zombies of the Japanese imagination, which tends to rather embrace a filtered version of its past, representing an ideal of a time that is past yet cannot be let loose without daring to fully lose what is such an essential part of Japan's tradition: honor, dedication, and the wish to serve a greater good.

Notes

1. A concise introduction into the history and cultural impact of the samurai is given in Schwentker, *Die Samurai*; Turnbull, *The Samurai*.
2. Kiyotada, *Jidaigeki eiga no shisō*. On the samurai film in particular, which dominated this genre, see Galloway, *Warring Clans, Flashing Blades* and Silver, *The Samurai Film*, 2006.
3. Bernardi, "The Early Development of the Gendaigeki Screenplay."
4. Japanese names are given according to the Japanese language, i.e., surnames followed by first names.
5. Desser, "Remaking Seven Samurai in World Cinema," 17–40.
6. On the role of horror and violence in Japanese film and society, see, among other works, Glaser, "'Further Down the Spiral," 27–32; Pühler, "Spiel ohne Grenzen," 37–47.
7. Jacob, "Tokugawa Ieyasu, Reichseiniger, Shōgun oder Japans Diktator?" 79–102.
8. Inazō, *Bushido*.
9. Shigeki, *Meiji Ishin*.
10. For a detailed discussion see Lutum, *Das Denken von Minakata Kumagusu und Yanagita Kunio*; Sukehiro, *Wakon yōsai no keifu*.
11. Naomi, "Fukuzawa Yukichis Datsu-a-ron (1885)," 210–24.
12. Junji, *Meiji kenpō taisei no kakuritsu*.
13. The Gen'yōsha (Black Ocean Society) and the Kokuryūkai (Amur Society), often falsely translated as Black Dragon Society, were probably the most well known of these societies. Their influence, however, was often overemphasized, as a report of the British Foreign Office from April 16, 1946, highlights: "The Genyosha [sic], the parent of this type of society, in its origin consisted chiefly of disgruntled ex-samurai who, seeing the futility of armed revolt to gain their goal of Japanese expansion in Asia, organized pressure groups by which they could exercise a decisive influence upon key members of the government, particularly in the Ministries of War and Foreign Affairs." Nelson T. Johnson, Confidential Report C4-004, April 16, 1946, National Archives UK, Foreign Office, Foreign Office files for Japan, 1946–1952, FO 371-54138, No. F-6420/95/23. A more detailed study of the two societies is provided in Jacob, *Japanism, Pan-Asianism and Terrorism*.
14. Toyotomi had tried to conquer Korea, and even dreamed of a Japanese Empire that would rule over China. His military campaign in the early 1590s, however, turned out rather unsuccessful in the end. Swope, *A Dragon's Head and a Serpent's Tail*; Lewis, ed. *The East Asian War, 1592–1598*.

15 Shichihei, *The Spirit of Japanese Capitalism and Selected Essays*, for example, describes "The Capitalist Logic of the Samurai" as one important aspect for the later capitalist development of Japan.
16 The suicide of the general also aroused some interest in US newspapers. See, for example, *Bridgeton Pioneer* (Bridgeton, NJ), October 3, 1912: 2; *The Call* (San Francisco, CA), September 15, 1912: 1; *The Evening Star* (Washington, DC), September 14, 1912: 1.
17 Mishima was also torn between tradition oriented nationalism and Western modernization and recognition. For an introduction about his life and work, see Jacob, "Mishima Yukio," 187–201.
18 MacArthur was particularly in this aim when he was considering the aims of his occupational government in Japan. Jacob, "MacArthur's Legacy," 207–27.
19 One example would be Terayama Shūji's film *Emperor Tomato Ketchup* (1971). See Jacob, "Emperor Tomato Ketchup," 153–70.
20 Harper, *Flowers of Hell*, 43.
21 Nakau, *Something Wicked from Japan*.
22 Foster, *The Book of Yōkai*. Lafcadio Hearn was one of the Westerners who dealt with these stories as well and identified some similarities to the zombies, known in the Western cultural hemisphere. Tomonori, "Rafukadio Hān to zonbi," 31–51.
23 While there are quite a lot of manga series that deal with the subject, readers themselves would also refer to themselves as zombies, as they sometimes turn into otaku, begin to live in an imagined world, related to manga and anime, and lose contact with reality. See exemplary Udagawa Takeo, *Manga zonbi* (Tokyo: Ōta, 1997). On the Japanese otaku culture, see Mizuko Ito, Daisuke Okabe, Izumi Tsuji, eds. *Fandom Unbound: Otaku Culture in a Connected World* (New Haven, CT: Yale University Press, 2012).
24 Hanazawa Kengo's *I am A Hero* (Ai amu a hīrō, 2009–17) is just one example that was also translated into English.
25 Bun'ei, "Zonbi no shigaku," 67–88. With regard to Japanese research on zombie cinema see Tomonori, "Zonbieiga kenkyūjoron," 13–26.
26 Rhodes, *White Zombie* discusses the film in some detail.
27 Asako, "'Howaito zonbi' ni okeru zonbi no byōsha," 138–9.
28 Asako, "Zonbieiga-shi saikō," 55–68.
29 Yuki, "Ningen dearu, dōbutsu ni naru koto, zonbi ni todomaru koto," 7.
30 For an introductory survey see Popkin, *A Concise History of the Haitian Revolution*.
31 Lauro, *The Transatlantic Zombie*, 28.
32 Lauro, *The Transatlantic Zombie*, 29.
33 Lauro, *The Transatlantic Zombie*, 29.
34 Jacob, "Die Meiji-Restauration und die Neuordnung Japans," 79–92.
35 Prorokova, "Romance as a Panacea and a New Generation of Intellectual Zombies in *Warm Bodies* and *iZombie*," 147–60.

36 It is interesting to note here that there is also a feminist approach toward the zombie genre, stressed by Yasayo, "Zonbi eiga no hirointachi," 141–65.
37 There is also a problem of the so-called zombie houses in some (rural) regions of Japan, which is in a way reflected in zombie films as well. Chihiro, "Shichōson ha, akiya zonbi to tatakau koto ga dekiru no ka?" 35–42.
38 The two had worked on other projects before and are a well-known duo in the genre.
39 The festival is an important event for film fans in East Asia and was first organized in 1997.
40 "Zombie-Splatter aus Fernost."
41 Tuck and Yang, "Decolonization Is Not a Metaphor," 4.
42 Uchida, *Brokers of Empire*.
43 Tuck and Yang, "Decolonization Is Not a Metaphor," 4.
44 Couldry and Mejias, *The Costs of Connection*, 70.
45 The Japanese government and Japanese nationalists would, replicating older imperialist narratives, argue in 1910 that the annexation was for the better and according to Korean *and* Japanese interests. For a contemporary Japanese view, see Iyenaga, "Japan's Annexation of Korea," 201–23.

Works Cited

Banno, Junji. *Meiji kenpō taisei no kakuritsu: Fukoku kyōhei to minryoku kyūyō*. Tokyo: Tōkyō Daigaku Shuppankai, 1992.

Bernardi, Joanne R. "The Early Development of the Gendaigeki Screenplay: Kaeriyama Norimasa, Kurihara Tōmas, Tanizaki Jun'ichirō and the Pure Film Movement." PhD Diss., Columbia University, New York, 1992.

Desser, David. "Remaking Seven Samurai in World Cinema." In *East Asian Cinemas: Exploring Transnational Connections on Film*, edited by Leon Hunt and Leung Wing-Fei, 17–40. London: I. B. Tauris, 2008.

Foster, Michael Dylan. *The Book of Yōkai: Mysterious Creatures of Japanese Folklore*. Berkeley, CA: University of California Press, 2015.

Fukuda, Asako. "'Howaito zonbi' ni okeru zonbi no byōsha." *Kontakuto zōn* 11 (2019): 122–42.

Fukuda, Asako. "Zonbieiga-shi saikō." *Ningen kankyōgaku* 25 (2016): 55–68.

Fukunaga, Yasayo. "Zonbi eiga no hirointachi: Manazashi ga toraeru monsutā no honshitsu." *Ferris Studies* 51 (2016): 141–65.

Fukuzawa, Naomi, "Fukuzawa Yukichis Datsu-a-ron (1885): Wegbereiter des japanischen Imperialismus oder zornige Enttauschung eines asiatischen Aufklarers?" *Tātonnemen* 13 (2011): 210–24.

Galloway, Patrick. *Warring Clans, Flashing Blades: A Samurai Film Companion*. Berkeley, CA: Stone Bridge Press, 2009.

Glaser, Tim. "'Further Down the Spiral.' Der japanische Spielfilm Uzumaki (2000) als Mittler zwischen Form und Furcht." In *Dawn of an Evil Millennium: Horror/Kultur im neuen Jahrtausend*, edited by Jörg van Bebber, 27–32. Marburg: Büchner, 2018.

Harper, Jim. *Flowers of Hell: The Modern Japanese Horror Film*. Hereford: Noir Publishing, 2008.

Hirakawa, Sukehiro. *Wakon yōsai no keifu: Uchi to soto kara no Meiji Nihon*. Tokyo: Kawade Shobō Shinsha, 1992.

Ito, Mizuko, Daisuke Okabe, and Izumi Tsuji, eds. *Fandom Unbound: Otaku Culture in a Connected World*. New Haven: Yale University Press, 2012.

Iyenaga, Toyokichi. "Japan's Annexation of Korea." *The Journal of Race Development* 3, no. 2 (1912): 201–23.

Jacob, Frank. "Die Meiji-Restauration und die Neuordnung Japans: Umverteilung und sozialer Wandel." *Traverse* 22, no. 1 (2015): 79–92.

Jacob, Frank. "Emperor Tomato Ketchup: The Child as Dictator of Mankind." In *The Child in Post-Apocalyptic Cinema*, edited by Debbie C. Olson, 153–70. Lanham: Lexington Books, 2015.

Jacob, Frank. *Japanism, Pan-Asianism and Terrorism: A Short History of the Amur Society (The Black Dragons) 1901–1945*. Bethesda: Academica Press, 2014.

Jacob, Frank. "MacArthur's Legacy: Japan and the Early Years of the Cold War." In *Peripheries of the Cold War*, edited by Frank Jacob, 207–27. Würzburg: Königshausen & Neumann, 2015.

Jacob, Frank. "Mishima Yukio: Aesthetics, Dualism, and Postwar Nationalism." In *Critical Insights: Modern Japanese Literature*, edited by Frank Jacob, 187–201. Hackensack: Salem Press, 2017.

Jacob, Frank. "Tokugawa Ieyasu, Reichseiniger, Shōgun oder Japans Diktator?" In *Diktaturen ohne Gewalt? Wie Diktatoren ihre Macht behaupten*, edited by Frank Jacob, 79–102. Würzburg: Königshausen & Neumann, 2013.

Johnson, Nelson T. Confidential Report C4-004, April 16, 1946, National Archives UK, Foreign Office, Foreign Office files for Japan, 1946–1952, FO 371-54138, No. F-6420/95/23.

Kiyomizu, Chihiro. "Shichōson ha, akiya zonbi to tatakau koto ga dekiru no ka? Gifu ken Seinō chiiki wo kēsu-toshite." *Nihon fudōsan gakkaishi* 30, no. 4 (2017): 35–42.

Kohara Bun'ei. "Zonbi no shigaku: 'Tsuiseki' to 'rōjō' no mochīfu ni tsuite." *IVY* 49 (2016): 67–88.

Lauro, Sarah Juliet. *The Transatlantic Zombie: Slavery, Rebellion, and Living Death*. New Brunswick: Rutgers University Press, 2015.

Lewis, James B., ed. *The East Asian War, 1592–1598: International Relations, Violence and Memory*. London: Routledge, 2015.

Lutum, Peter. *Das Denken von Minakata Kumagusu und Yanagita Kunio: Zwei Pioniere der japanischen Volkskunde im Spiegel der Leitmotive wakon-yōsai und wayō-setchū*. Münster: LIT, 2005.

Maruyama, Yuki. "Ningen dearu, dōbutsu ni naru koto, zonbi ni todomaru koto: Mitsu no ējenshī to kyakutaika." *Rikkyō Daigaku Amerika Kenkyūjo* 41 (2019): 7–29.

Nishiyama, Tomonori. "Rafukadio Hān to zonbi: Koizumi Yakumo no tabunkateki yōkaitachi." *Rikkyō Daigaku Amerika Kenkyūjo* 41 (2019): 31–51.

Nishiyama, Tomonori. "Zonbieiga kenkyūjoron: Adaputchon obu za dedo." *Saitama Gakuen Daigaku kiyō: Ningengakubu-hen* 18 (2018): 13–26.

Nitobe Inazō. *Bushido: The Soul of Japan*. Philadelphia: The Leeds & Biddle Co, 1900.

Popkin, Jeremy D. *A Concise History of the Haitian Revolution*. Oxford: Wiley-Blackwell, 2012.

Prorokova, Tatiana. "Romance as a Panacea and a New Generation of Intellectual Zombies in *Warm Bodies* and *iZombie*." In *All Around Monstrous: Monster Media in Their Historical Context*, edited by Verena Bernardi and Frank Jacob, 147–60. Wilmington: Vernon Press, 2019.

Pühler, Simon. "Spiel ohne Grenzen: Sadistische Gewalt als Ausdruck vager Ängste im Japan der Jahrtausendwende und in einer globalisierten Welt. Zu Kinji Fukasakus Battle Royale (2000)." In *Dawn of an Evil Millennium: Horror/Kultur im neuen Jahrtausend*, edited by Jörg van Bebber, 37–47. Marburg: Büchner, 2018.

Rhodes, Gary. *White Zombie: Anatomy of a Horror Film*. Jefferson: McFarland, 2006.

Schwentker, Wolfgang. *Die Samurai*. Munich: C.H. Beck, 2003.

Silver, Alain. *The Samurai Film*. New York: Abrams Press, 2006.

Swope, Kenneth M. *A Dragon's Head and a Serpent's Tail: Ming China and the First Great East Asian War, 1592–1598*. Norman: Oklahoma University Press, 2009.

Tōyama, Shigeki. *Meiji Ishin*. Tokyo: Iwanami Shoten, 2011.

Tsutsui, Kiyotada. *Jidaigeki eiga no shisō: Nosutarujī no yukue*. Tokyo: Uejji, 2008.

Tuck, Eve and K. Wayne Yang. "Decolonization Is Not a Metaphor." *Decolonization: Indigeneity, Education & Society* 1, no. 1 (2012): 1–40.

Turnbull, Stephen. *The Samurai*. Oxford: Osprey, 2016.

Uchida, Jun. *Brokers of Empire: Japanese Settler Colonialism in Korea, 1876–1945*. Cambridge: Harvard University Press, 2011.

Udagawa, Takeo. *Manga zonbi*. Tokyo: Ōta, 1997.

"Zombie-Splatter aus Fernost: Samurai Zombie lässt Köpfe rollen." https://www.moviepilot.de/news/samurai-zombie-laesst-koepfe-rollen-106568. Accessed September 1, 2020.

5

Crude Monsters in the "Extractive Zone": The Creaturely and Ecological Zombie

Josephine Taylor

> *What cultural and intellectual production makes us see, hear, and intimate the land differently? What do we really know about the invisible, the inanimate, and the nonhuman forms that creatively reside as afterlives of the colonial encounter?*
>
> —*The Extractive Zone: Social Ecologies and Decolonial Perspectives*, Macarena Gómez-Barris

The zombie permeates cultural production acting as the driving narrative force in shows such as *The Walking Dead* and *Z-Nation*. In the "Fracking Zombies" episode of *Z-Nation*, the central motivation of the only "human" characters is not just survival amid the zombie apocalypse but an access to gasoline. As the characters drive through a resource-depleted and ecologically devastated landscape, the line "we're out of gas" motivates the action of the episode. Strewn among the empty highways are abandoned automobiles alongside the somnambulistic rhythm of zombies, moving in and out unconsciously within the remnants of petroculture.[1] The characters' logical destination is to the nearest oil refinery, the Jersey Devil Refinery. What awaits them there is a "swarm" of zombies mechanically moving toward the reverberations of the refinery. On opening the oil storage tank, they are horrified to discover an indistinguishable mesh of limbs and flesh immersed within the black oil. This mergence between the undead and gasoline immediately presents itself as a corporeal metaphor for society's addiction to oil, a naturalization of our need for it as something intrinsic to human life and for survival.

But what is perhaps the most striking element of this scene, however, is how oil becomes flesh-like, merged with rotting yet animate human bodies.[2]

Such an image resonates with the strange and gothic registers crude oil often possesses in the literary imagination, connected to images of contagion, buried monstrosities, encounters with alien life forms, and an awakening of the dead. Imagining crude oil as an ecological zombie has an emancipatory potential that can incite an act of decolonization. This potential arises as a method for changing our relations to energy, leaving behind imperial extractive projects to more just and ethical engagement with the environment. Zombie figurations often act as a geopolitical index to registrations of petroculture in crisis and as a crisis. In the tension between the "always-on" zombie and the fears of system collapse due to the end of peak oil, the zombie arises when the lifeworld expectations of the capitalist core encounter the brutal realities of extractive violence elsewhere in the world-system's periphery. The metaphor of the zombie in this chapter is thus deeply bound to petroleum as a commodity and to the sites of extractive violence.

In this chapter, I explore China Miéville's *Covehithe* and Reza Negarestani's *Cyclonopedia*, where I focus on their depiction of oil and its infrastructure as an unthinking yet active entity, a collective force or "swarm" of the undead. This depiction resists the capitalist presentation of oil as a mere resource and commodity for human consumption. Such a process allows me to place the figure of the zombie within the petrocultural landscape, capturing oil as a resurgent figure of the walking dead. Like the critic Kerstin Oloff, I read the zombie as an essentially "ecological figure," what she terms "greening the zombie."[3] In addition to these ecological aspects of the zombie, I also suggest the zombie figure can be informed through Anat Pick's *Creaturely Poetics*, a non-anthropocentric aesthetics and ethics, forming what I term the creaturely zombie.

The geographical placement of the two narratives draws us toward what Macarena Gómez-Barris terms as the extractive zone and the peripheral spaces of the world-system, subject to neocolonial forces and regimes. What Gómez-Barris defines as the extractive view—seeing "territories as commodities, rendering land as for the taking"[4]—is what currently shapes energy politics and relations, and in particular the locations of these two fictions: Iran and the North Sea, Suffolk. They are locations that are dominated by imperial regimes of energy, rich with natural resources; the two texts thus magnify the destructive effects of extractive capitalism at the semi-peripheral and peripheral space. Sharae Deckard suggests extractivism "typically takes place in peripheralized zones, from which raw materials are removed and exported to cores for processing and production into commodities." Through the world-system of core and periphery, production of natural resources occurs in peripheralized zones to fuel consumer centers. Turning to the extractive zone in the literary imaginary, thus, offers a way of magnifying what occurs at the (semi-) periphery. The extractive view is challenged, however, through crude oil and its infrastructure becoming a powerful actor of its own in the texts, a zombie resurgence and rebellion against the reign of colonial forces and capital.

Drawing on what Kathryn Yusoff terms as "the afterlives of geology,"[5] I explore the creative manifestation of crude oil as a zombie in the literary imaginary, suggesting it is a process of decolonial artistic practice. For Yusoff, extraction is a colonial project, and thus perhaps the awakening of crude oil and its infrastructure as an agential and rebellious force can alternatively be read as a radical act of decolonization. Exploring the parallels between the process of zombification and fossil fuel extraction opens us to Yusoff's understanding of the afterlives of geology, what becomes inhuman matter, considered inert and thing-like. As Yusoff suggests, "geology is often assumed to be without subject (thinglike and inert) whereas biology is secured recognition of the organism (bodylike and sentient)."[6] Within the legacy and myth of the zombie and the violent histories of oil extraction, there is a connection between the objectification of life and matter, a colonization of both body and land. In such a process of categorization, the category of the human is intimately bound within the logic of colonialization. For Sylvia Wynter, the human is often defined according to the Western bourgeois conception of what is and what is not human."[7] What Wynter refers to as the coloniality of being, the Western white man, who becomes the measure of all things, has important implications for how both land and bodies become rendered as commodity.

As Yusoff further argues, "both enslaved, land and ecologies became subject to encoding as inhuman property, as a tactic of empire and European world-building."[8] The zombie, the Haitian slave, and crude oil itself are encoded as inhuman property, resources for the growth of empire. This relation is further illuminated through the ways crude oil is extracted from the ground, utilized and labored upon like the zombie who is awakened from the depths of the grave, mastered and controlled, to labor for the purposes of building an empire. Both crude oil and the zombie become extractable matter under the mastery of the white colonizer. Yusoff suggests, "extractable matter must be both passive (awaiting extraction and possessing properties) and able to be activated through the mastery of white men."[9] This passivity, however, is disturbed and challenged as crude oil in the texts becomes an ecological and creaturely zombie as planetary elements form a rebellious collective refusing to be harnessed as extractable matter. My formulation of the ecological zombie is drawn from the two separate traditions including both the figure of the Haitian zombie and its Euro-American construction in popular culture. I engage with both as a type of evolution, noting how these categories are different yet how both point toward an unruly and rebellious potential against extractive capital.

The act of reimaging crude oil outside the bounds of capital and colonial logic offers movement toward a decolonized and a non-anthropocentric perspective. As Melanie Doherty asks, "how do we think the non-human role of oil?"[10] Such creative reimaginings must begin with a defamiliarization from oil as a mere commodity, of its flow and movement defined by the actions of the market and its relations. Combining Doherty's question with the figure of the zombie points toward a non-anthropocentric understanding of energy, a movement that opens up to an unbound and liminal space which refutes the categorization imposed by capital. The process of de-objectivizing petroleum from capitalist logic is essential for building a movement toward decolonization. In what Yusoff terms as the "Age of Man," "Man is a dominant and dominating mode of subjectification—of nature, the Non-Western world, ecologies and the planet."[11] Under capitalist imperial regimes, in which man is the dominant mode of subjectification, ecological matter is rendered as a lifeless commodity. Yet, however, through the texts I analyze, the authors' creative exploration of oil as beyond the grasp of capital allows for petroleum to occupy its own autonomy outside the extractive view.

In Miéville's *Covehithe* and Negarestani's *Cyclonopedia*, we are told the nonhuman story of oil. Negarestani's theory fiction follows the paranoid notes and articles of the Iranian archaeologist Dr. Hamid Parsani, who draws the conclusion that oil is an earth-crawling entity with a subterranean logic of its own. Oil arises and awakens like the force of the undead in the narrative. Miéville similarly opens us to the surrealist and gothic aspects of oil and its infrastructure with his short story *Covehithe*. Set near the extraction site of the North Sea, *Covehithe* follows a father and his daughter lurking in forbidden territory where the oil rigs reside. As the narrative develops, we soon discover the oil rigs are live and animate beings, which, having healed on the ocean floor, now seek to drill new lands and to procreate. Defining petroleum as a zombie in these two narratives breaks the typical construction of life as inert, as subject to colonial and capitalist dynamics, and returns it a curious form of collective agency. Like the zombie, oil appears as "a strange being, at once alive and dead, grotesquely literal and blatantly artificial, and cannot be encompassed by any ordinary logic of representation."[12] The zombie is slippery and ungraspable, avoiding taxonomic distinctions moving through rot, decay, and contagion.

Yusoff discusses the dangers of these divisions, as she argues that "the language of materiality and its division between life and nonlife, and its alignment with concepts of the human and the inhuman, facilitated the divisions between subjects as humans and subjects priced as flesh (or inhuman matter)."[13] The creaturely and ecological zombie is therefore a direct challenge to the subject/object dichotomy that shaped the histories of slavery and the rendering of land as commodity under colonialism. Yusoff further notes on this slippage between the human and the inhuman, describing "how the inhuman is made to slide over personhood as a process of making the subjugated (as in the black body rendered as flesh and units of energy) is an unrecognised dynamic of geological life that rewrites a radically different text for the Anthropocene."[14] Through rewriting and revising what is an agential subject, endowed with human qualities, we can thus begin to challenge the violent divisions that push certain lives and subjects outside "the structures of cozy humanism."[15]

In both Negarestani's and Miéville's surrealist depiction of oil as an agential force, we become introduced to what Anat Pick defines as the creaturely: a non-anthropocentric project that follows a logic of flesh, exposing the animal or even vegetative aspects which lurk within the human itself.[16] Reading both oil and the zombie through Pick's creaturely prism draws together a material and corporeal way of being which refutes and challenges commodification. In the same way oil is often presented as a resource, a disposable body of material matter, the zombie has a history in which it is severed from the power of consciousness and agency. As Roger Luckhurst declares, "zombies are speechless, gormless, without memory of prior life or attachments, sinking into an indifferent mass and growing exponentially."[17] To trace the zombie to its origin of the Haitian slave, a myth that incorporates both slavery and resistance, we find alternatively a mode power and liberation in materiality.[18] Like Pick's advocation of a corporeal ethics, the zombie myth has "an undercurrent of rebellion"[19] in which the indistinguishable mass of bodies and flesh challenges the hegemonic order. In what follows, I adhere to Pick's creaturely practice, in which "man as the centre of the universe is no more, and a new history… the natural history of creatures—is born."[20]

Pick's creaturely poetics is centered on the work of the philosopher Simone Weil, whose core principle is that vulnerability is a marker of existence. Whatever one is, one is always subject to forces beyond control, and thus to injury pain and death. For Pick, "the idea of contact is not only central to the experience of reading Weil but is the very fabric of her thought."[21] Contact zones, cross-contamination, and spaces of indistinction are central themes of the zombie myth appearing through the fear and inevitability of contagion, the permeability of our fleshy borders, the danger of contact with more than human worlds. Negarestani's theorization of both oil and dust as contaminating collectives mirrors the movement of the zombie who proliferates and spreads through disease and contagion. *Cyclonopedia* draws us toward these abject domains— as oil and dust are shown to occupy subterranean complexes and underground terrains. He defines oil, the petropolitical undercurrents of the earth, as the "blobjective," and dust becomes "dustism," a nomadic entity "progressing at a cosmic level."[22] Crude oil produces "diseases, deluges and blinding smog [and] all employ dust as their primary agent."[23] Negarestani emphasizes the contagious quality of oil, describing it as possessing "tendencies for mass intoxication on pandemic scales."[24] Like Shaviro's description of the zombie, oil is similarly "a plague: it takes the form of a mass contagion, without any discernible point of origin."[25] Oil conceived as a mass contagion captures its unruly nature—its inability and refusal to be contained or captured. As critic Sarah Juliet Lauro suggests about the zombie,

> Just as the monster is never fully living nor entirely dead, it is never wholly terrifying but also pitiable, in between agent and object, master and subject, neither the capable captain nor merely his commanded craft—and this is precisely what makes it worthy of our critical attention.[26]

By occupying such a position, moving between subject and object, agential and individual yet material and collective, Negarestani's presentation of oil unravels capital's attempt to capture it as a commodity, and instead introduces a non-anthropocentric frame into our understanding.

If the zombie is, as Shaviro suggests, "all body"[27] so too is oil in Negarestani's narrative. Its power lies not in individual subjectivity or abstract thought but in its collective materiality. What Negarestani describes as the "thingness" of petroleum, its ability to make things move, is a power of corporeality which moves away from Enlightenment narratives of the atomized thinking subject, distinct from physical affect and movement. Unraveling the Enlightenment subject is an essential process of decolonization; like Yusoff suggests, "modern liberalism is forged through colonial violence."[28] Oil as an animate and collective force thus abolishes the "Cartesian" understanding of human life and biological matter. Pipeline politics are not dictated by the capitalist and neocolonial regime, but rather oil itself is shown to be the narrator: "the cartography of oil as an omnipresent entity narrates the dynamics of planetary events."[29] Oil creates its own "petropolitical network" in which political actors are its puppets, a "singular anorganic body with its own agendas." Negarestani goes on to describe oil as "hydrocarbon corpse juice: a post-apocalyptic entity composed of organic corpses, piled up and liquidated in sedimentary basins (mega-graveyards)."[30] This visualization of indistinguishable flesh and rotting corpses returns us to both the myth of the zombie and Pick's notion of the creaturely. Pick suggests the creaturely invokes a "rawness of nerves" and follows the "logic of flesh,"[31] creating what she terms as a corporeal ethics and aesthetics. Through Negarestani's emphasis of the corporeal aspects of oil as a collation of past living organisms crudely awakened by extraction machinery, we can begin to conceive of oil as a creaturely entity, leading to an exposure of what Pick describes as "the flesh and blood nature of reality."[32]

Negarestani's focus on corporeality, of bodily contact zones, and cross-contamination, challenges the dominance of the colonizer, allowing for new possible narratives to arise around subjectivity, autonomy, and agential power. It thus challenges liberal and philosophical conceptions of the human, provoking a new understanding of our position and relation to ecology and other species. For Wynter, the local concept of Man/Human has an imperial universality. As she notes, "the idea of Man at a particular moment of world history, the European Renaissance, was also the foundational step for building racism as we know it today."[33] In order to think and live decolonial practice, Wynter argues, it is necessary to unsettle and undo Western conceptions of the human. Negarestani's undoing of Western liberal conceptions of the human offers a mode of decolonial thinking in which new subjectivities are discovered.

The strange and almost grotesque amalgam of a creaturely petro-zombie allows for radically reshaped subjectivities beyond the grasp and force of colonial violence. Negarestani explores the agential power in the collective movement of crude oil. Oil is a "pipeline crawler"[34] moving through abject and underground terrains, decentering man and opening up new passageways of possible revolt and resistance. Like the Haitian Zombie, whose origins lay in the dialectic of slavery and resistance, Negarestani's depiction of oil is similarly connected to a unity of opposites between "enslavement and rebellion."[35] While, on the one hand, capital reduces oil to the status of an object, the same extractive process lends it a rebellious form of agency which takes up the pipeline as but one of its parts, always on the point of counteraction.

Dust takes on a similar zombie-like formation in the narrative; dust is, as Negarestani describes, "a demonic mobilisation"[36] in which "dust particles originate from dark corners never trodden before, different territories (fields of narration) and domains of invisible hazard."[37] Negarestani's focus on all the "dejected domains of being,"[38] including tombs, decay, rot, and dust, envisions a zombie-like collective. This mergence and process of cross-contamination captures the hybridity of the zombie, neither living nor dead, somewhat conscious yet deprived of reason and thought. There is, however, a resurgence and form of resistance that characterizes geological matter in the text; as Negarestani describes, "dust is the name of a rebellion marked by utter collectivity."[39] Like the zombie, dust, oil, and other geological formations are "inherently resistant."[40] The text is characterized by "a fantasy of rebellion against the hegemonic order,"[41] as geological matter and the earth itself are described as "rebel disciples of the sun."[42] Geology takes on a new meaning in the text as particles, organic matter, debris, and remains discover their own agential power. Abject forces thus come together as outsiders, peripheral residents who now take center stage. In Negarestani's description of the rebellious congregation of dust particles, we find a movement akin to the formation of the zombie:

> A dust particle collects its components from different milieus so distant from one another that they can operate for each other only as outsiders. When dust is utilised in creation to compose and concoct, it turns the object, or to be precise the created composition, into a fierce operative of horror, with a progressively thickening ominous plot or storyline… this emergence of new life forms and collective particles might be apprehender as an insider take over, the rise of a new people.[43]

Dust in this passage gives rise to a new people, a rebellious movement which emerges from forgotten corners and leftover remains. Dust creates an "awakening," one in which capitalist and anthropocentric control becomes destabilized. Dust and oil become zombie-like not through the American appropriation of the allegory to describe an empty consumerism but instead through the Haitian myth of resistance, what Lauro terms as "the counteroccupation of mythical space."[44] The agential, mythical, abject, and somewhat magical qualities attributed to oil and dust allow for a way of reconfiguring what we conceive as waste and commodity. This is oil's "magical revenge"[45] in the narrative, slipping from the grasp of colonial and capitalist domination and revealing itself to be an affective and rebellious movement of its own.

The anthropocentric usage and understanding of oil as fossil capital slowly becomes deconstructed in *Cyclonopedia*, for oil surfaces instead as something liberatory yet somewhat monstrous in the text. Similar to Vint's description of the zombie narrative which "challenges us to rethink life beyond the anthropocentrism of the liberal subject,"[46] Negarestani also breaks down Western ideals of humanism through his conception of geology as a sentient and animate agent. The corporeal aesthetic of oil as formerly living matter connects to Pick's creaturely project of breaking down species distinction in order to expose ourselves and other beings as material, temporal, and finite—oil in this literary work thus becomes a creaturely archive of the living and the dead, a zombie-like formation. Contact with oil, the living dead, becomes at once dangerous and emancipatory, freeing ourselves from the Enlightenment subject that is in many cases the source of oppression. As Lauro and Embry suggest in their Zombie Manifesto, "to truly move post human, we have to not shrink the body but the Enlightenment subject position."[47] The combined nexus of the creaturely, oil, and the zombie serves to rid ourselves of this Enlightenment subject position, the privileged subject who becomes the measure of all things. Instead the aesthetic and ethics of the creaturely alongside the petro-zombie "resists being a tool of capitalism, which is destructive rather than productive, which resists the rational, which becomes anti-individual, anti-subject."[48] *Cyclonopedia* creates an awakening of geological forces, rallying against the chains of Western capital and the domination of the colonizer.

The figure of the petro-zombie as a rebellious and unruly movement likewise permeates the pages of Miéville's short story *Covehithe*. The narrative magnifies the peripheral extraction zone of the North Sea, illuminating abandoned production spaces and exposing us to the decaying remnants of the extraction process. The eerie setting of an abandoned production lot, the absence of human presence, and a nearby graveyard create a gothic atmosphere as the two central characters' inquisitive curiosity takes them toward the oil rigs. They wait for the slow and mechanical movement of the oil rigs, as the infrastructure of petroculture becomes awakened, their monstrous steps moving through the seabed. They were "ruined, lost burnt, scuttled rigs [that] were healing on the ocean floor and coming back."[49] What is perceived as inanimate and controlled becomes chaotically reversed in the narrative. In *Covehithe*, crude oil and its infrastructure are not merely a backdrop to a metropolitan landscape or simply a form of capital defined by and subject to market relations; instead, it becomes alive, colliding with a world in which it was once an object of domination.

The crisis which unfolds in *Covehithe* of oil rigs collectively drilling at will and laying eggs on the seashore further recalls the movement of the zombie. As Jen Webb and Samuel Byrand describe, "zombies aren't social isolates—they seem to prefer to live in groups, within built environments… they actively colonise space for themselves—they seek to spread well beyond their local region and to dominate places."[50] As we have noted in Negarestani's *Cyclonopedia*, there is a sense of multiplicity, a gathering between ecological elements and infrastructure.

In this emergence of a multiplicity of oil rigs autonomously and collectively acting upon their own will, we find that they possess the uprising quality of the zombie, "the capacity to awaken, to throw of their bonds, to reclaim life amid the morbid ruins of capitalism."[51] The descriptions of the oil rig slowly moving out from the ocean encapsulate the methodical and rising movement of the zombie:

> It shook the coast with its steps. It walked through buildings, swatted trucks then tanks out of its way with ripped cables and pipes that flailed in efficient deadly motion, like ill-trained snakes, like too heavy feeding tentacles. It reached with corroded chains, wrenched obstacles from the earth. It dripped sea water, chemicals of industrial ruin and long-hoarded oil.[52]

The chaos in which the oil rig wrecks across the landscape enacts the zombie's power of "radical refusal and destruction of value."[53] This speculative encounter with energy infrastructure becomes a way of disturbing a system that follows a model of business-as-usual, as the rigs defy subordination, opening up new possibilities of alternative futures, a possible movement away from capitalist regimes. The oil rigs possess the disruptive dualism of the zombie, possessing what Shaviro describes "both as a monstrous symptom of a violent, manipulative, exploitative society and as a potential remedy for its ills—all this by virtue of their apocalyptically destructive, yet oddly innocuous, counterviolence."[54] It is difficult to discern whether the oil rigs autonomous drilling across the globe is a haunting specter of our past and future relation to petroleum, an incessant drive for more extraction, or whether it is a way of capturing oil and its infrastructure as possessing an agential power slipping from anthropocentric grasp.

This sense of opposition echoes Lauro's description of the legacy of the zombie as the dialectic of enslavement and rebellion. We witness the slow and zombie-like steps of the oil rig in Miéville's narrative as the characters await the rig's movements: "Another step—because these were clumsy steps with which it came... it waded."[55] The rig's mechanical and slow movements capture the laborious and mindless work of the Haitian slave zombie. Yet, as Lauro suggests, enslavement always entails the essence of rebellion ready on the point of being launched. For Lauro, "there is something forceful, even malevolent about the way the zombie undermines potential success of protest at the same time it embodies revolutionary drive."[56] The zombie appears to be trapped within this dialectic of slavery and rebellion, where the legacies of colonialism and the present force of neocolonial regimes encode and block access to freedom. Miéville's oil rigs are similarly caught between these oppositions for at no stage do we have a glimpse or access into the oil rigs' subjectivity; we perceive the oil rigs as only the observer where they are simultaneously an object of awe and conversely an impending threat to be exterminated.

The narrative moves back in time to the father's memories of working for the military in efforts to tackle the global awakening of oil infrastructure. The oil rigs demonstration of life, agency, and movement is automatically rendered as a deviant force which must be attacked, as is echoed of the commanding officers: "Should we attack?"[57] This collective awakening of oil rigs moving together as a multiplicity, drilling and spreading across different regions, and occupying space, is the rebellious force of the petro-zombie, moving outside the bounds and limits of anthropocentrism. They are, what Miéville describes as, "petrospectral presences";[58] like the zombie, they haunt and challenge, provoking questions around subjectivity and the bounds of what is to be considered normatively "human."

The creative reimaginings of crude oil and its infrastructure in both *Cyclonopedia* and *Covehithe* capture this move toward a new understanding of crude oil outside of capital and the market. The playful destruction of the subject/object domains allows for new possibilities to emerge: social, cultural, and structural transformations to our current energy regimes. As Vint suggests, "when humans refuse to be what liberal philosophy constituted as 'the human', new possibilities emerge, including new models of the relationship between individual and community."[59] These new models arise through the petro-zombie who emerges as a multiplicity, creating new forms of community between geological formations, debris, and leftover matter.

What could these new forms of communities and creative recodings of crude oil do in such a moment of what Sheena Wilson terms an "energy impasse"?[60] The energy impasse is a crucial turning point for an energy transition, but as Wilson suggests, it is also a moment of "atrophy of the imagination that blockades transformative action."[61] Wilson's remedy to this blockade is to turn to "the reintroduction of Other knowledge systems and world views, including but not limited to feminist and Indigenous knowledges, which can help us collaboratively imagine and collectively move toward socially just—decolonized and feminist—energy futures."[62] Among these categories it is possible to also find that of both the zombie and the creaturely, both of which are forms of Other's knowledge systems, outside the violence of colonialism. Working under the nexus of the creaturely, the zombie, and oil, we find an unusual fellowship which can transform our ways of thinking beyond the force and violence of neocolonialism and colonial legacies. Miéville's and Negarestani's creative reimagining of oil and its infrastructure as a powerful agent who thus refuses to be measured by the barrel, rejects the label of commodity, and challenges the systematic and structural violence of our global energy regimes. Turning to the extractive zone in the literary imaginary presented seeds of resistance and hope for an alternative from the present violence of energy production. The petro-zombie under the lens of the creaturely strikes as a new formation that conceives of just and perhaps a utopian understanding of energy beyond the imperialism of extractive capital.

Notes

1. I refer to "petrocultures" in the context of the research collective co-organized by Imre Szeman and Sheena Wilson. This collective illuminates how crude oil shapes the social and cultural imaginary of the twenty-first century. Their proposal is that energy transition is not just an economic or structural issue but a cultural one.
2. Many oil texts such as Daniel Yergin's *The Prize* and Peter Maas' *Crude World* often invoke oil through this corporeal imagery, entwining this resource within our veins and bodily needs. To do so, however, has problematic implications as it suggests oil is intrinsic to our functioning and survival, leading to a process of naturalization and therefore suggesting addiction to oil is a bodily phenomenon.
3. Oloff, "'Greening' The Zombie."
4. Gómez-Barris, *The Extractive Zone*, 5.
5. Yusoff, *A Billion Black Anthropocenes or None*, 3.
6. Yusoff, *A Billion Black Anthropocenes or None*, 9.
7. Wynter, "Unsettling the Coloniality of Being/Power/Truth/Freedom," 266.
8. Yusoff, *A Billion Black Anthropocenes or None*, 68.
9. Yusoff, *A Billion Black Anthropocenes or None*, 6.
10. Doherty, Barrett and Worden, *Oil Culture*, 371.
11. Yusoff, *A Billion Black Anthropocenes or None*, 54.
12. Shaviro, "Contagious Allegories," 9.
13. Yusoff, *A Billion Black Anthropocenes or None*, 9.
14. Yusoff, *A Billion Black Anthropocenes or None*, 72.
15. Yusoff, *A Billion Black Anthropocenes or None*, 9.
16. Pick, *Creaturely Poetics*, 6.
17. Luckhurst, *Zombies*, 7.
18. Sarah Juliet Lauro's collection on *The Transatlantic Zombie* traces the changes in zombie imagery, the way in which it has been appropriated, returning the image to its origins. This origin is located within folk tale from Haiti, "one that is deeply associated with the nation's history as a colony and the people's past as plantations slaves," Lauro, *The Transatlantic Zombie*, 3.

19 Lauro, *The Transatlantic Zombie*, 16.
20 Pick, *Creaturely Poetics*, 183.
21 Pick, *Creaturely Poetics*, 3.
22 Negarestani, *Cyclonopedia*, 89.
23 Negarestani, *Cyclonopedia*, 89.
24 Negarestani, *Cyclonopedia*, 17.
25 Shaviro, "Contagious Allegories," 9.
26 Lauro, *The Transatlantic Zombie*, xi.
27 Shaviro, "Contagious Allegories," 9.
28 Negarestani, *Cyclonopedia*, 19.
29 Negarestani, *Cyclonopedia*, 20.
30 Negarestani, *Cyclonopedia*, 27.
31 Pick, *Creaturely Poetics*, 3.
32 Pick, *Creaturely Poetics*, 13.
33 Wynter, "Unsettling the Coloniality of Being/Power/Truth/Freedom," 118.
34 Negarestani, *Cyclonopedia*, 28.
35 Lauro, *The Transatlantic Zombie*, 5.
36 Negarestani, *Cyclonopedia*, 117.
37 Negarestani, *Cyclonopedia*, 88.
38 Negarestani, *Cyclonopedia*, 183.
39 Negarestani, *Cyclonopedia*, 89.
40 Lauro, *The Transatlantic Zombie*, 32.
41 Lauro, *The Transatlantic Zombie*, 31.
42 Negarestani, *Cyclonopedia*, 88.
43 Negarestani, *Cyclonopedia*, 90.
44 Lauro claims that "the zombie is a twentieth century commodification of a people's narrative about their ancestors commodification under transatlantic slavery and its persistence in postcolony. In a way, then, the appropriation of the zombie myth in a display like Occupy Wall Street risks seeming like a kind of second-degree blackface, an appropriation of people's cultural narrative of struggle and empowerment for entertainment purposes." In Lauro, *The Transatlantic Zombie*, 11.
45 Shaviro, "Contagious Allegories," 9.
46 Vint, "Abject Posthumanism, Biopolitics, and Zombies," 175.
47 Lauro and Embry, "Zombie Manifesto," 400.
48 Lauro and Embry, "Zombie Manifesto," 407.
49 Miéville, *Three Moments of an Explosion*, 344.
50 Webb and Byrand, "Some Kind of Virus," 111.
51 McNally, "Ugly Beauty," 124.
52 Miéville, *Three Moments of an Explosion*, 343.
53 Shaviro, "Contagious Allegories," 8.
54 Shaviro, "Contagious Allegories," 9.

55 Miéville, *Three Moments of an Explosion*, 341.
56 Lauro, *The Transatlantic Zombie*, 199.
57 Miéville, *Three Moments of an Explosion*, 345.
58 Miéville, *Three Moments of an Explosion*, 345.
59 Vint, "Abject Posthumanism, Biopolitics, and Zombies," 178.
60 Wilson, "Energy Imaginaries," 377.
61 Wilson, "Energy Imaginaries," 377.
62 Wilson, "Energy Imaginaries," 378.

Works Cited

Deckard, Sharae. "Trains, Stone, and Energetics: African Resource Culture and the Neoliberal World-Ecology." In *World Literature, Neoliberalism, and the Culture of Discontent*, edited by Sharae Deckard and Stephen Shapiro, 239–62. London: Palgrave Macmillan, 2020.

Doherty, Melanie. "Oil and Dust, Theorising Reza Negarestani's Cyclonopedia." In *Oil Culture*, edited by Ross Barrett and Daniel Worden, 366–83. Minneapolis: University of Minnesota Press, 2014.

Gómez-Barris, Macarena. *The Extractive Zone, Social Ecologies and Decolonial Perspectives*. London: Duke University Press, 2017.

Hageman, Andrew. "Bringing Infrastructural Criticism to Speculative Fiction: China Miéville's 'Covehithe.'" *C21 Literature: Journal of 21st-Century Writings* 7, no. 1 (2019): 1–10.

Lauro, Sarah Juliet. *The Transatlantic Zombie: Slavery, Rebellion, and Living Death*. New Brunswick: Rutgers University Press, 2015.

Lauro, Sarah Juliet and Karen Embry. "Zombie Manifesto: The Non-Human Condition in the Era of Advanced Capitalism." In *Zombie Theory: A Reader*, edited by Sarah Juliet Lauro, 395–412. Minneapolis: University of Minnesota Press, 2017.

Luckhurst, Roger. *Zombies: A Cultural History*. London: Reaktion Books, 2015.

Marder, Michael. *Dust*. London: Bloomsbury Publishing, 2016.

McNally, David. "Ugly Beauty: Monstrous Dreams of Utopia." In *Zombie Theory: A Reader*, edited by Sarah Juliet Lauro, 124–36. Minneapolis: University of Minnesota Press, 2017.

Miéville, China. *Three Moments of Explosion Stories*. London: Macmillan, 2015.

Negarestani, Reza. *Cyclonopedia, Complicity with Anonymous Materials*. Melbourne: Re-Press, 2008.

Oloff, Kerstin. "'Greening' The Zombie: Caribbean Gothic, World-Ecology, and Socio-Ecological Degradation." *Green Letters: Studies in Ecocriticism* 16, no. 1 (2012): 31–45.

Oloff, Kerstin. "From Sugar to Oil: The Ecology of George A. Romero's Night of the Living Dead." *Journal of Postcolonial Writing* 53, no. 3 (2017): 316–28.

Pick, Anat. *Creaturely Poetics: Animality and Vulnerability in Literature and Film.* New York: Columbia University Press, 2011.
Shaviro, Steven. "Contagious Allegories: George Romero." In *Zombie Theory: A Reader*, edited by Sarah Juliet Lauro, 7–19. Minneapolis: University of Minnesota Press, 2017.
Vint, Sherryl. "Abject Posthumanism, Biopolitics, and Zombies." In *Zombie Theory: A Reader,* edited by Sarah Juliet Lauro, 171–82. Minneapolis: University of Minnesota Press, 2017.
Webb, Jen and Samuel Byrand. "Some Kind of Virus: The Zombie as Body and as Trope." In *Zombie Theory: A Reader*, edited by Sarah Juliet Lauro, 111–23. Minneapolis: University of Minnesota Press, 2017.
Wilson, Sheena. "Energy Imaginaries: Feminist and Decolonial Futures." In *Materialism and the Critique of Energy*, edited by Brent Bellamy and Jeff Diamanti, 377–412. Chicago: MCM Publishing, 2018.
Wynter, Sylvia. "Unsettling the Coloniality of Being/Power/Truth/Freedom: Towards the Human, after Man, Its Overrepresentation–An Argument." *CR: The New Centennial Review* 3 no. 3 (2003): 257–337. *Project MUSE*, doi:10.1353/ncr.2004.0015.
Yusoff, Kathryn. *A Billion Black Anthropocenes or None.* Minnesota: University of Minnesota Press, 2019.

6

Undead, Undeader, Undeadest: Narrating the Unevenness of Ecological Crisis in Nana Nkweti's "It Just Kills You Inside"

Fiona Farnsworth

"Boogeymen are real in Africa, folks"[1] begins Nana Nkweti's "It Just Kills You Inside." The story's narrator, Connor, refers knowingly to the occult "imaginings that rise up from the darkest of hearts": a bold opening gambit which invokes racist (and racialized) interpretations of Africa as a "dark continent" only to undercut them with an unmistakable tone of mockery. Of course, the nod to "the darkest of hearts" inverts and puns on Conrad's *Heart of Darkness*, widely criticized in postcolonial academic circles for its reductive portrayal of a homogenous, savage (and, indeed, "dark") Africa. Most famously, perhaps, Chinua Achebe critiques the novel as symptomatic of a need "in Western psychology to set Africa up as a foil to Europe, as a place of negations at once remote and vaguely familiar."[2] Moreover, in the heavy irony of statements like "This was Africa after all—the land of juju, obeah, and kamuti,"[3] it is possible to read shades of Binyavanga Wainaina's now-seminal "How to Write about Africa," in which the author issues a dictum to the aspiring author-cum-white savior: "Whichever angle you take, be sure to leave the strong impression that without your intervention... Africa is doomed."[4] This kind of "doom" narrative is mobilized in response to looming material threat. The implication satirized is, of course, that there is only one antidote to the inevitable decay (or outright, immediate destruction) presaged by such a narrative: the benevolent "intervention" of the white author. These opening sentences seem thus to gesture toward ongoing discourses surrounding the ways in which "Africa" is written and written about, and particularly in response to crisis and disaster. In doing so, they lay the groundwork for a zombie story which is less about zombies and more about stories: one which not only registers ecological crisis and its uneven impact throughout the world-system but foregrounds questions around the formal and aesthetic capacity of narrative to represent or obscure crisis immediately and long term.

At this juncture, I must acknowledge my positionality as a white scholar writing from and within the United Kingdom, and the privilege that affords me in global (racialized, capitalist) structures of inequality. This short story draws attention—even demands attention—to the politics of storytelling, and I have tried to be sensitive and attentive to this in my critical engagement with Nkweti's work. Nonetheless, because of the positionality highlighted above, the perspective I offer here is, in some ways, necessarily limited. My standpoint is not one of lived experience but of a literary scholar and interested reader, convinced of the discursive salience of Nkweti's work to the narration of the uneven effects of ecological crisis.

It is not always solely about how crisis is narrated, after all, but by whom it is narrated. Nkweti's narrator Connor (or "Con"—"short for [his] last name, Connor. Long on innuendo"[5]) is a "fixer." He works in "crisis management and communications"—in other words, he is flown to various locations around the world by governments and corporations to sanitize their public images in the wake of political, social, and environmental catastrophe. In 1991, Con is hired by French scientists based in Cameroon (on formerly colonized territory, expropriated in the "arbitrary and uncompensated alienation of some of the most fertile Bakweri land"[6]) to manage a media campaign that will initially silence public narratives surrounding a zombie outbreak. The text is nonlinear in its approach (a formal gesture toward the tension between the all-too predictable trajectory of environmental crisis and the apparent swiftness of its symptomatic disasters), and it moves between the earliest days of the outbreak and the crisis' development on a world stage, including the emergence of the "truth" about the outbreak in global consciousness when a spate of killings makes continued cover-up impossible, to the present day. This is presented alongside modulations in Con's personal life such as marriage and fatherhood, and a contemporary moment in which Con attempts to establish whether a zombie child was responsible for the death of the film star who adopted her. I address modes of storytelling contained within Nkweti's story—in particular, folklore and attendant mythos, and media and cultural production, alongside attention to the narrative properties of the text itself—through which the zombie is invoked in ways that are, though distinct, unmistakably and consistently imbricated. As such, Nkweti's narrative employs the contradictory figure of the zombie and its status of duality as a means through which to register and represent the ways in which "the tendency towards core-periphery polarization inherent in the logic of capital [entails] the unequal exchange not just of economic surpluses but of ecological ones too."[7] As Jennifer Wenzel asserts, for example, "A text need not announce concerns with the environment in its theme and plot to illuminate relationships among nature, culture, and power."[8] In this spirit, I contend that the "dialectic"[9] of Nkweti's zombies may be read in conjunction with, and as a registration of, the ongoing and uneven ramifications of environmental degradation and disaster.

I am working here with an understanding of "ecological crisis" informed by thinkers including Eric Cazdyn and Jason W. Moore. Cazdyn's piece "Disaster, Crisis, Revolution" investigates frequent and (he argues) erroneous conflation of "disaster" and "crisis" as terminologies, arguing that where the social implications of a "disaster" render it contingent and, often, predictable, "there is something necessary about a crisis, something true to the larger systemic form."[10] Although Cazdyn's work is wide-ranging in its approach to the arenas in which "disaster" might play out (he refers, for example, to "disaster" on the level of the individual for sufferers of HIV and cancer "when the logic of cells overproduces so that they no longer relate to the logic of the living body"[11]), it is his addressal of "crisis" that is most salient here. He states, "Crisis was always a condition of the short term. But now there seems to be the crisis of the long term."[12] Assuming such an understanding of crisis as a condition extended, ongoing, or continuous—indeed, as "playing out across a range of temporal scales"[13]—we might turn to Moore's suggestion that it may be productive "to think crisis as a process through which new ways of ordering the relations between humans and the rest of nature take shape."[14] The environmental angle I take is rooted similarly in Moore's work on capitalism as a "world-ecology," in which he asks that we contemplate "a unified theory of capitalism encompassing the accumulation of capital, the pursuit of power, and the co-production of nature."[15] Important here is a recognition of the fact that indigenous systems of knowledge in Africa have long understood human and nonhuman lives as ecologically inextricable: Cajetan Iheka asserts, for example, that "the relational positioning of the human to nonhumans is a model attribute of the stories and social practices of indigenous communities worth considering in an era of hypercapitalism."[16] Furthermore, reading the figure of the zombie as both resulting from *and* representing the material conditions of hypercapitalism, Kerstin Oloff has contended that while "the slow labouring zombie has long been understood as representing the exploitation of alienated workers" in Marxist criticism, "unless we grasp capitalism as a world-ecology, certain aspects of the trajectory of this figure... remain open to misreading."[17] Along these lines, I posit that Nkweti's zombies are not only mediated by the uneven impacts of ecological crisis throughout the capitalist world-system, nor are they exclusively a simple registration of such impacts, but also highlight the ways in which storytelling, mythology, and narrative may uphold and perpetuate the logics of capitalism as world-ecology.

Folklore and Myth

The instigative "disaster" of the story's zombie outbreak occurs at Lake Nyos, a volcanic crater lake in Cameroon, in 1986: "Natural disaster, bucolic lake goes acidic, belches up a cloud of CO_2 gas that asphyxiates villagers for miles 'round."[18] Geologists have speculatively attributed the real Nyos explosion to displacement of rising levels of carbon dioxide, and an eruption following a gradual build-up of gas[19]—both of which might be read as examples of Rob Nixon's "slow violence," or "a violence that occurs gradually and out of sight, a violence of delayed destruction that is dispersed across time and space."[20] Nonetheless, scientists have largely agreed that the eruption must have had a trigger, and this is the point upon which Nkweti's narrative pivots into the irreal, asking instead what might be at stake—environmentally, socially, morally—should the trigger have been not a landslide or a particularly aggressive storm but a nuclear test conducted in secret by an ex-colonial power. In the story, the chief scientist attributes it to Israeli military tests for a neutron bomb, an explanation that was indeed given credence at the time of and shortly after the explosion, Eugenia Shanklin explains, because it was thought to be "the newest weapon in the American arsenal, an experiment conducted on behalf of Israelis, who wished to see it demonstrated for possible use against Palestinians."[21] Con is unsure: "More likely, the French had done this themselves... and now were on to the slapdash ass-covering phase of the project."[22] Crucially, Con does not care to find out the truth. He is motivated by money, rather than by moral or ethical practice; he is representative of the same systems of colonial control that employ him; and, for him, identifying the specific colonial power responsible for an atrocity affects neither the narrative trajectory of his story nor his willingness to tell it.

Nkweti's narrative also extrapolates an alternative set of social and environmental ramifications. Chiefly, the gas cloud appears to have caused the rising of the dead, alongside "the usual complaints: heartburn, lesions, and neurological problems like monoplegia."[23] Key to this configuration is that the "incremental and accretive"[24] effects of the disaster resonate globally and over a range of temporal moments and periods: there is the initial gas cloud, resulting in nearly 2,000 deaths; physical displacement to refugee camps and other enduring ecological consequences of the decimation of fertile land and its nonhuman (and "other-than-human"[25]) inhabitants; the long-term health effects on victims which are at best disruptive and at worst life-limiting; and even hitherto unknown ramifications for climate and ecology. This is a perfect illustration of combined and uneven development, or the sensibility that "parts of the world undeveloped by capitalist modernization—or, indeed, *underdeveloped* by it—are nonetheless coeval contemporaries of the world-system's metropolitan centres":[26] the slow violence of environmental crisis is most visible in the areas of the world-system which contribute to it the least, and it is largely ignored by populations in the Global North until they are affected directly. A parallel scenario is also presented in reference to the Ebola virus, suggesting that cure research from the Global North is withheld from countries in the Global South until, in Con's words, "us good white folks start dying."[27] Inequities in global medical research are explicitly shown to follow a necropolitical logic in which life in the periphery and semi-periphery is valued lower, and "vast populations are subjected to conditions of life conferring upon them the status of *living dead*."[28]

The living dead victims of the Nyos disaster are also written into textual dialogue with extant zombie mythologies from Cameroonian indigenous peoples. These mythologies of zombies have much in common with the original Haitian *zombi*, a dialectic figure widely believed to have ancestral links to a number of West African tribal traditions, and understood to signify both "the positive, resistive return of the revenant and the specter enslaved, doomed to repeat."[29] Attention is drawn, in particular, to local tales from the Bakweri people: at the literal center point of the story, Con tells us of the *vekongi* who are "victims snared by *nyongo* witchcraft, doomed to a half-life: withered existence by day and entranced enslavement on the farmlands of their 'masters' by night."[30] Key continuities with the *zombi* are evident in the common theme of enslavement, and the understanding of the zombie as living dead therefore evokes the ancestral potential for revolt. Stephen Shapiro invokes the Bakweri explicitly in his discussion of recently "invented" zombie traditions as "new constructions that register globalizing conditions in local-seeming idioms,"[31] drawing upon the work of Edwin Ardener in demonstrating that "while the rise and fall of witchcraft discourse within the West Cameroon Bakweri synchronizes with the concomitant shape of economic cycles, the return of these beliefs in the first half of the twentieth century after German colonization and reorganization of communal plantations involves historically new aspects." In these new mythologies, zombies and zombification are understood to be a result of *nyongo*, a "dynamic, flexible, fluid and common form of witchcraft among the coastal and Grassfields peoples of Cameroon."[32] To this myth, John and Jean Comaroff add the following:

> Their land appropriated for the establishment of plantations manned largely by foreigners, the Bakweri found themselves crowded into inhospitable reserves… The living dead, many of them children, were said to be victims of the murderous greed of their own close kind; they were sent away to work in distant plantations, where witchmasters had built a town overflowing with modern consumer goods.[33]

The salient ideas of kinship highlighted by the Comaroffs are also invoked in Con's own familial relationships, which are crucial, albeit peripheral, to the plot of Nkweti's story. Con characterizes the *vekongi* as the "kissing cousins" of the Nyos victims. This phraseology refers to two things which are so similar as to appear related, thus troubling notions of family, lineage, and kinship. A lineage of this kind—shadowy, ghoulish—would be a narrative constructed around the ideological nexus of the "living dead": not biologically related but related in the sense of similarity by virtue of their biology. This finds further articulation—and further narrative mediation—in the bedtime stories that Con tells his daughter Chelsea. Chelsea demonstrates an early fascination with the monstrous, but figures like vampires are too tame for her tastes. Instead, her imagination latches onto tales of zombies and, more specifically, the *vekongi*, although notably these are still not figures of fear. In her vocal feedback to Con's stories, Chelsea even shortens *vekongi* to "*Kongi*" as a pet name for her "imaginary revenant relatives":[34] an expression of affection particularly illustrative of the ways in which the zombie may become divorced from its original context via the telling, appropriation, and retelling of particular myths.

This is particularly important because Chelsea's mother is Con's ex-wife Mambe, who is herself Bakweri, and yet it is from her American father that Chelsea hears stories of her zombified Bakweri "kin." Indeed, Con suggests that Mambe hates the exercise of these deliberately horrifying stories, but he ignores, and even belittles, her objections ("was I really going to listen to a woman who named our child after a British football team?").[35] Con refers to Mambe at one point in the story as a "conjure woman" because she features in a hallucinatory dreamscape that he experiences while anesthetized following a zombie-related injury. While use of this terminology signifies certainly a problematic exoticization of Mambe, it is also indicative of Con's lack of situated understanding of the stories he tells or the ways in which they might be read euhemeristically as irreal registrations of displacement under colonial occupation. Even on a prosaic level, inaccuracies are present in Con's narrative, which suggest that he is neither as well informed nor as attentive as he considers himself; for example, he refers to "the Bakweri tribe of North Cameroon,"[36] despite the fact that the Bakweri people are found chiefly in the south.[37]

These are not Con's tales to tell, and yet he assumes responsibility for their narration and appropriates them for his own purposes—the fact that these purposes are paternal rather than mercenary is of comparatively little significance. This is particularly striking considering that Chelsea's response is not one of fear. For her, these stories are demonstrably "a dress rehearsal for facing life's terrors head-on"[38] rather than nemeses she must confront with any physical immediacy—she can sleep safely because she registers the figures in her bedtime stories not as "irreal" but as *un*real. The detachment Chelsea exhibits is also of significance in the story's overall commentary on the nature of narrative, because it evidences a false dichotomy enacted between the "backwoods relatives," for whom relatives lost to *nyongo* are all too (ir)real, and the "civilized," for whom such experiences are merely "ridiculous notions."[39] While it seems that Con does not himself subscribe to such a division between the "civilized" ("city folk," characterized by their readership of global news media such as *Jeune Afrique* and *Le Monde*) and the "backwoods" (principally associated with the local and parochial, who are presented as uninterested in and even afraid of the world beyond), the fact that he employs the terms at all, even mockingly, suggests that he has no qualms about exploiting it nonetheless.

In a similar vein, folklore and attendant beliefs resonate throughout the story beyond Cameroon. The story culminates in direct address:

> This is what we tell you. The only truth you'll ever know. And you'll accept it because you once set out sugar cookies for Santa, you trust deeply in the power of your voice and your vote, and expect that when you die, when you are nothing but bone and bliss, there lies a new beginning, a sweet hereafter.[40]

An uneasy comparison is evoked between belief in the myths of childhood— "sugar cookies for Santa"—and belief in the crucial components of democracy— "your voice and your vote"—as similarly facile and naïve. We return here to the "doom narrative" with an unforgiving sense of irony: the naïve expectation of "a new beginning, a sweet hereafter" recalls Kafka's maxim (as quoted by Jonathan Franzen) that "There is infinite hope, but not for us."[41] Once more, the naiveté invoked is indicative of the structural unevenness of combined and uneven development. The conditions that make possible a deep trust "in the power of your voice and your vote" are also necessarily those in which such power is at least credible, if not actualized. Instead, the voices of those designated "Other" are systematically silenced in a racialized, patriarchal, capitalist world-system; and voter suppression is in evidence across marginalized populations within national electorates, from the insidious barriers of bureaucracy[42] to the overt action of military and political coup.

Media and Cultural Production

Wenzel suggests in *The Disposition of Nature* that our urgent attention must focus upon "recognizing the work that literature and cultural imagining do *all the time* in naturalizing ideas about nature and shaping constituencies of caring and regimes of visibility."[43] For Nkweti's work, to recognize this work is necessarily to attend to the various forms of storytelling implicated in this one text: not simply cultural production and global media within "It Just Kills You Inside" but "It Just Kills You Inside" *as* a cultural production that is itself shaped by position and interaction within the world-literary system. I have noted the registration of the tension between the slow violence of climate change and the ostensible suddenness of the Nyos disaster and the "resurrections" it occasions. However, perhaps more pertinent is the Warwick Research Collective (WReC) understanding of the unreliable narrator as another of a number of "irrealist" formal features,[44] in which they suggest that such irrealist features are "discernible wherever literary works are composed that mediate the lived experience of capitalism's bewildering creative destruction (or destructive creation)."[45] The story begins, in fact, with the tongue-in-cheek subtitle *"Based on true events."* As such, a shadow of doubt is cast over the veracity of the story from the beginning. Later, it turns out that "Connor" is our narrator's last name: the nickname "Con" is therefore nominally significant not only because of its pun on an act of intentional duplicity but because it constructs another wall between reader and "truth." How do we put our faith in a narrator whose name we do not know? And yet, Con seems to suggest, trust in unreliable narrators (and their unreliable narratives) is characteristic of engagement with crisis media and, in particular, media pertaining to crises linked explicitly to legacies of colonial violence. In this configuration, "crisis management" and "communications" have come to be synonymous. The "crisis" to be "managed" is not the ecological degradation from the burst oil pipeline or the loss of life inflicted by Big Pharma; it is the optics of such events in the sphere of public news media in the Global North, the fickle nature of consumer loyalty, and the ensuing possibility of financial detriment for company sales. For corporations and corrupt governments, the crisis is not ontological. The crisis is capital.

One of the foremost ways in which Nkweti's text interrogates the capacity of narrative and narrator to register crisis is by calling upon existing cultural production. S. J. Lauro explains that as the zombie became more popular and more prevalent in film and pulp fiction particularly, it transformed into "a more varied signifier" associated with, among other salient social concerns, the "rapacious hunger of a capitalistic and increasingly corporate society."[46] Through this modulation, themes of contagion and infection have become associated with the plots of contemporary zombie fictions in the Global North; see, for example, Romero's commonly theorized *Night of the Living Dead* film series by George Romero, comics and their televisual adaptations like *The Walking Dead*, or the pathogenic fungus *Orphiocordyceps unilateralis* that turns the infected into "hungries" in M. R. Carey's *The Girl with All the Gifts*.[47] Nkweti creates an intertextual link with these kinds of cultural production in a brief reference to *Resurrection Hill*—a diegetic blockbuster in which the adoptive father of the zombie child Anasta is the star, and which is suggested to be very much the kind of "B" movie that Con scorns. However, Nkweti's work engages with ideas of contagion only to refuse them emphatically, and therefore writes into a third "transformation" (to borrow Lauro's phraseology) of the zombie, one which recognizes the historical trajectory of "appropriation of a myth that, ironically or aptly, was *itself* about appropriation—specifically the appropriation of life and labour under colonial slavery,"[48] but which also reconsiders how the zombie figure might be used in a contemporary global imaginary to think through the unevenness of capitalism's economic and ecological effects. When Con is bitten by a zombie—his second face-to-face interaction—an overenthusiastic guard cuts off the injured hand, "trying to 'staunch the contagion,' keep it from stir-frying [Con's] brain pan."[49] Con tells Mambe that the disease is "not airborne, blood-borne. You either got it at Nyos or you didn't," but the statement is accompanied by uncertainty; who, he asks, is he trying to convince? With such rhetorical questions left unspoken but entirely legible to readers via narrative focalization, there is no way to discern the "truth" about the outbreak. In addition to its cinematic description, this scene is notable for its intertextual derision of the guard's "*Dawn of the Dead* hysteria"[50]—another nod to the ultra-prevalence of "whitewashed" newer zombie narratives, in which the zombie figure becomes "a more varied signifier capable of incarnating fears of disease and the body's vulnerability"[51] and its origins in resistance to enslavement are all but erased.

Indeed, the zombies in Nkweti's story are both narrative and narrativized in part via the mechanism of naming. We know already, for example, that the nickname "Con" plays on the narrator's profession as a fabricator of public relations fodder and that he refers to Mambe as "Maim" after detailing the physical violence he experienced at her hands ("She had a good throwing arm, that one")[52] which resulted in visible scarification. However, in relation to the zombies in the story, the issue is not of naming but of renaming. When we are introduced to the first zombie Con meets—"Test Subject 13" of Orliac's underground experiments—is nicknamed "Lazarus," in reference to the biblical figure who is resurrected by Christ. The zombie who bites Con is nicknamed "Namaan," again recalling a (lesser-known) biblical figure: this time the commander of the Aramean forces in the Book of Kings, who is "a powerful warrior but leprous, and thus disqualified from various kinds of social interactions."[53] Finally, the zombie child to whom Con seems to feel some kind of emotional bond is named Anasta, likely derived from the Ancient Greek *anastasis*, meaning "resurrection." Each of these acts of renaming recalls dually the renaming of African countries as part of colonial projects of remapping and dispossession—this is true of Cameroon itself, renamed by a fifteenth-century Portuguese trader[54]—and the prescriptive enforcing of Christian names on colonized and enslaved peoples. As well as acting in an allegorical capacity, renaming here obscures the human lived experiences of the victims of Nyos prior to their zombification. It is significant, too, that this renaming occurs at the hands of scientists, recalling pseudoscientific eugenicist logics which frequently provided the racist (and racialized) justification for colonial rule.

Nevertheless, Con is uneasy of Lazarus precisely because of his aura of the uncanny. Although Lazarus bears little resemblance to popular media portrayals of zombies as "shambolic shufflers, gray-fleshed and caterwauling like amateur sopranos,"[55] his skin is nonetheless "part nacreous, part necrotic," and he moves marginally slower than the living: he is "still undead, undeader, undeadest."[56] Nkweti's use of polyptoton evokes a linguistic and material tension between the states of "human" and "non-human," as well as between the various conditions of "living" and "unliving." This seems testament to the role of the zombie in complicating broadly understood binaries: if these are not absolute adjectives—if it is no longer the case that one is either "living" or "dead" but can, instead, fall somewhere in between—then does it not follow that this might occur on a spectrum, that one might be comparatively "undeader" than another, or even the "undeadest" of all?

Such questions bring us to the death of the famous movie star. In the nonlinear narrative of the story, this is the thread that occurs in the contemporary moment; and it provides the impetus behind Con's storytelling, since the death occurred ostensibly at the hands (or teeth) of Anasta, the zombie child adopted by the movie star and her husband. Con's task is to establish whether Anasta was indeed responsible, and to drip-feed more palatable stories to global media. In the death of the movie star at the hands of her child, and in conjunction with the text's other registrations of ecological crisis, the zombie's original association with rebellion and resistance is invoked and the existential threat is inverted: when the child murders the parental figure, the capacity of the parental figure to contribute to environmental degradation is mortally limited. This is amplified in the very fact of the movie star as parental figure: as Iheka notes, Hollywood's "primary paradigm remains excessive consumption through the making of capital-intensive films and the use of high-energy technologies with a considerable ecological footprint,"[57] and so the movie star is inextricably aligned with an extractive industry that actively perpetuates the unevenness of ecological crisis by making continental Africa "the disposable factory and junkyard for [its] contaminative practices."[58] It also recalls the Comaroffs' description of many *nyongo* victims as both children and "victims of the murderous greed of their own close kind":[59] current and future children face existential threat from climate change, because of the industry and (in)action of previous generations. Compounding this, the zombified appear not to age, thus condemning the "children of Nyos" to live longer in a world marked by destruction.

However, as Lauro points out, "the irresolution of the zombie's dialectic (not master/slave but slave/rebel-slave) continues to thwart attempts to read the figure as wholly resistive."[60] Such "irresolution" emerges in the narrative when it is revealed that Anasta was not responsible for her adoptive mother's death; rather, a militant religious group (the "Born-Agains") staged the attack, "siccing dogs on the screen idol to drum up anger."[61] However, the orchestration of the attack is deemed too violent and inflammatory a story and, instead, Con is instructed to falsify a narrative in which the movie star suffers "Death by Automotive Misadventure." This is deemed "plausible enough given Cameroon's notoriously treacherous roadways."[62] While Stephanie LeMenager reminds us that our contemporary "liveness, as in seeming to be alive, now relies heavily upon oil,"[63] it is perhaps pertinent here to remember that oil is often also associated with impending death: it is made up of decayed biomatter; its extraction and its use are environmentally devastating; above all, it is finite. Along with the earlier explicit references to crisis management following oil spills, the onomatopoeically rich reference to "sticky crude imaginings that ooze up,"[64] and a brief interjection regarding "Hollywood pooh-bahs and Saudi sheikhs flush with petrodollars and paranoia," the narrative of automotive fatality ensures that the text is formally and aesthetically saturated with oil.

On the subject of the capacity or, indeed, the purpose of narrative in registering environmental and social crises, then, LeMenager highlights the instability of a perceived causal chain from "media à empathy à action."[65] Such a notion is engaged with similarly by Wenzel in her "skepticism that images and narratives work in such straight lines"[66] and by Iheka in his contention that while African ecomedia "allow us to visualize the impacts of environmental degradation, and urge us to reorient our cultural habits to address the problem of climate change," they are nonetheless also "purveyors of ecological degradation that disproportionately imperil Africa's ecologies."[67] In "It Just Kills You Inside," the mechanisms through which pathos might be mobilized as a force for structural change are demonstrably inadequate, but, again, this inadequacy is conditioned by capital. This is perhaps most clearly illustrated in the news headlines that pepper Con's narrative for satirical effect—for example, "African Super Virus Kills, Regenerates Dozens!"[68] upon the initial finding of Lazarus and "African Super Virus the Secret of Eternal Life!"[69] These headlines are conventional in their abrupt, punchy syntax and their exclamatory form, and they highlight once more both the temporal discrepancy between the "ongoing" nature of crisis and the suddenness of its appearance in media, and the extent to which narrative can be formally manipulated.

Conclusion

Entangled with the broader narratives of global destruction is a more intimate kind of "disaster." Gradually, Con reveals that he has been diagnosed with terminal cancer, but he also suggests that the loss of his child and wife has "snuffed out" the "deep spark" of his identity.[70] As such, he characterizes himself as a "dead man walking"—seemingly playing with a notional idea that he is "zombified" as a result of the knowledge of his own impending doom. Notably, though, it is only on this individual level that he seems able to register the dynamics of disaster. Otherwise, he justifies his actions on the basis of the "greater good": "Can you even imagine what would have happened to those teeter-tottering African GDPs if the truth had gotten out?"[71] As in much of the text, the sincerity of this statement is debatable, and we might well wonder whether Con writes to convince us—or indeed, himself—or to parody those tropes. Nevertheless, the introduction of an attempt to justify complicity in colonial violence—whatever its level of sincerity—undermines moments in which Con professes to have a clean conscience. He says, "Look, I'm fine with what I did... I'm sure this might make me a monster to some. But I've met real monsters, and trust me, I don't come close,"[72] but in anticipating the perception of his actions as monstrous, Con doth protest too much. If—as seems likely—the "real monsters" are the corrupt officials, governments, and corporations whose capital fuels the narrative action and funds the stories Con spins, then he is patently complicit. Also suggestive is the fact that he invokes his daughter again here—"I sleep like a baby. Like Chelsea"[73]—as though a guilty intrusion over which he does not quite have total narrative control. An additional line of enquiry is illuminated in terms of narrative's capacity to incite action or to justify inaction—that of the stories we tell ourselves.

The stories we read and the stories we tell are important, whether they are the bedtime stories we invent (or appropriate) for our children or the news media we consume on a rolling basis. However, Nkweti's story confronts us with the possibility that narrative is also drastically limited in its capacity to represent and in its capacity to effect change, and this configuration plays, of course, on neocolonial dynamics. For example, Con's assertion that "A lot of Africans were different... These folks have touched the slithery underbelly of darkness, so they never quite bought the snake oils [he] was selling"[74] is quite as ensconced in well-worn colonial discourses of "darkness" and "savagery" as are those that he mocks for their archaism ("bloodthirsty natives (Exterminate all the Brutes!)").[75] Thus, the story—though written by a Black Cameroonian American woman—focalizes (and satirizes) the perspective of a white American man in telling a story about telling stories about Africa and about the uneven reverberations of crises throughout world ecology. As such, it registers and responds to an urgent intersection between ecological crisis and the mastery of narrative and narrator, and it introduces zombie figures and tropes in order to think through the short- and long term under the threat of climate change's slow violence: who lives, who dies, and for whom existence is read as "a form of death-in-life."[76]

Notes

1 Nkweti, "It Just Kills You Inside," 83.
2 Achebe, "An Image of Africa," 15.
3 Nkweti, "It Just Kills You Inside," 83.
4 Wainaina, "How to Write about Africa."

5   Nkweti, "It Just Kills You Inside," 97.
6   Kofele-Kale, "Asserting Permanent Sovereignty over Ancestral Lands," 106.
7   Niblett, "World-Economy, World-Ecology, World Literature," 16.
8   Wenzel, *The Disposition of Nature*, 12.
9   Lauro, *The Transatlantic Zombie*, 30.
10 Cazdyn, "Disaster, Crisis, Revolution," 649.
11 Cazdyn, "Disaster, Crisis, Revolution," 648.
12 Cazdyn, "Disaster, Crisis, Revolution," 658.
13 Nixon, *Slow Violence and the Environmentalism of the Poor*, 2.
14 Nixon, *Slow Violence and the Environmentalism of the Poor*, 2.
15 Moore, "Crisis," 100.
16 Iheka, *Naturalizing Africa*, 8.
17 Oloff, "From Sugar to Oil," 317.
18 Nkweti, "It Just Kills You Inside," 85.
19 Kling et al., "The 1986 Lake Nyos Gas Disaster in Cameroon, West Africa," 173.
20 Nixon, *Slow Violence and the Environmentalism of the Poor*, 2.
21 Shanklin, "Exploding Lakes in Myth and Reality: An African Case Study," 170.
22 Nkweti, "It Just Kills You Inside," 85.
23 Nkweti, "It Just Kills You Inside," 85.
24 Nixon, *Slow Violence and the Environmentalism of the Poor*, 2.
25 Iheka, *Naturalizing Africa*, 7.
26 WReC, *Combined and Uneven Development*, 62.
27 Nkweti, "It Just Kills You Inside," 89.
28 Mbembe, "Necropolitics," 40.
29 Lauro, *The Transatlantic Zombie*, 2.
30 Nkweti, "It Just Kills You Inside," 93.
31 Shapiro, "Transvaal, Transylvania," 33.
32 Nyamnjoh, "Images of Nyongo amongst Bamenda Grassfielders in Whiteman Kontri," 242.
33 Comaroff and Comaroff, "Alien-Nation," 795.
34 Nkweti, "It Just Kills You Inside," 93.
35 Nkweti, "It Just Kills You Inside," 93.
36 Nkweti, "It Just Kills You Inside," 93.
37 Mbaku, *Culture and Customs of Cameroon*, 13.
38 Nkweti, "It Just Kills You Inside," 93.
39 Nkweti, "It Just Kills You Inside," 93.
40 Nkweti, "It Just Kills You Inside," 93.
41 Franzen, "What if We Stopped Pretending?"
42 See, for example, criticisms of the newly introduced Elections Bill 2021–22 in the UK, which would require electorate to display photo ID before voting in polling stations.
43 Wenzel, *The Disposition of Nature*, 17.

44 WReC, *Combined and Uneven Development*, 51.
45 WReC, *Combined and Uneven Development*, 51.
46 Lauro, "Introduction," x.
47 Carey, *The Girl with All the Gifts*, 52.
48 Lauro, "Introduction," x.
49 Nkweti, "It Just Kills You Inside," 97.
50 Nkweti, "It Just Kills You Inside," 97.
51 Lauro, "Introduction," x.
52 Nkweti, "It Just Kills You Inside," 93.
53 Bodner, *The Theology of the Book of Kings*, 142.
54 Kimeria, "The Most Unusual Ways Many African Countries Got Their Names."
55 Nkweti, "It Just Kills You Inside," 88.
56 Nkweti, "It Just Kills You Inside," 88.
57 Iheka, *African Ecomedia*, 221.
58 Iheka, *African Ecomedia*, 221.
59 Comaroff and Comaroff, "Alien-Nation," 795.
60 Lauro, *The Transatlantic Zombie*, 33.
61 Nkweti, "It Just Kills You Inside," 103.
62 Nkweti, "It Just Kills You Inside," 102.
63 LeMenager, *Living Oil*, 6.
64 Nkweti, "It Just Kills You Inside," 9.
65 Nkweti, "It Just Kills You Inside," 17.
66 Wenzel, *The Disposition of Nature*, 14.
67 Iheka, *African Ecomedia*, 221.
68 Nkweti, "It Just Kills You Inside," 88.
69 Nkweti, "It Just Kills You Inside," 89.
70 Nkweti, "It Just Kills You Inside," 103.
71 Nkweti, "It Just Kills You Inside," 101.
72 Nkweti, "It Just Kills You Inside," 101.
73 Nkweti, "It Just Kills You Inside," 101.
74 Nkweti, "It Just Kills You Inside," 101.
75 Nkweti, "It Just Kills You Inside," 89.
76 Mbembe, "Necropolitics," 21.

Works Cited

Achebe, Chinua. "An Image of Africa: Racism in Conrad's Heart of Darkness." *The Massachusetts Review* 57, no. 1 (Spring 2016): 14–27.

Bodner, Keith. *The Theology of the Book of Kings*. Old Testament Theology. Cambridge: Cambridge University Press, 2019.

Carey, M. R. *The Girl with All the Gifts*. London: Orbit, 2014. Kindle E-book.
Cazdyn, Eric. "Disaster, Crisis, Revolution." *South Atlantic Quarterly* 106, no. 4 (2007): 647–62.
Comaroff, Jean and John L. Comaroff. "Alien-Nation: Zombies, Immigrants, and Millennial Capitalism." *The South Atlantic Quarterly* 101, no. 4 (2002): 779–805. https://muse.jhu.edu/article/39105.
Franzen, Jonathan. "What if We Stopped Pretending?" Web, *The New Yorker*, September 8, 2019. https://www.newyorker.com/culture/cultural-comment/what-if-we-stopped-pretending. Accessed August 23, 2021.
Iheka, Cajetan. *African Ecomedia: Network Forms, Planetary Politics*. Durham: Duke University Press, 2021.
Iheka, Cajetan. *Naturalizing Africa: Ecological Violence, Agency, and Postcolonial Resistance in African Literature*. Cambridge: Cambridge University Press, 2017.
Kimeria, Ciku. "The Most Unusual Ways Many African Countries Got Their Names." Web, *Quartz Africa*, October 6, 2019. https://qz.com/africa/1722919/how-many-african-countries-got-their-names/. Accessed August 25, 2021.
Kling, George W., Michael A. Clark, Glen N. Wagner, Harry R. Compton, Alan M. Humphrey, Joseph D. Devine, William C. Evans, John P. Lockwood, Michele L. Tuttle, and Edward D. Koenigsberg. "The 1986 Lake Nyos Gas Disaster in Cameroon, West Africa." *Science* 236, no. 4798 (1987): 169–75.
Kofele-Kale, Ndiva. "Asserting Permanent Sovereignty over Ancestral Lands: The Bakweri Land Litigation against Cameroon." *Annual Survey of International & Comparative Law* 13, no. 1 (2007): 103–56.
Lauro, Sarah Juliet. *The Transatlantic Zombie*. Ithaca: Rutgers University Press, 2015.
Lauro, Sarah Juliet. "Introduction: Wander and Wonder in Zombieland." In *Zombie Theory: A Reader*, edited by Sarah Juliet Lauro, vii–xxiv. Minneapolis: University of Minnesota Press, 2017.
LeMenager, Stephanie. *Living Oil: Petroleum Culture in the American Century*. New York: Oxford University Press, 2014.
Mbaku, John Mukum. *Culture and Customs of Cameroon*. Westport, CT and London: Greenwood Press, 2005.
Mbembe, Achille. "Necropolitics." *Public Culture* 15, no. 1 (2003): 11–40.
Moore, Jason W. "Crisis." In *Fueling Culture: 101 Words for Energy and Environment*, edited by Jennifer Wenzel, Patricia Yaeger and Imre Szeman, 99–102. New York: Fordham University Press, 2017.
Niblett, Michael. "World-Economy, World-Ecology, World Literature." *Green Letters* 16, no. 1 (2012): 15–30.
Nixon, Rob. *Slow Violence and the Environmentalism of the Poor*. Cambridge, MA: Harvard University Press, 2011.
Nkweti, Nana. "It Just Kills You Inside." In *Walking on Cowrie Shells*, 83–103. Minneapolis, MI: Graywolf Press, 2021.
Nyamnjoh, Francis B. "Images of Nyongo Amongst Bamenda Grassfielders in Whiteman Kontri." *Citizenship Studies* 9, no. 3 (July 1, 2005): 241–69.

Oloff, Kerstin. "From Sugar to Oil: The Ecology of George A. Romero's Night of the Living Dead." *Journal of Postcolonial Writing* 53, no. 3 (May 4, 2017): 316–28.

Shanklin, Eugenia. "Exploding Lakes in Myth and Reality: An African Case Study." In *Myth and Geology*, edited by L. Piccardi and W. B. Masse, 165–76. Geological Society Special Publication. London: The Geological Society, 2007.

Shapiro, Stephen. "Transvaal, Transylvania: Dracula's World-System and Gothic Periodicity." [In English]. *Gothic Studies* 10, no. 1 (May 2008): 29–47.

Wainaina, Binyavanga. "How to Write about Africa." Web, *Granta*, 92, May 2, 2019, 2005. https://granta.com/how-to-write-about-africa/. Accessed September 29, 2020.

Wenzel, Jennifer. *The Disposition of Nature*. New York: Fordham University Press, 2019.

WReC. *Combined and Uneven Development: Towards a New Theory of World-Literature*. Liverpool: Liverpool University Press, 2015.

Zombie Proletkino: Labor, Race, and Genre in Pedro Costa's *Casa de Lava*

Thomas Waller

Recent scholarship has attempted to read the wave-like rises and falls of genre production under the sign of the capitalist world economy, tracing a direct correspondence between the patterned repetition of specific sets of cultural forms and the cyclical rhythms of long-wave capital accumulation. If genres are typically understood as exemplary cultural indices for specific moments in history—such as punk rock for the youth subculture of 1970s Britain or serialized realism for the long nineteenth century—then this scholarship rather asks why it is that certain genres and styles tend to reappear in clusters over the *longue durée* in apparently heterogeneous locations and at discontinuous points in time. Stephen Shapiro, for instance, has shown how gothic narrative devices tendentially recur during periods of primitive capitalist accumulation to respond to the violence and dispossession engendered by cyclical reconfigurations in the world market.[1] In a similar vein, Sharae Deckard has encouraged us to seek out homologies between literary fictions in the late neoliberal era and texts produced in earlier historical moments in which financialization had also been ascendant.[2] Whereas most materialist approaches to cultural production operate at the level of capitalist *periodization*, and thus strive to differentiate the cultural forms of a given temporal phase from those of another, these critics instead place the emphasis on *periodicity*: "the quality or character of being periodic, the tendency to recur at intervals."[3] This shift of focus, in turn, offers a way out of the limitations of earlier variants of cultural materialism that had relied too heavily on a vertical and overly linear base-superstructure model, for here cultural forms are considered not as reflective or simply representational but as *constitutive* and *co-productive* moments in capitalist value production.[4] Genres, as more or less coherent bundles of cultural forms that bring together diverse social audiences through symbolic conventions, might then be understood as endowed with a certain internal logic that predisposes them to appear and reappear across similar moments in capitalism's long spiral to register analogous yet historically specific social conditions.

The internal logic of the zombie genre is deeply rooted in the categories of labor and race. As has been well documented, the figure of the zombie has its origins in the Haitian experience of slavery and the plantation economy during the era of European capitalist expansion in the seventeenth century. The hemispheric Caribbean at this time functioned as a "haven of pirates and buccaneers," "the Wild West of the era," as northwest European powers began to fight for control over the region's labor and resources.[5] By the middle of the century, the French had taken definitive control of what was later to become Haiti, and over the next 200 years would import large amounts of West African slave labor to cultivate cash crops of coffee and sugar, leading to the "abysmal demographic collapse" of the island's Taíno indigenous population.[6] The uprooting and resettlement of cultures enacted by this traffic of human cargo across the middle passage resulted in the formation of a complex creolized religion named vodou in Haiti. The figure of the zombie as it is commonly understood is a product of this creolized Haitian belief system, where it can signify either a bodiless spirit or a soulless body. Due to its historical links to racialized slave labor, Kieran M. Murphy has characterized the zombie as "a figure of mourning that incarnates the fear experienced by plantation slaves, that is, the fear of the first modern industrial workers."[7] Similarly, Kerstin Oloff has argued that the zombie is imbued with "the memory of the first experience of industrial exploitation[...] as well as the experience of the ecological dimension of modernity, intensified by the plantations."[8] In both senses, the zombie is "inseparable from the violent history of the modern capitalist world-system."

The emergence of the zombie in popular film culture coincides with the US occupation of Haiti between 1915 and 1934. This period saw the production of gothic American fictions such as W. B. Seabrook's novel *The Magic Island* (1929), which was highly influential in popularizing the concept of the zombie for a commercial mass audience. Oloff has perceptively remarked that the appearance of the zombie in this text is intimately bound up with "the uneven landscape of labor and ecology produced by capitalism," as the narrator's tale of Haitian zombies is set against an incongruous backdrop of "cane fields in juxtaposition with the gleaming symbol of industrial modernity, Hasco [the Haitian-American Sugar Corporation]."[9] This connection between racialized labor, the sugar industry, and the figure of the zombie is also explored in several of the period's major cinematic releases. Most famous in this respect is the factory scene in Victor Halperin's *White Zombie* (1932), in which Black zombie workers can be seen laboring in a primitive sugar mill ill-suited to the pace and demands of modern industry. Also notable is Jacques Tourneur's *I Walked with a Zombie* (1943), which takes place on a British West Indian sugar plantation and features a memorable sequence in which the zombified wife of the plantation owner is taken to a vodou houmfort held by the workers in a dark and eerie setting of rustling cane fields. To this extent, the first images of zombie cinema can be read as meditations on the racialized system of labor exploitation that underpinned the production of sugar in the Caribbean during the late colonial era.

However, the appearance of the zombie in early Hollywood film culture ultimately had less to do with the experiences of workers on Caribbean sugar plantations than it did with the interests of US capitalists in the first half of the twentieth century, who were suffering from one of the worst economic recessions in modern history. "Hollywood," writes Joshua Clover, "sings to its audiences the story of their waking lives moved to the faraway-near of allegory."[10] In these terms, the proliferation of zombies on US movie screens in the 1930s and 1940s can be read as a cultural anxiety on the part of moviegoers themselves in the Great Depression era, for which the figure of the Black zombie served as an allegorical remedy. As Shapiro has argued:

> The initial zombie cinema typified by *White Zombie* (1932) and *I Walked with a Zombie* (1943) seems fascinated by the possibility of American hemispheric imperialism as an enabling solution to the Depression era's failures. These movies seem to wonder if colonized, foreign workers, illustrated by the barely animate zombie, could provide the consumer goods that economic doldrums, wartime rationing, and mass, domestic unemployment were otherwise not allowing Americans to purchase.[11]

This allegorical reading of the early zombie as a racialized economic fix suggests that the internal logic of the zombie genre might predispose it to appear at moments during which crises of labor and consumption are experienced most acutely. The genre's narrative obsession with work and industry would then be the visual register in which it communicates this logic to its community of consumers. In what follows, I want to begin to test out this hypothesis through a reading of Portuguese director Pedro Costa's film *Casa de Lava* (1994).

Pedro Costa and Neoliberal World-Culture

Highly regarded among film critics for his cinephile style of referencing, his political commitment to marginalized populations, and the slow, measured pace of his films' aesthetics, Costa is well known for defying generic categorization. As Emma Fajgenbaum writes, attempts to define Costa's films in terms of conventional categories such as cinematic modes, subject matter, and geo-cultural context "have a disconcerting tendency to destabilize the categories themselves."[12] Over a career spanning three decades and seven feature-films, Costa has experimented with an eclectic range of genres and styles, from the moody noir of his first feature *O Sangue* (1989) to the *cinema vérité* of the Fontainhas Trilogy (1997–2006) and the zombie genre itself in *Casa de Lava*. But while the trajectory of Costa's *oeuvre* in this way flits between cinematic modes from one film to the next, it should also be noted that these generic shifts often happen within the films themselves, so that a work such as *Ossos* (1997) can be read as a piece of docufiction as much as it reactivates the genres of quest and melodrama. Recent attempts to categorize Costa's work under the banner of "slow cinema" have emphasized his use of long duration shots, contemplative close-ups, and minimalist narratives as potential criteria for classification,[13] though such criticism risks losing sight of the sheer multiplicity of Costa's generic engagements through an emphasis on his art-house cinematic techniques. What is remarkable about Costa's films is their ability to both take up and destabilize several cinematic genres at once, without exclusively identifying themselves with any one tradition in particular.

This promiscuous approach to genre and cinematic form is unsurprising once we consider the culturally hybrid character of semiperipheral zones in the capitalist world-system, of which Costa's native Portugal is a prime example. While core-like and peripheral regions of the world-system are defined by their relatively homogeneous combination of production processes, semiperipheries stand out for their socially uneven composition which contains a mixture of both core-like and peripheral aspects. To this extent, Immanuel Wallerstein describes semiperipheral zones as caught up in an economic double bind: "Under pressure from core states and putting pressure on peripheral states, their major concern is to keep themselves from slipping into the periphery and to do what they can to advance towards the core."[14] Far from a mere residual category, however, the semiperiphery represents a necessary structural element in a world-economy insofar as it mediates social relations between core and periphery by functioning as a "collection point"[15] or "transistor space"[16] that *translates* the commodities of one sphere into the other. As Deckard and Shapiro have recently argued, this liminal socioeconomic status means that "the semiperipheries are the zones where political economy receives its greatest cultural inflection."[17] In his canonical essay "Between Prospero and Caliban: Colonialism, Postcolonialism, and Inter-identity" (2002), Portuguese sociologist Boaventura de Sousa Santos describes Portugal as precisely one of these transistor spaces, where cultural hybridity is born from a situation of combined and uneven development:

> Portugal is and has been since the seventeenth century a semiperipheral country in the modern capitalist world-system.... Although this condition has evolved across centuries, it has kept its basic features: an intermediate economic development and a position of intermediation between the center and the periphery of the world economy; a state which, being both product and producer of that intermediate position, never assumed fully the characteristics of the modern state of the core countries...; cultural processes and systems of representation that do not adjust well to the typical binarisms of western modernity—such as culture/nature, civilized/uncivilized, modern/traditional—and may therefore be considered originally hybrid, even if ultimately merely different... Portuguese culture is a borderland culture. It has no content. It does have form, however, and this form is the borderland zone.[18]

It thus seems only natural that the work of one of Portugal's most famous directors should display such a heightened sensitivity to the admixing of style and genre. Insofar as the uneven composition of his films' aesthetics works to register to the semiperipheral character of Portuguese society, Costa's *oeuvre* presents itself as an exemplary instance of "world-culture" properly speaking, understood as the cultural production of the capitalist world-system.[19]

But in spite of the generic discontinuities of Costa's filmography, it is still possible to highlight some recurring themes and preoccupations, the most prominent of which being his interest in the issue of Cape Verdean labor migration to Portugal. Jacques Rancière, for example, has argued that the central subject of Costa's films "is also one at the heart of contemporary politics—the fate of the exploited, of those who have come from the former African colonies to work on Portuguese construction sites."[20] Indeed, the poverty as well as marginalization of the Cape Verdean diaspora in Portugal is a topic to which Costa has continually returned in his work, most famously in his Fontainhas Trilogy, which explores the impoverishment of Cape Verdean immigrants living in the Fontainhas shanty town in Lisbon, right up to its demolition by the Portuguese government in the first decade of the new millennium (an event dramatized in *No Quarto da Vanda* [2000], the penultimate film of the trilogy).

Costa has repeatedly stated in interviews his belief in filmmaking as a political vocation with a crucial role to play in the class struggle, such as when he claims, "Most of mankind's stories—I mean the stories of the lower classes—either have been told wrongly or haven't been told at all, so cinema has to step in."[21] To this extent, Emilie Bickerton has proposed that Costa's work be understood as part of a new genre of postindustrial *proletkino* that reboots the working-class commitment of earlier filmmakers such as Sergei Eisenstein and Jean Renoir to address the reconfigured class identities of the late neoliberal era.[22] Noting the similarities between his filmography and those of directors such as Ken Loach, Richard Guédiguian, and the Dardennes brothers, Bickerton argues that Costa's focus on the "marginals and outcasts, the surplus-labor flotsam and jetsam of Europe's past" bespeaks a resurgence in consciousness of labor at a time when "the working class and its organizations, from trade unions to political parties, have never been politically weaker."[23] This contradiction is then registered in Costa's films by the substitution of the isolated, atomized individual worker for the collective subject of early *proletkino*, which Bickerton describes as a necessary transformation given the de-industrializations, de-unifications, and the rightward shifts of former social-democratic and communist parties that have unfolded in Western Europe since the 1970s.[24] While labeling Costa's work as postindustrial *proletkino* risks downplaying the generic pluralities of his work, it does helpfully capture Costa's political affinities with the economically marginalized. Both Costa's engagement with the issue of postcolonial migrant labor and his vexed relationship with cinematic genre are forcefully combined in his second feature film, *Casa de Lava*.

Absent Zombies

Casa de Lava has been described by Costa himself as a remake of Jacques Tourneur's *I Walked with a Zombie*.[25] In an interview with the Portuguese press at the time of *Casa de Lava*'s domestic release, he characterized it as "*um filme sonâmbulo, muito 'zombie'*" (a sleepwalking film, very "zombie").[26] Indeed, just like the early Hollywood zombie films, *Casa de Lava* is centrally preoccupied with the injustices of colonialism and racialized labor flows. It begins with a shot of Cape Verdean construction workers piling into a Lisbon building works, engaging in the sort of light-hearted back-and-forths proper to workplace camaraderie. The industrial atmosphere, the mass of quick-moving workers, and the backdrop of exposed construction beams have led Emma Fajgenbaum to liken this scene to one of cinema's earliest sequences—Louis Lumière's "Workers Leaving the Lumière Factory" (1895)—only this time, in reverse.[27] This opening scene is then cut short by the switch to a close-up of one of the workers in particular, Leão (Isaach de Bankolé), who is seen looking down from a height at the bustling construction site, wearing a mind-numbed expression and with the whirring of machinery nagging impatiently in the background. While we never see the incident itself, we learn from one of his colleagues that Leão has fallen from this height and seriously injured himself—due to the narrative ellipsis, this fall could have been either accidental or voluntary.

Seven weeks later, Leão is found lying comatose in a Lisbon hospital bed under the watchful supervision of a nurse named Mariana (Inês de Medeiros). After an anonymous letter, and check, arrives calling for Leão's return to his home in the Cape Verde islands, Mariana volunteers to escort him and is subsequently sent off to the volcanic island of Fogo to tend to her patient and deliver him over to his relatives. But when no one on the island appears to have ever seen Leão before, Mariana begins to neglect her custodial duties and becomes fascinated by the island's singular community of inhabitants. Even in this remote landscape, however, Mariana cannot escape the realities of postcolonial migrant labor, as one night she meets a group of musicians who are preparing to travel to Lisbon's Sacavém district in search of well-paid construction work, and who want to know if Mariana has ever been there and what the neighborhood looks like. But Mariana seems somehow frustrated and confused at why these musicians would want to travel all the way to a location from which she has only just arrived, and she ends up storming off in a huff, leaving their questions unanswered. It falls to the island's fiddle playing old man to sum up this crossing of paths: "*É o destino, a Mariana chega e nós partimos*" (it's destiny, Mariana arrives and we depart).

The more direct affinities between *Casa de Lava* and *I Walked with a Zombie* can be found in the two films' narrative proximity. Both films, for example, feature white, female protagonists who travel as nurses to a remote part of the colonized world and there take an active interest in the lives of the local community. In Tourneur's film, the heroine is Betsy Connell (Frances Dee), a Canadian nurse who is dispatched to the Caribbean island of Saint Sebastian to tend to Jessica Holland (Christine Gordon), the invalid wife of a sugar plantation owner. Dissatisfied with the doctor's suggested treatments for Jessica's illness, and suspecting that she might have been placed under a zombifying spell, Betsy turns to the island's local magical belief system for help and takes Jessica to a vodou houmfort amid the cane fields to be cured. The film ends after Jessica has been led to her death by Carrefour (Darby Jones), a listless black zombie who stalks the edges of the film. Nuno Barradas Jorge has explored in depth the narrative connection between the two films, noting that Costa "relied substantially on Jacques Tourneur's film as a central work of adaptation" and urging us to understand *Casa de Lava* as a piece of "distant referencing" that reworks both the narrative structure of Tourneur's film and its chief political concerns by tacitly adapting them to a different time and place.[28] As it reproduces the narrative binary of local colonized community and white European outsider, *Casa de Lava* thus presents itself as a postcolonial remake of *I Walked with a Zombie*, and the comatose state of Leão can in this sense be read as a condition of zombification closely linked to his status as a postcolonial migrant worker.

Nevertheless, *Casa de Lava* is a film conspicuously void of all reanimated or cannibalistic corpses, even eschewing Tourneur's interest in the zombie figure's origins in vodou practices and beliefs. For this reason, its relationship to the zombie genre as a whole is notably less forthcoming, perhaps surprisingly given the canonical status of Tourneur's film and its formative influence on Costa. As Jorge notes, the original script for *Casa de Lava* had signaled a much closer narrative and aesthetic relationship to *I Walked with a Zombie* than would eventually materialize in the final film, as it included characters more recognizably zombie-like in appearance and planned to reproduce some of the "sharp chiaroscuro cinematography and eerie nocturnal atmosphere" that characterized Tourneur's earlier film.[29] During the second stage of the pre-production process, however, the decision was made to move filming away from mainland Portugal to the island of Fogo in Cape Verde, and this resulted in a departure from the more conventional "American" zombie film imagined in the film's original screenplay. Upon arrival in Fogo, Costa began using improvisational techniques that gave more screen time to his untrained local actors and crucially decided to veer away from the original plans for a monochromatic, eerie cinematography toward a grittier realism marked by stark colors, candid close-ups, and a documentary-like style of visual narrative. The zombie motif also underwent significant alterations during this process. Whereas the earlier script had planned to include a zombie more in line with the figure in Tourneur's film, as filming progressed the zombie theme was transformed by Costa into a type of "apathetic condition" associated with mental instability to be transposed onto the psyches of the film's tormented cast of characters.[30]

In *I Walked with a Zombie*, there are two zombie characters: Jessica and Carrefour. These two zombie characters are telescoped in *Casa de Lava* by the figure of the Black construction worker Leão, whose comatose state during the first half of the film references the zombification of Jessica in *I Walked with a Zombie*, while the close-up shots of his face when he awakens from his coma and the images of him stumbling zombie-like across Fogo's volcanic landscape recall similar scenes in Tourneur's film when Carrefour is subjected to the white gaze of the movie camera. But these aesthetic references to *I Walked with a Zombie* are complicated by the fact that Leão's zombified state is never associated with witchcraft, magical beliefs, or religious superstition: in simple narrative terms, *Casa de Lava* merely relates Leão's awakening from a coma after he has been returned from Lisbon to his home in Cape Verde. This rejection of the magical imaginary of the zombie genre in favor of a more realist cinematic style tallies with Bickerton's conception of Costa's work as postindustrial *proletkino*, which is also defined by its use of nonprofessional actors and documentary-like cinematic realism.[31] It thus becomes clear how *Casa de Lava* emerges as a kind of aesthetic negation of Tourneur's film, one that is intricately tied up with the two films' locational politics, but also registered at the level of cinematic form through the opposition between Costa's realism and the modernist gothicism of *I Walked with a Zombie*.

At the same time, however, and in spite of its commitment to some renewed form of realism, *Casa de Lava* is littered with verbal allusions to the returning dead and visual references to the aesthetics of canonical zombie cinema, so that the film appears to be staking a claim to the same zombie tradition from which it had only just distanced itself. The moment when Leão awakens from his coma, for example, is signaled to the viewer through a close-up shot in which his eyes are opened suddenly and stretched wide as if he were not emerging from a coma but from the deep sleep of death itself. Likewise, in one of the film's iconic final scenes, we see Leão pursuing Mariana over Fogo's blackened volcanic landscape, on crutches due to his state of convalescence, and with a limping gait that cannot but call to mind the slow yet implacably menacing movements of the walking dead as they pursue their human prey. Hilary Owen has also observed that Mariana's first appearance in the film is communicated to the viewer "through a series of heavily gothicized images," as she is surprised by an elderly patient in her death throes who suddenly awakens and grabs hold of Mariana's face. The scene is presented in such a way that all we see are Mariana's face and hair "being gripped by a pair of disconnected, visibly blood-stained white hands, appearing disembodied as if reaching from the grave."[32] These visual signals to the cultural imaginary of zombie cinema are then matched by more explicit references to the returning dead in the dialogue of the film. "*Até morto se ri*" (even in death he laughs), remarks one of the film's peripheral characters in a cryptic allusion to both Leão's catatonic state and the frenetic efforts of Mariana to find someone on the island who might be able to identify this paperless construction worker.

One night at a party, the island's fiddle-playing old man similarly whispers to Mariana: "*Aqui nem os mortos descansam. Devia ouvi-los como eu*" (not even the dead rest here. You must be able to hear them like I do). But the moment at which these verbal and visual references to the undead collide most forcefully comes when a local boy named Tano sneaks into the hospital at night and approaches the bed where Leão is laid comatose. As Tano lingers over the patient, inspecting his curious state of restful unconsciousness, Leão suddenly awakens and clutches the boy's arm, who subsequently manages to break free and escape out the door. The next morning, Tano is found asleep on the beach, and when Mariana enquires what has happened to the boy, his sister tells her: "*O morto quer matar o Tano*" (the dead man wants to kill Tano). The fact that Tano is found with bite marks on his arm further holds out the promise of the zombie motif, while the film's realist visual register would simultaneously seem to foreclose this possibility. In this way, *Casa de Lava* is torn between two opposing tendencies: on the one hand, to destabilize the tropes of the zombie genre through a cinematic realism that pretends to represent postcolonial Cape Verde in a manner entirely void of romanticism or magical overtones, and on the other, to align itself with this same genre through implicit or "distant" references to zombies in both the film's aesthetics and the dialogue between its characters.

Down to Earth

But if this vexed relationship to the zombie genre can be explained with reference to Costa's tendency to move fluidly between cinematic styles, and to the culturally hybrid character of semiperipheral spaces more generally, it nevertheless leaves unanswered the question of why Costa chose to work with (and against) the zombie genre on this film in particular, and at this specific point in time. According to Costa, the motivation behind filming *Casa de Lava* came from a feeling of deep resentment for the social transformation of Portuguese society during the 1990s:

> *Este filme é filho de desgosto. Ele guarda profundos vestígios disso. Desgosto com o país, com o miserável humilhação política, social, artística, deste povo passivo*

e mau... Para nós, cineastas portugueses, foi o momento de começar a sofrer a violência de um poder inculto e arrogante. E tomei a decisão de me afastar de casa.

[This film is a product of disgust. It is profoundly marked by this feeling. Disgust with the country, with the miserable political, social and artistic humiliations of this passive and rotten people. We Portuguese filmmakers began to suffer the violence of a coarse and arrogant power. And I decided to get out of there.][33]

The "miserable" atmosphere Costa is describing here is a reference to the free market and reprivatizing Social Democrat governments of Aníbal Cavaco Silva (1985–95), which succeeded in restructuring Portuguese society along the lines of the neoliberal policies set out by the European Economic Community (EEC) toward the end of the 1980s. The period of Cavaquismo, as it came to be known, was characterized, above all, by a reversal of the revolutionary nationalizations that followed the overthrow of the Portuguese fascist dictatorship in 1974. After Portugal gained membership to the EEC in 1986, Silva started to remove clauses protecting public assets from the volatilities of the free market, reduced by half the market share of state-owned banks, and sold off a widening tranche of other enterprises under the auspices of limiting the public debt.[34] The liberalization of trade with the rest of Europe further drove Portugal toward more labor-intensive forms of industry that were less productive than other sectors, and by the end of the decade real wages in Portugal accordingly lagged well behind the regional average, with Portuguese workers in 1998 earning less than the two thirds of the EU average, and only 71 percent of workers in Spain.[35] Jacques Lemière has argued that Costa's decision to move filming from mainland Portugal to the Cape Verde islands in *Casa de Lava* was an implicit rejection of the "illusions" of consumerism underpinning this period of Cavaquismo in Portugal, and thus at once also an artistic protest against the neoliberalization of Portuguese society.[36] Given the zombie genre's own elective affinity to crises of labor and consumption, it is then a remarkable fact that Costa should turn to Tourneur's film in particular at this historical juncture as a vehicle for his feelings of discontent.

A further correspondence between *Casa de Lava* and early Hollywood zombie cinema lies in the issue of racialized labor flows. For just as the barely animate Black zombie in Tourneur's film offers an allegorical remedy for the economic doldrums of the Great Depression, so does the figure of the Cape Verdean construction worker in *Casa de Lava* contain its own crisis-ridden history of labor and race. From the late 1950s, deskilled Portuguese laborers had begun to migrate elsewhere in industrialized Europe in search of comparatively more lucrative work in the construction—cleaning and catering industries of countries such as Germany, France, and Belgium. Despite mild economic growth rates and rising urbanization, this mass exodus of labor power created a vacuum in the domestic economy which the Portuguese state sought to fill with imported labor from its African colonies. Accordingly, during the 1960s, masses of Cape Verdeans were recruited as an economic fix intended to provide a replacement for the hemorrhaging of the Portuguese working class.[37] This is then the historical terrain negotiated by *Casa de Lava* in its treatment of the flows of Cape Verdean labor migration to Portugal and their centrality to the expansion of the Portuguese construction industry. To the extent that the comatose Leão functions as the film's migrant labor zombie, *Casa de Lava* returns us to the original problematic of Hollywood zombie cinema: the allegorical figuration of the barely animate zombie as a racialized economic fix. These parallels between *Casa de Lava* and *I Walked with a Zombie* might then suggest a generic periodicity that predisposes zombie texts to reappear during moments when the combination of these categories is economically enforced or politically desired.

But whereas the early Hollywood zombie films imagined this racialized labor as a solution to the economic crisis of the Great Depression, *Casa de Lava* seems to expose this type of economic fix as an illusion drawn from the world-system's axial division of labor, since the mass recruitment of Cape Verdeans for the Portuguese economy from the 1960s onward could hardly prevent the cascading of real wages and labor productivity that arrived in the neoliberal 1990s. With welfare securities stripped and markets deregulated, the continued flows of Cape Verdean migrant labor during the era of Cavaquismo simply served to swell a surplus population the state cared little to look after, crowding already-crowded district shanty towns that would ultimately be demolished. The fall of Leão on the Lisbon building works is an apt metaphor for these migrants and the marginalized that were allowed to slip through the cracks at the same time as it visualizes crises of labor in times of postindustrial stagnation. "Down to Earth," the English title of *Casa de Lava*, does well to capture this sense of loss and decline, while also referencing Costa's attempts to escape the "illusions" of neoliberalism by moving production from the Portuguese mainland to Fogo's volcanic landscape. The Portuguese title, on the other hand, carries the hope that things might be different. It comes from a scene of the film in which Mariana finds a letter written by a political prisoner who was held at Cape Verde's infamous Tarrafal prison camp during the days of the Portuguese dictatorship. This letter, addressed to the prisoner's lover, is filled with the promises he hopes to deliver on once the revolution has arrived and he is released from incarceration. "*Eu gostava de te oferecer 100,000 cigarros*," he writes, "*ma dúzia de vestidos daqueles mais modernos, uma automóvel, a casinha de lava que tu…*" (I want to offer you 100,000 cigarettes, a dozen of the most modern dresses, a car, a little house of lava that you…). But at this point the letter breaks off. The film's title is the promise of a revolution yet to come.

Notes

1. Shapiro, "Transvaal, Transylvania."
2. Deckard, "Capitalism's Long Spiral," 90–1.
3. Deckard, "Capitalism's Long Spiral," 90; Shapiro, "From Capitalist to Communist Abstraction," 1250.
4. Shapiro, "The Cultural Fix," 102.
5. Wallerstein, *The Modern World-System II*, 157.
6. Braudel, *The Perspective of the World*, 393.
7. Murphy, "White Zombie," 48.
8. Oloff, "'Greening' The Zombie," 42.
9. Oloff, "'Greening' The Zombie," 36.
10. Clover, *The Matrix*, 72–3.
11. Shapiro, "Zombie Health Care," 198.
12. Fajgenbaum, "Cinema as Disquiet," 137.
13. Luca and Jorge, *Slow Cinema*.
14. Wallerstein, *World-Systems Analysis*, 29.
15. Wallerstein, *The Modern World-System I*, 351–2.
16. Shapiro, *The Culture and Commerce of the Early American Novel*, 37.
17. Deckard and Shapiro, "World-Culture and the Neoliberal World-System: An Introduction," 10–11.
18. Santos, "Between Prospero and Caliban," 9–10.
19. Deckard and Shapiro, "World-Culture and the Neoliberal World-System."
20. Rancière, *The Intervals of Cinema*, 127.
21. Quoted in Fajgenbaum, "Cinema as Disquiet," 139.
22. Bickerton, "A New Proletkino?" 107–25.
23. Bickerton, "A New Proletkino?" 109.
24. Bickerton, "A New Proletkino?" 123, 109–10.
25. Quoted in Corless, "Crossing the Threshold," 28–31.
26. Câmara, "Convalescer na Ilha dos Mortos," 2–4. All translations are mine unless specified otherwise.
27. Fajgenbaum, "Cinema as Disquiet," 144.
28. Jorge, "Pedro Costa on the Island of the Dead," 254–5.

29 Jorge, "Pedro Costa on the Island of the Dead," 255–6.
30 Jorge, "Pedro Costa on the Island of the Dead," 258–60.
31 Bickerton, "A New Proletkino," 125, *passim*.
32 Owen, "White Faces/Black Masks," 190.
33 Quoted in Lemière, "'Terra a Terra'," 50.
34 Finn, "Luso-Anomalies," 14–15.
35 Finn, "Luso-Anomalies," 15.
36 Lemière, "'Terra a Terra'," 52. See also Jorge "Pedro Costa on the Island of the Dead," 261.
37 Batalha, *The Cape Verdean Diaspora in Portugal*, 133–4.

Works Cited

Batalha, Luís. *The Cape Verdean Diaspora in Portugal: Colonial Subjects in a Postcolonial World*. Lanham: Lexington Books, 2004.

Bickerton, Emilie. "A New Proletkino?" *New Left Review*, 109 (January/February 2018): 107–25.

Braudel, Fernand. *The Perspective of the World: Civilization and Capitalism, 15th–18th Century*, vol. III. Translated by. S. Reynolds. London: Fontana Press, 1985.

Câmara, Vasco. "Convalescer na Ilha dos Mortos." *Público* (February 10, 1995): 2–4.

Casa de Lava. [Film] Dir. Pedro Costa, Portugal/France, 1994.

Clover, Joshua. *The Matrix*. London: British Film Institute, 2004.

Corless, Kieron. "Crossing the Threshold." *Sight & Sound* 19, no 10 (2009): 28–31.

Deckard, Sharae. "Capitalism's Long Spiral: Periodicity, Temporality and the Global Contemporary in World Literature." In *Literature and the Global Contemporary*, edited by Sarah Brouillette, Mathias Nilges and Emilio Sauri, 83–102. Cham: Palgrave Macmillan, 2017.

Deckard, Sharae and Stephen Shapiro. "World-Culture and the Neoliberal World-System: An Introduction." In *World Literature, Neoliberalism and the Culture of Discontent*, edited by Sharae Deckard and Stephen Shapiro, 1–48. Cham: Palgrave Macmillan, 2019.

Fajgenbaum, Emma. "Cinema as Disquiet: The Ghostly Realism of Pedro Costa." *New Left Review*, 116/117 (March/June 2019): 137–59.

Finn, Daniel. "Luso-Anomalies." *New Left Review*, 106 (July/August 2017): 5–32.

I Walked with a Zombie. [Film] Dir. Jacques Tourneur, Los Angeles: RKO Pictures, 1943.

Jorge, Nuno Barradas. "Pedro Costa on the Island of the Dead: Distant Referencing and the Making of *Casa de Lava* (1995)." *Adaptation* 7, no. 3 (2014): 253–64.

Lemière, Jacques. "'Terra a Terra': Portugal e Cabo Verde no cinema do Pedro Costa (1994–2000)." *Devires* 5, no. 1 (2008): 46–57.

Luca, Tiago de and Nuno Barradas Jorge eds. *Slow Cinema*. Edinburgh: Edinburgh University Press, 2016.

Murphy, Kieran M. "White Zombie." *Contemporary French and Francophone Studies* 15, no. 1 (2011): 47–55.

Oloff, Kerstin. "'Greening' The Zombie: Caribbean Gothic, World-Ecology, and Socio-Ecological Degradation." *Green Letters* 16, no. 1 (2012): 31–45.

Owen, Hilary. "White Faces/Black Masks: The White Woman's Burden in Pedro Costa's *Down to Earth*." In *Portugal's Global Cinema: Industry, History and Culture*, edited by Mariana Liz, 185–204. London and New York: I.B. Tauris, 2018.

Rancière, Jacques. *The Intervals of Cinema*. London and New York: Verso, 2014.

Santos, Boaventura de Sousa. "Between Prospero and Caliban: Colonialism, Postcolonialism, and Inter-identity." *Luso-Brazilian Review* 39, no. 2 (2002): 9–43.

Shapiro, Stephen. "Transvaal, Transylvania: *Dracula*'s World-System and Gothic Periodicity." *Gothic Studies* 10, no. 1 (2008): 29–47.

Shapiro, Stephen. "From Capitalist to Communist Abstraction: *The Pale King*'s Cultural Fix." *Textual Practice* 28, no. 7 (2014): 1249–71.

Shapiro, Stephen. *The Culture and Commerce of the Early American Novel: Reading the Atlantic World-system*. University Park, PA: Pennsylvania State University Press, 2008.

Shapiro, Stephen. "Zombie Health Care." in *This Year's Work at the Zombie Research Center*, edited by Edward P. Comentale and Aaron Jaffe, 193–226. Bloomington: Indiana University Press, 2014.

Shapiro, Stephen. "The Cultural Fix: Capital, Genre and the Times of American Studies." in *The Fictions of American Capitalism: Working Fictions and the Economic Novel*, edited by Jacques-Henri Coste and Vincent Dussol, 89–108. Cham: Palgrave Macmillan, 2020.

Wallerstein, Immanuel. *The Modern World-System I: Capitalist Agriculture and the Origins of the European World-Economy in the Sixteenth Century*. San Diego: Academic Press, 1974.

Wallerstein, Immanuel. *The Modern World-System II: Mercantilism and the Consolidation of the European World-Economy, 1600–1750*. New York: Academic Press, 1980.

Wallerstein, Immanuel. *World-Systems Analysis: An Introduction*. Durham and London: Duke University Press, 2004.

8

"It Feels Like I'm Giving My Body Something It Needs in an Intense and Powerful Way": Netflix, *Santa Clarita Diet*, and the Neoliberal Feminist Encounter with Pleasure Politics

Roxanne Douglas

The word "zombie" is likely to evoke an image of horrific decay: a walking corpse conjuring the mindlessness of consumerism or the advancing march of late-stage capitalism, despite the decay in its system. It is less likely to evoke, one supposes, Drew Barrymore looking pretty foxy. *Santa Clarita Diet* (2017–19) is a Netflix original show where Sheila (Barrymore), a downtrodden wife and real estate agent, mysteriously becomes a zombie. However, she is not the shuffling, mindless ghoul of early George Romero canon; she is what I call a "cognizant zombie." Emerging around the same period that the term "mental load" came into popular usage among feminists,[1] the "cognizant zombie" demonstrates how women are grappling with the biological thresholds of youth and pleasure at the same time as coming to terms with the failed promise of neoliberal slogans of "having it all." Shows like *Santa Clarita* appropriate the figure of the zombie to exemplify the tension between individuality and an alternative language of collective rebellion that neoliberal feminism fails to offer. In this chapter, I argue that *Santa Clarita* alerts us to neoliberal feminist anxieties around women's agency and desires under late-stage capitalism, particularly around (peri)menopause. At the same time, the presence of the "cognizant zombie" is also a useful tool to think through the nature of our relationship with Netflix's programming and interface through the lens of digital coloniality. Viewer time and attention, in no uncertain terms, is a source from which streaming services extract value.

The "cognizant zombie" has arrived in Anglophone media in recent years, and she is almost always a woman: for instance, Liv in television series *iZombie* (2015–19) solves murders after being zombified by getting a new job as a mortician in order to imbibe the memories from crime victims' brains. I choose the word "cognizant" here to reflect the gendered aspects of "being cognizant" of others and their needs, or "being cognizant" of the consequences of impulsive actions. As a "cognizant zombie," Sheila has to manage her household, her family, her (attractive) appearance, and her job at the same time as discovering and managing her new compulsion to eat human flesh. This is directly counter to the revolutionary potential that zombies, according to David McNally, "possess… for revelry and revolt… As viewers, we (or at least many of us) derive a deep pleasure from images of fantastic beings wreaking havoc upon polite citizens of well-ordered society. And, here, we can locate part of the utopian charge animating zombie rebellions."[2] This potential for "revelry and revolt" is actively resisted by "cognizant zombies," who are particular in their drive to do good in society, despite their own destructive compulsions. Romero's later films such as *Land of the Dead* (2005) do show zombies who "are pretending to be alive" by repeating behaviors that they performed before zombification, and are able to strategically attack the human protagonists, but Netflix's Sheila strives to live a fairly normal life. The difference between Sheila and, say, *Land of the Dead*'s Big Daddy is that Sheila deliberately redirects her flesh-eating compulsions into what she and her husband perceive to be productive kills for the good of wider society. Both Liv and Sheila essentially go back to who they were before their zombification and endeavor to continue to play their role in the social system. This is entirely counter to the revolutionary history of the zombie, as discussed at length in this volume, and the purpose of the zombie as a tool to think with in the international imagination about the destruction of society. The "cognizant zombie" then encapsulates how, as Sarah Juliet Lauro and Karen Embry point out, "capitalism depends on our sense of ourselves as having individual consciousnesses to prohibit the development of a revolutionary collective and to bolster the attitude that drives it: every man for himself… to move posthuman, to lay humanism and its legacy of power and oppression in the grave, we have to undo our primary systems of differentiation: subject/object, me/you."[3]

The first season of *Santa Clarita* follows Sheila and her very understanding husband Joel (Timothy Olyphant) as they negotiate the most ethical way to satisfy her desire for live flesh. The show carefully establishes that this is a biological need, implying that were it "just" a physical drive, then she would just have to control herself. Nevertheless, she settles on eating neo-Nazis as a way of using her powers for the good of society. Sheila, as a zombie with morals in mind, brings into frame broader questions of control and of the individual, particularly for women and people of color in the neoliberal, late-capitalist world. Feminism since the 1990s has anxiously grappled with the tensions between acknowledging the individual agential subject and developing a collective strategy based on shared experience and struggle.[4] Having and utilizing choice—especially in balancing the needs of oneself and of the minoritized social group to which one might belong—is the gold standard of freedom according to neoliberal ideologies. Christina Scharff argues that

> in a neoliberal postfeminist era, young women are positioned as beneficiaries of increased opportunities. Now able to work, consume, and control reproduction, young women are called upon to manage their lives independently. This neoliberal, individualist imperative does not sit well with perceptions of feminism as involving collective struggle. Young women reject feminism because they regard it as a collective movement which robs them of the opportunity to navigate their lives.[5]

Sheila's zombification is paradoxically a plight and an opportunity. She becomes more assertive at work, in her marriage, and "independently manages" her cravings. Yet, Sheila is not the young subject that Scharff is talking about. Here, a white woman's renegotiation of the way in which she consumes and becomes hyper-productive in the workplace is framed by the relative neglect of (peri) menopausal women's issues within mainstream feminism, as well as menopausal women's relative invisibility in media and power structures. Absent from *Santa Clarita* is the hoard to which the zombie normally belongs. The neoliberal feminist anxieties in *Santa Clarita* prioritize the pleasure, and social impact, of the individual women—she does not have a hoard or collective struggle to identify with, nor is she beholden to any master other than her drives. There is only Sheila, and her ever more impulsive choices.

Neta Alexander asks, "but what exactly do we choose, when we choose choice?... is it still possible to differentiate between our choices and the choices the algorithm is making on our behalf?"[6] The anxious social moralizing of *The Santa Clarita Diet* also alerts us to our relationship to Netflix's strategies to generate content. Netflix not only instrumentalizes a viewer's desire to "binge" but, in fact, creates the very desires we understand to be our own. Alexander argues that subscribers to Netflix

> have remained unaware of the ways in which their choices shape the preferences of others—and vice versa. In a narcissistic manner, they confuse the "You" in

"Recommended for You" with a unique, complex individual rather than with a group of strangers who all happened to have made similar choices. Ironically, the fact that Cinematch's criteria for recommendations remain hidden serves to sustain the myth of personalization... we simply assume that Netflix knows us. The god resides in the machine.[7]

In this way, our relationship with the Netflix interface evokes the zombie hoard; indeed, Alexander I. Stingl and Sabrina M. Weiss ask, "if you are part of a swarm, are you still you, and are you still free?"[8] The paradox is that, both in neoliberal feminist "lean in" sensibilities and Netflix's appeal to the unique "You" in its recommendation system, we are all parts of a collective, group, or a type, while being encouraged to feel and behave like individuals. Jeffrey Jerome Cohen notes that "we live in an age that has rightly given up on Unified Theory, an age when we realize that history (like 'individuality', 'subjectivity', 'gender', and 'culture') is composed of a multitude of fragments, rather than of smooth epistemological wholes."[9] The white, middle-class, alive-looking zombie, then, cannot provide us with "epistemological wholes"—*Santa Clarita* is no zombie feminist manifesto—but she can alert us to our blindspots about what it means to be a desiring and desirable agent during late-stage capitalism.

At the intersection of the above themes are questions of autonomy, of pleasure, and of desire. Nick Couldry and Ulises A. Mejias trace the genealogy of tools of colonialism from the physical—"the telegraph pole, the Christian cross, and the rifle"—and map this onto the digital means of generating capital.[10] They point out that the indigenous activists during the Idle No More campaign with "every tweet, Facebook post, blog post, Instagram photo, YouTube video, and email we made... the largest corporations in the world... more money to reinforce the system of settler colonialism."[11] Couldry and Mejias then trace this trajectory onto an app which is "a program to bypass the part of the brain that regulates thirst, reminding you to drink regularly to meet predefined quotas while tracking your progress."[12] At the time of writing many women input data about potential menstrual symptoms into "period tracking" apps which "remind" or "notify" users that they might menstruate soon, and gives advice on how best to care for one's body at each stage of the menstrual cycle. Couldry and Mejias conjugate the ideological and violent tools of colonialism onto the ways in which technology and social media companies have quantified human embodied experience and behavior to the point where basic needs are not only served but bypassed and constructed by programs to which we, willingly, provide crucial data. It follows that the North American Menopause

Society (NAMS) has developed a mobile app, *MenoPro*, which, according to their website, is designed

> to help you and your clinician work together to personalize treatment decisions on the basis of your personal preferences... The app has two modes, one for clinicians and one for women, to facilitate shared decision making.[13]

Much like Couldry and Mejias' reading of the water consumption app, this app presents a complex dynamic of agency and choice, of being informed while also making decisions about one's own body alongside another person who is connected to you digitally through an app. Quoting JoAnn Pinkerton of the NAMS, Calhoun notes that "we tell people who are grieving not to make major changes for a year. I don't think anybody's ever said: 'Don't make a major decision when you're perimenopausal.'"[14] There is a cultural uneasiness around the decisions that (peri)menopausal women might make, because, like the zombie, they are perceived as volatile due to biological changes.

At the same time, the Global South is becoming a part of Netflix's viewership, a new vista from which it can extract viewing data. Louis Brennan indeed cites Netflix's "mastery of local contexts."[15] According to the *Harvard Business Review*, in 2018 Netflix had a presence in 190 countries, and was working on "improving its mobile experience, including... streaming efficiency for cellular networks."[16] For the end user, this may feel like the "You" which Alexander identifies is approaching consumable content more easily, perhaps democratizing digital content. However, being able to engage with steaming services as and when the impulse strikes expands the remit of the ways that content creators and distributors such as Netflix can gather data. It doesn't take much to read the shuffling zombie onto the ability to access mobile streaming, which by necessity will draw the user's attention away from their immediate surroundings to focus on one single product: the streamed media. This ambulatory separation of attention and body speaks to Couldry and Majias' concerns about technology and the colonization of our attention and bodies, which the zombie in many ways exemplifies. It follows that "Netflix sees such content production as not just local-for-local, but also local-for-global."[17] In other words, one market's data drives content generation which can be used in other markets. The complex individuated yet clustered customer-taste and experience model recalls how "zombies never appear in the singular... Zombies, as a consequence, are about relations, about togetherness and about 'how to be together.'"[18]

The folkloric Haitian zombie had a master to whom it was enslaved, for the Anglophone "cognizant zombie" she has no apparent master, and yet on a metatextual level these texts are constructing our consumption behaviors on our behalf—while Sheila describes a new sense of agency emerging from her zombification, she still must consume, and consume, and consume, despite the consequences. Couldry and Mejias point out that the collection of our data and integration of technology into daily life is not simply a case of aligning any and all oppression as subalternity but rather that "the underlying function remains the same as under historical colonialism: to acquire large-scale resources from which economic value can be extracted."[19] For women, this means that questions about "having it all" are characterized by "cognizant zombies" like Sheila, whose managed condition still does not exempt her from mental loads, emotional labor, and workplace politics. Indeed, her zombification in some ways makes her a more effective and successful real estate agent and mother. Being effective in society, according to Linda Zerilli, has "historically governed every iteration of the 'woman question': what is a woman *for*?"[20] Zerilli points out that early feminism's calls for women's rights made the case for social utility: "be it in terms of difference or equality, the ballot [women's suffrage] was not an end in itself but a means to an end: the betterment of society."[21] That is to say that there was an argument that it was expedient to give women rights for the good of all people: white women, although not colonized subjects, leveraged the idea that they were "large-scale resources from which economic value can be extracted."[22]

In the United States, the women's suffrage movement and the abolition movement are historically linked. While not strictly analogous struggles, Angela Davis (1983) explains that the 1830s represented a time where white women's economical and familial roles were being redefined due to the Industrial Revolution, around the same time in 1831 "the year of Nat Turner's revolt, the organized abolitionist movement was born."[23] Problematically, white women compared their lot to slavery, either on the basis of low wages and poor working conditions or "literally in their effort to express the oppressive nature of marriage."[24] Fredrick Douglass also recognized "that women were indispensable within the abolition movement" due to their numbers.[25] Likewise, activists for women's suffrage recognized that while they petitioned for the liberation of enslaved Black people, they were simultaneously making a case for women's participation in politics.[26] In other words, each cause recognized the political resources that the other could provide. The colonial history of the United States, and therefore the Haitian zombie folklore, is a specter at the edges of *Santa Clarita*—the very first shots of the first episode depict manicured lawns in a desert environment, signaling the colonial occupation of the United States as a whole, as well as middle-class suburbia's encroachment on the natural environment. Joel and Sheila are real estate agents who quite literally deal in capital, and the name of the Santa Clarita Valley signals a history of European colonization.

Inheriting this history, *Santa Clarita* is in some ways a problematic experiment in what would happen if the Haitian zombie nightmare was visited onto the perimenopausal white suburban woman. For enslaved Haitians, zombie folklore at the most fundamental level represented an end to life without an end to enslavement. The zombie, in this instance, is a culturally significant resource from which value can be extracted to serve the needs of women's neoliberal anxieties: for instance, much of the comedy in the show is derived from observing a super-strong woman with the ability to eat people control her rage when she faces sexism or belittlement. We do not fail to notice that the emotional labor and mental load of day-to-day household management still falls upon a woman, even if she is undead. Reminiscent of the suffrage activists that Davis described who aligned marriage with enslavement, Shelia's characterization problematically aligns the plight of enslaved and colonized peoples with her concerns over being a successful businesswoman, mother, and remaining desirable to her husband while her body slowly deteriorates.

One of the most problematic signals of this alignment in the show is with the introduction of Loki (DeObia Oparei), a Black man whom Sheila initially attempts to kill for food. She does this because her police officer neighbor, Dan (Ricardo Chavira), blackmails her and points out that Loki is a felon that he wants to "disappear." The establishment of the federal prison system's legacies of enslavement is well documented in the Netflix film *13th*, directed by Ava DuVernay, released only a year before *Santa Clarita*. Shelia accidentally turns Loki into a zombie, and in his first appearance as a member of the undead he is in a bar, gently singing a folksy, acoustic version of Cat Steven's 1971 *Moonshadow*. This appearance is comedic, with Joel and Sheila armored in preparation to kill him, initially subverting expectations that Loki will be even more violent in his zombie form. *Moonshadow*'s lyrics include the symbolic loss of hands, eyes, the mouth, and so on, gesturing toward the zombie's eventual deterioration; however, the part which Loki sings also contains references to land and plows: "And if I ever lose my hands / Lose my plow, lose my land / Oh, if I ever lose my hands / Oh, if, I won't have to work no more." *Moonshadow* is not a song about enslavement; however, the symbolic weight of these lyrics is especially glaring when put in context of the rest of the episode.

Earlier in the episode, Shelia hides the fact that she lost a toe from Joel, and confides in Loki about this, since he is the only other zombie that she knows. It is no surprise that Shelia and Loki build a connection on the basis of their shared experience, which turns romantic for him. Shelia rejects Loki's advances, and he plans to kill Joel as a consequence. This places Loki in the long-standing racist cinematic tradition, that is, the rapacious Black man from who white women must be protected. This echoes the sentiments of pulpy monster films such as *King Kong* (1933) and *I Walked with a Zombie* (1943), where white women are associated with, or find affinity with, Black-coded subjects. Shelia and Joel kill Loki in the same episode, releasing Shelia from her symbolic affinity with the Black zombie, moving the narrative onto matters of scientific intervention into Sheila's state. Lola Olufemi points out:

> White feminist neo-liberal politics focuses on the self as vehicle for self-improvement and personal gain at the expense of others.... This model works best for wealthy white women, who are able to replace men in a capital structure.... It invisibilises the women of colour, low paid workers and migrant women who must suffer so that others may "succeed." It makes their exploitation a natural part of other women's achievements.[27]

In other words, Loki's character as a Black male zombie exemplifies the vexed neoliberal philosophy that there is a struggle that is shared between all women, but here instead of women the struggle could be shared between the "only people like us in the world."[28] Yet, Sheila and, in some ways, Joel experience "personal gain" and "self-improvement" as Loki's character is used as a vehicle for them to better understand Sheila's condition and to help them solidify honesty and trust in their own relationship.[29] Loki's character is never revisited, nor is there any sense of guilt or concern over his demise, especially as he was the only other known zombie in the show at the time: Loki's exploitation as a narrative tool becomes "a natural part of [Sheila and Joel's] achievements."[30]

The question of agency and zombification has been historically feminized in the popular imagination: as previously mentioned *I Walked with a Zombie* reveals that a white woman is zombified and is thus without agency, likewise *White Zombie* (1932), recognized as the first zombie feature film, sees a woman (Madge Bellamy) become a vodou zombie at the hands of a white master (Bela Lugosi), with the film's theatrical poster touting that "he made her perform his every desire!" Almost 100 years later, *Aim for the Head* (2011), a pulpy poetry collection about zombies, uses the image of a 1950s housewife reimagined as a zombie as its front cover, again evoking the problematic alignment of white middle-class women's concerns about marriage and enslavement. We can trace a legacy of this feminization in a 1931 pulp-fiction short story "Salt is Not for

Slaves" by G. W. Hutter, which tells the story of a Black woman, Marie, who recalls the Haitian slave revolution of a 150 years prior to a male, presumably white, narrator. Marie appears human as long as she does not consume any salt; if she does eat salt, she will become a zombie and rush immediately toward her grave, like her peers did over a century before. Marie appears as "old as the island," and her survival depends on resisting food that is seasoned with salt due to a curse that her old master had put on all his slaves.[31] This curse ensures that they would never get sick or die, and thus his slaves would remain valuable assets that never need to be replenished. Without salt, it is implied, food simply is fuel, rather than a vector for pleasure.

Marie's story in "Salt is Not for Slaves" from the neoliberal perspective is one of having been the "beneficiary" of an opportunity in that the curse granted her a long life without sickness.[32] Yet, she remains in her raced and classed position, and so is doomed to work until she dies and is certainly not liberated by her supernatural status. Marie is not quite a "cognizant zombie" in that she does not have to manipulate a desire to eat human flesh for the good of society; however, she does remain part of the system, working in kitchens and performing the same tasks that she would have done a century and a half prior. Likewise, she survives to become an older woman, unlike her male lover, because she manages her condition carefully; Hutter writes that "she had tried to kill [a servant when he tripped] because a little salt had fallen on her... her rage was as inexplicable to me as it had been to him."[33] Marie is both a figure of denial ("salt is not for slaves," after all) and excess in emotion. Thus the "cognizant zombie" in *Santa Clarita* represents an inherited monstrous potential of the older women, especially in her sexual desires and capacity for anger and violence (and arguably the power this bestows upon her), qualities which are not typically assigned to older women.

Stingl and Weiss point out that

> the condition of being *already dead* is the condition of... The *new chronic*... their state of being as the ones who are *already dead* is a state that is currently "in management"... people who are in constant crisis, where crisis has turned into the new normal. The future of crisis as continued crisis or as "crisis to come."[34]

There has been much critical ink spilled and feminist discourse over the erasure of "women of a certain age"—even the colloquialisms regarding this group being vague—which may represent a metaphorical "undead" quality to existing in society as a (peri)menopausal woman. Likewise, it is significant that Marie's exact age is vague: "her years," according to Hutter, "were impossible to reckon."[35]

At the same time there are numerous headlines about death and sickness at the onset of menopause and use of Hormone Replacement Therapy (HRT), a typical medical intervention to ease the symptoms of menopause: "We don't know menopausal hormone therapy causes breast cancer, but the evidence continues to suggest a link"; "Menopause? Start estrogen [sic] replacement therapy sooner, to reduce heart disease"; "Breast cancer risk from using HRT is 'twice what was thought'"; and "Menopause experts say compounded HRT is unsafe" are all real and recent headlines published in *The Conversation* and *The Guardian*.[36] There is a cultural narrative in the Anglophone world of erasure, silence, and death around the condition of menopause. The female body becomes a "new chronic" anticipating the "crisis to come."[37] This indeed holds true for Sheila, inasmuch as there is no cure for her "condition," yet a scientist, played by Portia de Rossi, develops a "serum" which ceases, or at least slows, the decaying of Sheila's flesh.

Lauro and Embry point out that "our fascination with the zombie is, in part, a celebration of its immortality and a recognition of ourselves as enslaved to our bodies."[38] There is a similar metaphor available to us in the body of the (peri) menopausal woman. Testimonials from women who experienced menopause published in *The Guardian* discuss symptoms and experiences which align with Sheila's in *Santa Clarita*, such as surges of adrenaline, surges of sexual appetite (including one woman starting an affair), that they no longer bend to the will of others quite so freely, and become more "themselves."[39] Sheila depicts the "revelry and revolt" of giving in to one's hormonal impulses and forgoing gendered restraint for the perimenopausal woman.[40] But, there are also symptoms which put us in the mind of the zombie. For instance, NAMS describes how "decreased water and fat content of the skin as well as reduced sweat and oil production contribute to dryness."[41] According to mortician Caitlin Doughty, "skin often becomes dehydrated after death. The once plump, living skin shrivels and retracts."[42] The perimenopausal body takes on qualities of both living and dead flesh. Several women also report sleep deprivation, making (peri)menopausal women akin to those who, quite literally, go "bump in the night." As a result of this sleep deprivation alongside a normal daily work schedule, they report how "the fatigue was really hard to deal with and was coupled with short-term memory issues," perhaps evoking the horror of the loss of cognition in the traditional zombie.[43]

It is worth noting here that the Netflix model of releasing entire series on one day and the "autoplay" function invites binge-viewing habits, which then often result in bouts of insomnia or sleep deprivation for the end user. Casey J. McCormick argues that binge-watching is integral to Netflix's original *House of*

Cards: "the show's thematic emphasis on addiction, power, and bodily exhaustion draws attention to the physical and psychological components of a TV binge… the viewer must confront the intensity of her immersion while in the midst of the consumption process."[44] This is applicable to *Santa Clarita*, especially given "that cultural attitudes toward binge-viewing complicate its negative connotations, as viewers engage in self-aware, often ironic discourse regarding loss of control."[45] In "Salt is Not for Slaves," Marie, once she has told her story to the narrator, reveals that her life will end because "a few grains [of salt] hit my tongue" when the other servant tripped with some at the beginning of the story.[46] The passage that follows reads: "'but what difference does it make how it happened? I have eaten and the curse is upon me. Perhaps a little more will hasten the time.' She licked her hands hungrily, then ran her tongue over the grass. I shuddered and rose to my feet."[47] Seeing an older Black woman indulge in eating salt without decorum and licking it from the grass, a sensual, almost sexual act, leaves the white male narrator perturbed. Likewise, we often see Sheila battling for control over her desires. This is especially self-consciously ironic given the show's discussions and pastiches of diet culture.

Santa Clarita was first advertised through trailers and posters which heavily reference diet advertisements. One trailer sees Barrymore in a red dress and red lipstick against a white background; she confides in the viewer by leaning forward to whisper that the "secret" to how she feels "younger, more energetic and sexier" is, as we might guess, "the Santa Clarita Diet."[48] The comedy in the ad comes from our recognition of the horrors of the diet industry, and the culture of virtuous self-denial surrounding it. Indeed, the series cites this virtue culture with montages with cheerful music of Sheila preparing smoothies, subverted by the fact that it is human flesh, and talking about her new high-protein diet with her friends. In contrast to the cleanliness of the diet-style marketing materials, we regularly see Sheila smeared with blood. In particular, when Joel kills their neighbor, Dan, Sheila resolves that she will dispose of the body by eating it. We see her in a bloodied bathroom, and slouched in her comfortable clothes, gnawing on parts of Dan. The parallels of hiding one's "failure" when one binges by hiding in the bathroom are all evident in these shots, perhaps even reflecting the binges of someone with an eating disorder. Sheila belches and experiences pleasure in her excess; nevertheless, she needs to consume to excess in this instance to keep her husband out of jail. McCormick points out that "the popularity of binging has engendered an entire discourse on the transformation of TV that recalls some of the most central debates in media studies: passive versus active consumption, narrative interactivity, and the shifting power dynamics among media producers and consumers."⁴⁹ In other words, Sheila's binge behavior, as pleasurable as it is to her, presents us with questions about power and agency when we consider the circumstances of the narrative.

Lauro and Embry point out that the zombie is a "boundary figure.... through the simultaneous occupation of a body that is both living and dead, [it] creates a dilemma for power relations and risks destroying social dynamics that have remained... largely unchallenged in the current economic superstructure."⁵⁰ But, how much does Sheila and the "cognizant zombie" actually threaten these economic and patriarchal structures? In an interview to promote the second season of *Santa Clarita*, Barrymore is asked if she is good at dieting, to which she gives a long reply which begins with her emphatically stating that she hates diets, yet she goes on to recount that

> when I first started the show I was 145lbs, and my life was kind of falling apart... I used this show as a wakeup call for myself, and I said "Victor can I lose 20lbs over the course of the show, and like, you know change my eyebrows and the height of my shoes and my body language and the attitude, and go from someone whose you know, kind of naïve and unhappy to someone who is empowered and alive."... then Season 2 I let it all go, and Victor was like "by the way, we're picking up in the scene we left off in."⁵¹

Barrymore links her diet with gaining a sense of control over a life that she states was "falling apart," referring to her marriage breaking down around the time of the first season's production. She then ties her body (exercise, dieting) to the show's production to motivate herself, instrumentalizing the contractual obligations that this would entail to look a certain way. Here, Barrymore exerts control by relinquishing agency: by the end of this story, she is obliged to lose weight to film the second season of the show. For Barrymore, her body is very much at the behest of outside forces, despite implying ownership of this process. This is arguably similar to the process of "binge-watching" via Netflix or other streaming services, where an act of choice—choosing a show or film to watch—impacts the body, as argued by McCormick.

Being a zombie enables Sheila to renegotiate the boundaries of her desires and the possibilities of her body, but this is not without complication. For example, in the first episode Sheila is being sexually harassed by her coworker Gary. She starts to pretend to comply in order to get out of the situation: she sucks his finger, mimicking fellatio. After some tension builds, she bites his finger off and then proceeds to eat him. The choreography of her killing and eating him is like a sex scene: she moans, she pushes him to the ground, and she rips his shirt open. We then follow her husband, Joel, coming home to find her with entrails hanging out her mouth at Gary's groin, mimicking being caught *in flagrante*. The scene comically cuts to Sheila saying, "oh Joel, I really want to make this work." At face value, Sheila was partaking in the "revelry and revolt" of zombification by exacting revenge on her rapacious colleague, but, on the other hand, actually using her zombie super-strength has grievous consequences, as she and Joel continuously try to evade the police following this murder.[52] Sheila has physical power and she is more in tune with her desires thanks to her zombification, but as a "cognizant zombie" she still is subject to the same restrictions that she always was; her zombie status is one which she has to hide, as many women hide the symptoms of (peri)menopause, and does not grant her any more systemic agency, nor the ability to shirk the system.

According to Jerome Cohen, "the folkloric zombie is a reduction of person to body: an utterly dehumanized laborer, compelled relentlessly to toil, brutally subjugated even in death."[53] While there is no master for the "cognizant zombie," the toil does not end. This encapsulates the nightmare of Sheila's situation: at the end of Season 1, when Sheila starts to lose control of her impulses, she chains herself in the basement to protect others, but she continues to take work calls, calls in takeout for her husband and daughter, and coordinates their schedules. Problematic or not, this is the nightmare of the Haitian zombie visited on suburban white women. Instead of being a madwoman in the attic, she is an organized woman in the basement, unable to shirk the gendered mental load. What do these distinctions say to us about agency and choice for women "of a certain age"? Donna Haraway argues that a "slightly perverse shift of perspective might better enable us to contest for meanings, as well as for other forms of power and pleasure in technologically mediated societies."[54] Sheila and the "cognizant zombie" are promising tools to think with because they confound and break down rigid imaginative categories; Sheila is at once dead and alive, a desiring agent and trapped because of her hunger, assertive and feminine, and yet, despite her "lean in" sensibilities, she does not provide the promise of cut-and-dry solutions that neoliberal and liberal feminisms demand, suggesting that perhaps there is more to the vexation between the individual and collective negotiation of desire and duty.

The Santa Clarita Diet was canceled by Netflix in 2019, and is perhaps a zombified show in its own right. While it will not get a fourth season (nor a resolution to a cliff-hanger ending), it is available to stream at the behest of a viewer, dormant in the digital realm of Netflix's servers, ready to reanimate at any moment. Its cancellation seems counterintuitive on the surface given that it was a "fan favorite" and received critical accolade.[55] However, as much as Netflix has been integrated into many people's lives, it is not a public service—it is a business like any other. *Santa Clarita* was canceled despite its popularity with existing users because it was not attracting enough *new* users. Like the zombie hoard, Netflix's expansion model's "underlying function remains the same as under historical colonialism: to acquire large-scale resources from which economic value can be extracted."[56] Netflix creates desirable content not for "you" but to create new viewers. Like the zombie, Netflix "is a machine that performs but two functions: it consumes," our data and viewing habits, "and it makes more consumers" from those viewing habits.[57] In our Netflix "binges," we not only feed ourselves content but unwittingly point Netflix in the direction of new "resources from which economic value can be extracted."[58]

Notes

1. In 2017, *The Guardian* republished a comic as *The Gender Wars of Household Chores: A Feminist Comic* by the web artist known as "Emma," which explained the feminist concept of "the mental load," suggesting that the term was coming into Anglophone popular feminist consciousness around this period.
2. McNally, *Monsters of the Market*, 253–4.
3. Lauro and Embry, "A Zombie Manifesto," 106.
4. Spivak, "Feminism 2000."
5. Scharff, *Repudiating Feminism*, 1.
6. Alexander, "Catered to Your Future Self," 85.
7. Alexander, "Catered to Your Future Self," 86.
8. Stingl and Weiss, "Between Shell and Ghost," 94.
9. Cohen, "Monster Culture (Seven Theses)," 3.
10. Couldry and Mejias, *The Costs of Connection*, ix.
11. Couldry and Mejias, *The Costs of Connection*, ix–x.
12. Couldry and Mejias, *The Costs of Connection*, x.
13. "*MenoPro* Mobile App."
14. "Surviving Perimenopause."
15. Brennan, "How Netflix Expanded to 190 Countries in 7 Years."
16. Brennan, "How Netflix Expanded to 190 Countries in 7 Years."
17. Brennan, "How Netflix Expanded to 190 Countries in 7 Years."
18. Stingl and Weiss, "Between Shell and Ghost," 90.

19 Couldry and Mejias, *The Costs of Connection*, xi.
20 Zerilli, *Feminism and the Abyss of Freedom*, 8.
21 Zerilli, *Feminism and the Abyss of Freedom*, 6–7.
22 Couldry and Mejias, *The Costs of Connection*, xi.
23 Davis, *Women, Race & Class*, 32–3.
24 Davis, *Women, Race & Class*, 33.
25 Davis, *Women, Race & Class*, 30.
26 Davis, *Women, Race & Class*, 39.
27 Olufemi, "Introduction," 4.
28 Fresco, "How Much Vomit?".
29 Olufemi, "Introduction," 4.
30 Olufemi, "Introduction," 4.
31 Hutter, "Salt Is Not for Slaves," 369.
32 Scharff, *Repudiating Feminism*, 1.
33 Hutter, "Salt Is Not for Slaves," 370.
34 Stingl and Weiss, "Between Shell and Ghost," 95.
35 Hutter, "Salt Is Not for Slaves," 369.
36 de Freitas, "We Don't Know Menopausal Hormone Therapy Causes Breast Cancer"; Keaveny, "Menopause? Start Estrogen Replacement Therapy Sooner"; Boseley, "Breast Cancer Risk from Using HRT Is 'Twice What Was Thought'"; Hill, "Menopause Experts Say Compounded HRT Is Unsafe."
37 Stingl and Weiss, "Between Shell and Ghost," 95.
38 Lauro and Embry, "A Zombie Manifesto," 88.
39 Osborne and Bannock, "I Miss What I Used to Be Like."
40 McNally, *Monsters of the Market*, 253–4.
41 "Menopause FAQs."
42 Doughty, *Will My Cat Eat My Eyeballs?* 182.
43 Osborne and Bannock, "I Miss What I Used to Be Like."
44 McCormick, "Forward Is the Battle Cry," 105.
45 McCormick, "Forward Is the Battle Cry," 105.
46 Hutter, "Salt Is Not for Slaves," 382.
47 Hutter, "Salt Is Not for Slaves," 383.
48 *SANTA CLARITA DIET Season 1 TRAILER (2017)*.
49 McCormick, "Forward Is the Battle Cry," 101.
50 Lauro and Embry, "A Zombie Manifesto," 90.
51 *Drew Barrymore Season 2 "Diet" Struggle Was Real*.
52 McNally, *Monsters of the Market*, 253.
53 Cohen, "Undead (A Zombie Oriented Ontology)," 404.
54 Haraway, "A Cyborg Manifesto," 15.
55 Robinson, "Here's the Real Reason Why Netflix Cancelled Santa Clarita Diet."

56 Couldry and Mejias, *The Costs of Connection*, xi.
57 Lauro and Embry, "A Zombie Manifesto," 99.
58 Couldry and Mejias, *The Costs of Connection*, xi.

Works Cited

Alexander, Neta. "Catered to Your Future Self: Netflix's 'Predictive Personalization' and the Mathematization of Taste." In *The Netflix Effect: Technology and Entertainment in the 21st Century*, edited by Kevin McDonald and Daniel Smith-Rowsey, 81–97. New York: Bloomsbury Academic, an imprint of Bloomsbury Publishing Inc, 2016.

Boseley, Sarah. "Breast Cancer Risk from Using HRT Is 'Twice What Was Thought.'" News. *The Guardian*, August 29, 2019. https://www.theguardian.com/science/2019/aug/29/breast-cancer-risk-from-using-hrt-is-twice-what-was-thought. Accessed March 26, 2020.

Brennan, Louis. "How Netflix Expanded to 190 Countries in 7 Years." Business. *Harvard Business Review*, October 12, 2018. https://hbr.org/2018/10/how-netflix-expanded-to-190-countries-in-7-years. Accessed March 26, 2020.

Calhoun, Ada. "Surviving Perimenopause: 'I Was Overwhelmed and Full of Rage. Why Was I So Badly Prepared?'" *The Guardian*, March 1, 2020. https://www.theguardian.com/society/2020/mar/01/surviving-perimenopause-i-was-overwhelmed-and-full-of-rage-why-was-i-so-badly-prepared. Accessed March 26, 2020.

Cohen, Jeffrey Jerome. "Monster Culture (Seven Theses)." In *Monster Theory*, 3–25. Minneapolis: University of Minnesota Press, 1996.

Cohen, Jeffrey Jerome. "Undead (A Zombie Oriented Ontology)." *Journal of the Fantastic in the Arts* 23, no. 3 (86) (2012): 397–412.

Couldry, Nick and Ulises Ali Mejias. *The Costs of Connection: How Data Is Colonizing Human Life and Appropriating It for Capitalism*. (Culture and Economic Life.) Stanford, CA: Stanford University Press, 2019.

Davis, Angela Y. *Women, Race & Class*. New York: Vintage Books, 1983.

Doughty, Caitlin. *Will My Cat Eat My Eyeballs?: Big Questions from Tiny Mortals about Death*. London: Weidenfeld & Nicolson, 2019.

Drew Barrymore Season 2 "Diet" Struggle Was Real. United States: CBS, 2018. https://www.youtube.com/watch?v=ZkyjoeLNOyk&t=2s. Accessed March 27, 2020.

DuVernay, Ava. *13th*. Documentary. Netflix, 2016.

Freitas, Will de. "We Don't Know Menopausal Hormone Therapy Causes Breast Cancer, but the Evidence Continues to Suggest a Link." *The Conversation*, September 3, 2019. https://theconversation.com/we-dont-know-menopausal-hormone-therapy-causes-breast-cancer-but-the-evidence-continues-to-suggest-a-link-122721. Accessed March 26, 2020.

Fresco, Victor. *Santa Clarita Diet*. United States: Netflix, 2017–19.

Haraway, Donna Jeanne. "A Cyborg Manifesto: Science, Technology and Socialist-Feminism in the Late Twentieth Century." In *Manifestly Haraway*, 3–90. Minneapolis: University of Minnesota Press, 2016.

Hill, Amelia. "Menopause Experts Say Compounded HRT Is Unsafe." *The Guardian*, August 26, 2019. https://www.theguardian.com/society/2019/aug/26/menopause-experts-say-compounded-hrt-is-unsafe. Accessed March 26, 2020.

Hutter, G. W. "Salt Is Not for Slaves." In *The Book of the Living Dead*, edited by John Richard Stephens, 369–83. New York: Berkley Books, 2010.

I Walked with a Zombie. [Film] Dir. Jacques Tourner, Los Angeles: RKO Pictures, 1943.

Keaveny, Paul. "Menopause? Start Estrogen Replacement Therapy Sooner, to Reduce Heart Disease." *The Conversation*, June 4, 2019. https://theconversation.com/menopause-start-estrogen-replacement-therapy-sooner-to-reduce-heart-disease-116890. Accessed March 26, 2019.

King Kong. [Film] Dirs. Merian C. and Ernest B. Schoedsack, Los Angeles: RKO Radio Pictures, 1933.

Land of the Dead. [Film] Dir. George A. Romero, California: Universal Pictures, 2005.

Lauro, Sarah Juliet and Karen Embry. "A Zombie Manifesto: The Nonhuman Condition in the Era of Advanced Capitalism." *Boundary 2* 35, no. 1 (March 1, 2008): 85–108.

McCormick, Casey J. "'Forward Is the Battle Cry:' Binge-Viewing Netflix's *House of Cards*." In *The Netflix Effect: Technology and Entertainment in the 21st Century*, edited by Kevin McDonald and Daniel Smith-Rowsey, 101–16. New York: Bloomsbury Academic, 2016.

McNally, David. *Monsters of the Market: Zombies, Vampires, and Global Capitalism*. Chicago, IL: Haymarket Books, 2012.

The North American Menopause Society. "Menopause FAQs: Understanding the Symptoms." https://www.menopause.org/for-women/expert-answers-to-frequently-asked-questions-about-menopause/menopause-faqs-understanding-the-symptoms. Accessed March 26, 2020.

The North American Menopause Society. "*MenoPro* Mobile App: A Mobile App for Women Bothered by Menopause Symptoms." https://www.menopause.org/for-women/-i-menopro-i-mobile-app. Accessed March 26, 2020.

Olufemi, Lola. *Feminism, Interrupted: Disrupting Power*. 1–9. London: Pluto Press, 2020.

Osborne, Hilary and Caroline Bannock. "'I Miss What I Used to Be Like': Women's Stories of the Menopause." *The Guardian*, August 25, 2019. https://www.theguardian.com/society/2019/aug/25/i-miss-what-i-used-to-be-like-womens-stories-of-the-menopause. Accessed March 26, 2020.

Robinson, Abby. "Here's the Real Reason Why Netflix Cancelled Santa Clarita Diet." Magazine. *Digital Spy*, May 2, 2019. https://www.digitalspy.com/tv/ustv/a27341559/santa-clarita-diet-cancelled-why-netflix/. Accessed March 26, 2020.

SANTA CLARITA DIET Season 1 TRAILER (2017) Drew Barrymore Netflix Series. YouTube Video, 2017. https://www.youtube.com/watch?v=kbXfhW6E6eI. Accessed June 16, 2019.

Scharff, Christina. *Repudiating Feminism: Young Women in a Neoliberal World*. Abingdon, OX: Routledge, 2016.

Spivak, Gayatri Chakravorty. "Feminism 2000: One Step beyond?" *Feminist Review*, no. 64 (2000): 113–16.

Stevens, Cat. *Moonshadow*. Single. London: Island Records, 1970.

Stingl, Alexander and Sabrina Weiss. "Between Shell and Ghost: A Hauntology of Zombies in the Social Imaginary." In *Vergemeinschaftung in Zeiten Der Zombie-Apokalypse: Gesellschaftskonstruktionen Am Fantastischen Anderen*, edited by Michael Dellwing and Martin Harbusch, 69–122. Wiesbaden: Springer, 2015.

White Zombie. [Film] Dir. Victor Halperin, Hollywood: United Artists, 1932.

Zerilli, Linda M. G. *Feminism and the Abyss of Freedom*. Chicago: University of Chicago Press, 2005.

Part Three

Zombie Decolonial

9

De/Zombification as Decolonial Critique: Beyond Man, Nature, and the Posthuman in Folklore and Fiction from South Africa

Rebecca Duncan

[O]ur present struggles with respect to race, class, gender, sexual orientation, ethnicity, struggles of the environment, global warming, severe climate change, the sharply unequal distribution of the earth's resources... are all differing facets of the... central ethnoclass Man vs Human struggle
—Sylvia Wynter, "Unsettling the Coloniality of Being"

Introduction

In the essay from which the above epigraph is taken, Sylvia Wynter examines how a mode of being designated "the human" emerges from the revolutions that have shaped the Eurocentric paradigm of knowledge since the long sixteenth century. This category of humanity is bound up, she argues, with unfolding social and ecological shifts; it must thus be "unsettl[ed]" to meet the challenges of the planetary present.[1] Taking its cue from similar observations, a developing strand of literary criticism has begun to propose that speculative fiction might provide a vocabulary for alternative, *posthuman* forms of existence. The argument that follows here engages with this ongoing conversation, but—focusing on the figure of the South African zombie—suggests that from vantages across the African continent, it is not sufficient simply to rethink the human in more accommodating terms. Instead, it is necessary to address *how* this category has been implemented over the history of what Walter D. Mignolo calls "modernity/coloniality,"[2] to suppress alternative forms of being and knowing in the interest of identifying exploitable and expendable lives and environments on a planetary scale. The human, in other words, requires *decolonization*, and this chapter proposes that the zombie as it is deployed in fiction from contemporary South Africa might facilitate such a project.

To make this argument, I draw from Latin American and Caribbean thinkers associated with the "decolonial option,"[3] and in doing so join with recent scholarship that examines and develops their work in African contexts. For Sabelo J. Ndlovu-Gatsheni, who has written extensively on topics in this vein, decolonial thinking offers the conceptual tools for making visible how—despite formal decolonization across Africa in the twentieth century—"the domains of culture, the psyche, mind, language, aesthetics, religion and many others have remained colonized."[4] As a result, the decolonial perspective also "exposes the fact that Euro-American epistemologies are exhausted opening up an opportune moment for... decolonial epistemologies from the South."[5] Thus, Ndlovu-Gatsheni writes, "decoloniality [i]s a necessary liberatory language of the future for Africa."[6] The discussion below examines the figure of the zombie in light of this possibility and proceeds in two phases: first, I outline how actually existing occult narratives of zombification, proliferating across the sub-Saharan region, register the social and ecological effects of the human as a colonial institution, and how such discourses also potentiate a decolonial critique. Second, I bring this discussion to bear on South African author Masande Ntshanga's *The Reactive*,[7] a novel that carries the imprint of African zombie lore, and which—I argue—capitalizes on its decolonial potential in a way that may be illuminating more widely across postcolonial literary mobilizations of the undead.

The Coloniality of Man and Nature

In Wynter's "Unsettling the Coloniality of Being/Power/Truth/Freedom," the author considers how what she calls "Man1" and "Man2" appear—respectively—during the Renaissance and the Enlightenment. Broadly, these concepts designate a vision of the human as rational subject, a construct that gains its definition in opposition to a postulated and subordinate object domain. This version of humanity underpins the emergence of first the physical- and then the biological sciences, and—given the universal purchase ascribed to these disciplines—is taken to be universal in turn, becoming "overrepresented."[8]

"Man," on Wynter's account, thus occupies the epistemic position described by Mignolo—drawing on Santiago Castro-Gómez—as the "zero point":[9] conceived as the rational master of all he surveys, this human provides a dislocated and all-encompassing god's-eye-view of the world, having been lifted out of the history in which he is shaped.

It is in part the objective of Wynter's essay to redress this dehistoricization. The author shows how the binary paradigm in which Man takes shape codevelops with racializing narratives that first appear during the colonization of the Americas—the moment that, inaugurating a transoceanic division of labor, also marks the inauguration of capital as world-system. Writing of this context, Aníbal Quijano identifies what he calls the "coloniality of power,"[10] a term that sheds light on how categories of racial difference—themselves rooted in pre-existing patriarchy—are mobilized for capitalist ends to organize the transnational distribution of paid and unpaid work. Building on Quijano, Wynter illuminates how these hierarchies of race enable the construction of Man as rational subject, ontologically distinct from an object world. She describes too how that same vision of Man is deployed across the history of modernity to ratify the treatment of certain, racialized lives as if they were objects: exploitable or expendable according to capital's demands. Summing up this point, she writes that in the colonial context "systemic stigmatization, social inferiorization, and dynamically produced material deprivation... serv[ed] both to 'verify' the overrepresentation of 'Man' as if it were the human, and to legitimate the subordination of the world and well-being of the [colonized] to those of the [colonizers]."[11]

The human as Man is thus central to the processes of domination that have shaped geopolitical relations across five centuries of modernity. This conception is equally implicated, as Wynter's epigraph suggests, in the conditions of socio-ecological inequality that characterize the global present. Writing in the domain of environmental history, Jason W. Moore locates the Eurocentric paradigm of Man at the root of currently unfolding planetary emergency. Harnessed by capital, Man becomes a mechanism for "cheapening" the potential "work/energy" of humans and extra-human nature,[12] enabling lives and environments that ostensibly fall outside the category of humanity to be conceptually congealed into a freely appropriable resource. Thus, for Moore, the capitalist world economy is more properly a "*world-ecology*, joining power, nature and accumulation in a dialectical and unstable unity."[13] The effects of this long-maintained conjunction are currently visible not only in deleterious planetary transformations but also in the radically uneven, gendered, and racialized distribution of these caustic shifts. As Moore notes, it is "women, neo-colonial populations and people of color" who disproportionately suffer the effects of present crises,[14] which must thus be understood as "systemically combin[ing] greenhouse gas pollution with... patriarchy, and climate apartheid."[15]

Zombie/i Posthumanism

In this uneven present, the product of a logic which expels "the majority of humans... from Humanity," the possibility of "planetary justice" requires—as Moore notes—that we "dismantle... the tyranny of Man and Nature."[16] It is with this imperative that we might turn to the zombie, since critics responding to the postmillennial rise of commercial zombie fiction have proposed that such texts have the potential precisely to unmake the human. Influentially, Sarah Juliet Lauro and Karen Embry have argued in their "Zombie Manifesto" that the zombie represents "the only imaginable spectre that could really be posthuman."[17] Critical posthumanism, Pramod K. Nayar writes, "involves a rethinking of the very idea of subjectivity."[18] The theoretical postulate Lauro and Embry call the "zombii" is intended to enable this revision through an extreme refusal "to reconcile subject and object."[19] Importantly, this argument relies on a conception of capital and ideology that suggests even "the individual is a fiction conjured by the economic structure."[20] Animate but without consciousness, the zombii represents a mode of being posthuman in a world where human consciousness itself is an effect of capital. Hence, write the authors, "when we truly become posthuman, we won't even *know* it."[21]

Though widely cited, Lauro and Embry's analysis is not without its difficulties, and sits uneasily alongside the history of enslavement, in which—the authors themselves note—the contemporary zombie is rooted (more on this below). There is a sense, after all, in which the zombii, a mindless nonsubject, resembles the colonial construction of colonized peoples, whose lives are rendered "cheap," in Moore's terminology, precisely on the grounds they are not fully rational. It is striking, also, that Wynter's own assessment of what lies beyond Man is not a "nullified" subject,[22] but a subject to which a richer consciousness is ascribed. The objective of her interrogation is—pointedly—to "secur[e]... the full cognitive and behavioural autonomy of the human species."[23] Indeed, posthumanism generally—and paradoxically—risks replicating the logic of Man. Though one of its key precepts is, as Nayar notes, that "the universal category of the 'human' is not really universal at all,"[24] the critical field nonetheless retains the generalizing language of humanity, and so lends itself to prescriptions that, similarly general, reproduce the dislocated god's-eye-view perspective of Eurocentric epistemology. "If today it is meaningless to universalize... Man/Human," writes Mignolo with Catherine Walsh, "it is equally limiting to conceptualise [the] posthuman beyond the regional scope of actors, institutions, and languages."[25]

The point sheds critical light on the zombii, which is explicitly offered as the "truly posthumanist" subject.[26] Part of what drives this universalizing impulse is the total efficacy Lauro and Embry ascribe to the forms of knowledge sustaining capitalist accumulation. Their argument leaves little room, in other words, for the possibility that other modes of being and knowing might persist, even in the face of capital's epistemic impositions. In this way the analysis overlooks the real endurance of indigenous cultures and belief systems in colonized regions, and thus potentiates the uncomfortable effect of reinforcing colonial silencing and suppression.

Decolonizing the Human

Mignolo's own account offers an alternative to the zombii's delineation of capital and epistemology: for him, modernity/coloniality—though universal in aspiration—is always fractured by what he calls "the colonial difference."[27] This is the position occupied by those excluded from the category of Man, and which thus provides a vantage from which Eurocentric knowledge and the material states of precarity it produces in combination with capital, appear not natural and universal but brutal, located, and arbitrary. While it is subject to colonizing epistemology, experience in the colonial difference is also informed, on the one hand, by the lived violence of objectification and, on the other, by "ways of life and... thinking that have been disqualified... since the Renaissance."[28] The point here is that forms of consciousness emergent in the colonial difference facilitate a different mode of "thinking geo- and body-politically,"[29] which in turn makes possible not only a *revision* but a *decolonization* of the human. This takes place when those historically expelled from this category apprehend the material and epistemic violence in which it is implicated, and when, beginning from the lived—and thus located—experience of marginalization, they draw on local histories and knowledges to enact nonuniversal modes of being. Across the rest of this chapter, I will suggest that, considered from a different perspective to the posthumanist approach taken by Lauro and Embry, the figure of the zombie might enable a decolonial engagement with the Eurocentric category of humanity. I will develop this idea via Ntshanga's novel below; at this juncture, it is necessary to turn briefly to the figure of the zombie in Africa and its contemporary resurgence.

Zombies on the African Continent

The origins of the contemporary zombie are usually located in the Haitian slave economy, where it emerges amid the transoceanic capitalist relations that constitute early coloniality. This zombie, writes Kerstin Oloff, is a "soulless body... raised from the grave" at the behest of sorcerer, who then mercilessly exploits the animate corpse.[30] As Oloff notes, Haitian zombies clearly encode the "experience of brutal enslavement" within the plantation system;[31] however, the source of Caribbean zombie figures lies in West Africa, in beliefs transported across the Atlantic with peoples seized from that region. Though not uniform, African zombie lore—like its Haitian counterpart—is predicated on the "primary belief... that the soul can be influenced" from outside the body by magical forces,[32] and thus reflects the animist principle that Harry Garuba locates as fundamental to epistemologies and cosmological formations throughout the sub-Saharan region. African animism, writes Garuba, entails a "locking" of spirit within matter. In a reversal of the Eurocentric impulse to divide consciousness from the substance of nature, "animist thought spiritualises the object world," understanding these two spheres as inextricably interwoven.[33] Implicitly linking this worldview to zombie-like figures in colonial-era Tswana culture, John and Jean Comaroff note that "*sefifi*"—a "state of non-being," which "speaks... of empty shells of humanity"[34]—is induced through the malicious manipulation of a self that, as on Garuba's account, is "not confined to the corporeal body," but instead "range[s] over... the sum total of its relations, presences, [and] enterprises."[35] This relational form of personhood—starkly distinct from Eurocentric Man—can thus be accessed through people's "footprints," for example, or through "magical operations on their houses, their clothes or their animal's."[36]

A number of critics have noted such threats are on the rise across sub-Saharan Africa, and have been since the late twentieth century. The Comaroffs describe how, in post-apartheid South Africa, "longstanding notions of witchcraft... have come to embrace zombie-making, the brutal reduction of others... to instruments of production; to insensible beings stored, like tools... at the homes of their creators."[37] As in earlier Caribbean iterations, contemporary African zombies also respond, as David McNally argues, to "sites where labouring bodies are at risk," and thus they too might be considered an effect of "capitalist modernity": an occult apprehension "of the corporeal power on which capital feeds."[38] It would be a mistake, however, to interpret zombie figures as cyphers for exploitation generally. As Oloff and the Comaroffs stress, the zombie is a response to *shifts* in the nature and configuration of capital accumulation on a global scale. In colonial Haiti, the zombie appears with the initiation of global capitalist relations. In contemporary Africa, these transformations are the result of postcolonial neoliberalization, which, across the continent, has most often taken the form of Structural Adjustment—self-imposed, in the post-apartheid context. Throughout Africa, in other words, the neoliberal agenda is experienced as privatization and deregulation that—by opening domestic economies to foreign control—also effectively extends the power dynamic and material conditions of colonial rule. Even as these measures have made vast flows of transnational capital visible to African citizens, they have also—despite the promises of formal decolonization—rendered wealth locally inaccessible through, for example, the casualization of the labor market and strategic underemployment. The figure of the undead laborer emerges amid this deepening postcolonial inequality, registering its disorientating effects as a state of magically imposed corporeal objectification.

Making a similar point, Stephen Shapiro has shown that "catachrestic" Gothic figures appear in European literary production on the advent of industrialization, as capitalist penetration violently breaks up pre-existing patterns of life.[39] Oloff's account of the Haitian zombie builds on this analysis, but—following Moore—emphasizes that because capital is not only a social but a socio-ecological formation, the experiences encoded in tales of undead workers relate to changes in the extra-human biosphere, as well as in the organization of human lives.[40] The observation seems pertinent, too, in respect to contemporary zombie lore on the African continent, where deleterious shifts to the labor market are unfolding in a context Gabrielle Hecht describes as the "African Anthropocene":[41] one characterized by intense multinational extractivism and the disproportionate accumulation of these (and other) industries' toxic effects. The lexicon of heightened threat in which discourses of zombification operate might thus be understood as registering a reality rendered acutely precarious not only by social transformations but also by processes of environmental plunder with which these are entangled, and, to the extent that it makes palpable the violence of these conditions, the zombie possesses a proto-critical charge. Asserting this point, McNally emphasizes African occult narratives' "*defetishising*" potential[42]—their capacity for exposing the material degradations on which capital depends. I would also point out, however, that the zombie addresses this violence *from within the colonial difference*, and so reflects a lived experience of exclusion from the domain of humanity. Beyond a critique of capital, zombie lore on the African continent might thus also make possible a decolonial engagement with the mode of being that Wynter identifies as Man. It indexes the effects of this category from the zone of objectification that lies outside its borders, and does so—importantly—with recourse to indigenous cosmological frameworks, thus foregrounding the endurance of knowledge systems forcibly suppressed through the operation of coloniality.

It is with all of this in mind that I turn now to Ntshanga's *The Reactive*. Although it does not deal explicitly with the figure of the undead laborer, this narrative can nonetheless be understood as offering an analogous literary response to social and environmental precarity from the vantage point of neoliberalizing South Africa. Further, as I will show, the novel capitalizes on the critical—and specifically decolonial—potential inherent in occult interpretations of socio-ecological shifts, and is legible in this sense as an example of what the Warwick Research Collective (WReC) have termed "critical irrealism" after Michael Löwy.[43] Across the novel, a dynamic of de/zombification makes visible, in the first instance, how socio-ecological inequalities continue to be organized by the racialized and ecocidal logic of Man, and in the second they chart the unraveling of this logic through a reconstitution of personhood within the framework of African animism.

Socio-Ecological Inequality and Irrealism in *The Reactive*

Ntshanga's *The Reactive* is set in Cape Town in 2003 and presents a vision of South Africa more generally in which the post-apartheid onset of neoliberalization is registered as a widescale (though not total) deepening of the racialized socioeconomic/ecological inequalities cultivated under formal white minority rule. Though he has himself escaped the poverty into which he was born, Nathi—the twenty-something narrator-protagonist—returns at the narrative's end to his family in the township of Du Noon: a place where the shacks are described tellingly as "like time capsules."[44] Old hardships are vividly evident here as profound poverty, but also as an attendant environmental inequality, visible—for example—in the variegated distribution of water and sanitation infrastructure: Nathi queues for the settlement's communal tap and spends his first days assisting his uncle in building a new pit latrine.

In the run-up to this concluding phase of the novel, action takes place, as Lara Buxbaum notes, at the height of South Africa's AIDS epidemic, before the state roll-out of Anti-Retroviral (ARV) therapy.[45] This situation is mobilized alongside ongoing (environmental) inequality to expose an uneven access to health care: part of the plot revolves around how Nathi—who is himself HIV positive—sells the medication made available to him through his private insurance on the black market. It is in this strand of the novel—which otherwise engages with a recognizable Cape Town—that an irrealist impulse becomes visible, linking the text to actually existing occult interpretations of conspicuous wealth amid resilient poverty in a neoliberalizing South Africa. Tales of undead laborers, as the Comaroffs argue, function to explain the influx of foreign capital into the still deeply unequal post-apartheid nation; *The Reactive* offers an analogous narrative of quasi-magical enrichment when a mysterious buyer makes a large and unanticipated advance payment for a substantial order of ARVs. This is no ordinary client; rather, he seems to enter Ntshanga's novel from the domain of speculative fiction. Known initially as "the ugly man," it turns out that beneath the tin mask he wears habitually, he has no face at all, only "skinless meat, gleaming in full view."[46]

Together with his capacity for bestowing fabulous wealth at will, the ugly man's disturbing and fantastically realized anonymity renders him—like posited zombie-makers—a catachrestic symbol for the inscrutable operation of the post-apartheid economy. In fact, he situates himself in this position when he refers to the underground trade in ARVs as "a social service"—a comment that both illuminates the caustic effects of privatized health care and suggests the black market doubles official channels of (uneven) distribution.[47] Later, this connection to popular occult interpretations of inequality is affirmed: amid the poverty of Du Noon, Nathi recounts how the community rounds on the salesman of a pyramid scheme (another occultist response to inaccessible post-apartheid wealth). Before he is attacked, this youth "addresses the crowd, shouting about the coming of a man without a face.... He says we'll no longer be slaves, when the faceless man comes."[48]

Zombie Aesthetics

Against this backdrop of bewildering socio-ecological precarity, the narrative follows Nathi and his friends Ruan and Cecilia (Cissie) as they drift through their days in a state of drug- and alcohol-fueled lethargy. Midway through the novel, it is revealed that the protagonist's HIV status is the result of self-infection, performed in the virology lab where he has worked, as an attempt to manage his grief over his brother Luthando's death. The fatality of Nathi's action looms large in the story from the outset. The three friends often play "Last Life," for example: a game in which they imagine Nathi's "last year on the planet."[49] Existing so explicitly in the force-field of his own mortality, Nathi exemplifies a kind of living death, and Cecelia makes this point overtly when she reminds him that "flesh is... meant to go off from the beginning."[50] Across the narrative, this sense of an impending end is expanded in an ecological register, as the characters regularly contemplate the destruction of the earth's biosphere. This catastrophic ecological vision appears inflected by the AIDS crisis, when in a telling moment Nathi relates "how the Earth was gutted open with so many new graves for paupers, that when the clouds parted, they revealed a view... that looked like a giant honeycomb."[51] Combining the social effects of neoliberalization with the language of extractivism, these lines offer a perspective on the world-ecology from the South African vantage, highlighting the uneven post-apartheid distribution of both social and ecological vulnerability. Further, though, they resonate in their apocalypticism with the protagonist's own approaching death, augmenting this so that all the characters in the narrative come to live in the shadow of biospheric collapse.

This infiltration of life by death is underscored, on the one hand, as Nathi self-medicates in a way that deadens his emotions, and on the other through an aesthetics of embodiment, which overemphasizes a form of objectified physicality. Introducing himself and his friends, and adopting the dispassionately descriptive register that is characteristic of his narration more generally, Nathi recounts his daily routine:

> Like always, the three of us... wake up sometime before noon and take two ibuprofens each. Then we go back to sleep, wake up again an hour later, and take another two from the 800-milligram pack. Then Cissie turns on the stove to cook up a batch of glue, and the three of us wander around mutely after that... caroming off each other's limbs.[52]

As it subordinates psychic experience to the actions and positioning of the material body, the passage articulates the anesthetizing effect of the chemicals the characters imbibe, but it also gestures toward a peculiarly reified form of subjectivity. Indeed, Ntshanga's vision of the three friends as silent bodies that, atom-like, ricochet off one another subliminally recalls Hollywood scenes of the shambling undead. This connection is rendered more palpable still when, high on "Industrial" (glue), Nathi appears in the zombie's signature stance, his consciousness overtly reduced to a series of mechanical impulses: "my mind instructs me to glide," he tells, "so I push my arms out... balancing with my hands and trying not to slip."[53]

Zombification and the Coloniality of Being

Together with the detached tone of Nathi's first-person narration, the novel's persistent prioritization of corporeal materiality over emotive life coheres as an aesthetics of zombification, which—like African occult discourses around the undead—can be understood as conveying a subjective experience of objectification. This state of being is linked to the characters' drug use, but is also situated in relation to the colonial difference. It is important in this sense that Nathi feels "scrutinised... and inadequate" in his job at the lab, where his colleagues have "skin that could flush red," and where his boss—a French AIDS researcher with an *"oblige noblesse"*—perceives the protagonist as "just another of his Africans."[54] Considered in this context, the sense of reified physicality that pervades Nathi's narrative resonates with Frantz Fanon's famous account of racialization as effecting "[a] slow composition of my *self* as a body."[55] Fanon's point is that, because racist dehumanization is woven into the fabric of Eurocentric knowledge and culture, the paradigm of selfhood constituted within these parameters can only ever provide colonized peoples with a "third person consciousness," in which one relates to oneself as, in Fanon's words, "an object in the midst of other objects."[56] Taking place in a scientific institution, Nathi's sense of alienation—his apprehension of his position in the colonial difference—speaks directly to the racialized principle encoded in hegemonized Eurocentric epistemology, the social and ecological effects of which the narrative has traced elsewhere as post-apartheid neoliberalization is shown to entrench the human and environmental inequity instantiated under white minority rule.

Ultimately, Nathi's drug use can be understood as what Fanon himself calls an "immunization of the emotions" in the face of violent objectification.[57] Most immediately, however, it is tied to Luthando's death, which occurs after the ceremonial circumcision through which young Xhosa men are initiated into adulthood. Nathi feels responsible for this tragedy, having not fulfilled his promise to accompany his brother in the ritual. For Ronit Frenkel, the protagonist's guilt and grief over this situation operate primarily on an interpersonal level.[58] However, it seems important that Luthando's memory is also linked overtly to the psychic effects of apartheid race politics, a connection made explicit when he angrily tells Nathi that "everything... about [him] was white."[59] The incident resonates with a later moment, when the protagonist recounts how his estrangement from Xhosa culture is heightened by elders who treat him "like anyone else—not a Model C who didn't know his clan name from his asshole."[60] Significantly, Nathi's allusion here locates his feeling of cultural alienation as the effect of institutionalized coloniality: post-apartheid Model C schools—where he is educated—were formerly reserved for white pupils, and have recently been critiqued for their covert perpetuation of apartheid's cultural politics.[61] The wider field of associations in which Luthando is situated thus suggests that as the protagonist's drug-use numbs the loss of his brother, it can also be understood as a response to the racialized culture in which Nathi gains his sense of self. Narcotic-fueled lethargy thus overlays and compounds the aesthetic of corporeal objectification via which the narrative articulates the experience of material and epistemic relegation from what Wynter has described as the category of Man.

Decolonizing the Human: Reactivity

Self-induced detachment is not, however, the protagonist's only recourse. Indeed, the act of slow suicide on which the narrative turns is framed as an attempted escape from numbness. "I infected myself with HIV," Nathi explains; "That's how I became reactive.... I gave my own body something it couldn't flee from."[62] Buxbaum proposes that Nathi's "infection is his method of forcing the experience of vulnerability on himself."[63] In the radically uneven context of post-apartheid South Africa, vulnerability is, as Buxbaum notes, a systemically produced "passive state,"[64] but she argues further that, under these conditions, acts of self-imposed risk in fictional narrative contest passivity by affirming the lively interdependency of existence. "[B]y actively risking vulnerability," she writes, characters "relinquish an attachment to embodied subjectivity as hermetically sealed off from others and the world."[65] Viewed in this light, Nathi's exposure to the HIV virus becomes a strategy for addressing the experience of objectification in the colonial difference, and one that—unlike self-medication—does not reinforce a condition of inertia and alienation.

Reactivity can thus be read as figuring a mode of existence not shaped by the paradigm of coloniality. In fact, Ntshanga's novel frequently calls the self-evidence of the human into question: Ruan wants to upload his consciousness, for example, and Cissie believes the destruction of the individual is sufficient for the end of the world. It is against this interrogative background, and following immediately on from the account of self-infection, that Nathi leaves Cape Town for Du Noon to undergo the initiation he has been avoiding since Luthando's death—a choice through which, as Frenkel notes, "Ntshanga offers traditional Southern African rituals and belief systems as a recourse."[66] Indeed, the significance of Xhosa cosmology is accentuated by the role of Nosizi—a diviner—on whose prompting the protagonist is brought back to partake in the ceremony. For Frenkel, initiation catalyzes "a sort of transformative healing process for Nathi,"[67] and the specific form this takes in the narrative is a shift in the protagonist's sense of self and his relation to the world. This is evidenced most vividly by his embarking on a new relationship immediately after his initiation. His connection with Esona is instant; the two feel from the outset as if they are "forehead to forehead."[68] As Buxbaum points out, the novel's final sex scene emphasizes this mutual intimacy, articulating a vibrancy of sensation that contrasts with Nathi's former numbness ("her fingernails tickle my underside like the tip of an ivy leaf")[69] while also expressing a sense of subjective "dissolution"[70] as Nathi experiences orgasm as a "melt[ing]" into the body of his partner.[71] Buxbaum argues that the encounter affirms the subjective interdependence introduced into the narrative via Nathi's reactive status. It is important also, however, that this model of the self is concretized through the protagonist's formal initiation into Xhosa society, and thus gains a cultural inflection.

As the Comaroffs have shown, personhood is precisely understood as relational in the context of African belief systems, predicated as these are—Garuba argues—on an animist principle. Viewed in this light, the mode of being Nathi occupies at the close of the novel can be understood not only as a *revision* of an objectifying racialized paradigm but more specifically as a *decolonization* of this paradigm's conception of the human. Ntshanga's narrative both maps out the material and epistemic effects of Wynter's principle of Man and reconfigures the categories through which this operates, in a way that re-centers the cosmology of those expelled from humanity proper into the colonial difference. The relational mode of being that emerges is apparent in Nathi's relationship with Esona; but Xhosa culture is also shown to provide a perspective on extra-human nature, which emphasizes socio-ecological interdependency through spiritualization. Nathi recalls how, as a child in his grandmother's village, he learned of animal spirits "with bodies tall as men," and how in this place he also acquired "the idea that the natural world was without borders."[72]

Conclusion: De/Zombification

I have argued that Ntshanga mobilizes an aesthetics of zombification to convey the subjective experience of objectification under socio-ecological conditions of post-apartheid coloniality—a narrative strategy that resonates with the figures of dehumanization circulating through popular African discourses of the occult. Rather than unraveling the subject-object divide (as in Lauro and Embry's posthumanist analysis), this zombie aesthetic registers the *persistence* of the human as a mechanism for organizing social and ecological relations. It is worth noting, too, that the affirmation of a Xhosa worldview implicit in *The Reactive* further sets Ntshanga's account apart from Lauro and Embry's, which—we will recall—hinges on the total efficacy of (colonial) capital's cultural and epistemic impositions. Rooted in Xhosa culture, the personhood on which Ntshanga's novel ends is resistant to universalization; as a result, the text reconfigures Man in a way that refuses the violent overrepresentation characteristic of this category in Eurocentric discourse.

Thus, *The Reactive*'s decolonization of the human does not emerge from the novel's zombie aesthetic itself; it takes place instead as the logic of objectification is redressed through Nathi's initiation. Indeed, to the extent that—as Frenkel writes—the ceremony marks the protagonist's decision "to live,"[73] Nathi's re-engagement with Xhosa cosmology functions—literally—to distance the impending end of his life. After the ritual is complete, Nathi learns of his uncharacteristically strong defensive response to the virus: "I was still reactive," he explains, "just slow to develop the syndrome."[74] The threat of death—in the shadow of which he has appeared zombie-like across the text—is thus tempered, and coinciding with this development, his initiation into Xhosa personhood functions as a critical de-zombifying event: a key moment in the trajectory of the plot, which brings the protagonist—and by extension also extra-human nature—out of a state of objecthood produced through coloniality, and into a fuller, more vibrant form of life. This narrative turn suggests that, from the historical vantage of those relegated from the domain of Man, the consciousless, objectified body of the zombie cannot function as a critical figure for thinking beyond the human, but only replicates the negation of subjectivity on which the human depends for its coherence. To dismantle this category requires instead a sensitivity to its failures—to the forms of being and knowing that endure even after its violent imposition.

Notes

1. Wynter, "Unsettling the Coloniality of Being/Power/Truth/Freedom," 268.
2. Mignolo, "Epistemic Disobedience, Independent Thought and Decolonial Freedom," 167.
3. Mignolo and Walsh, *On Decoloniality*, 127.
4. Ndlovu-Gatsheni, "Decoloniality as the Future of Africa," 485.
5. Ndlovu-Gatsheni, "Decoloniality as the Future of Africa," 492.
6. Ndlovu-Gatsheni, "Decoloniality as the Future of Africa," 485.
7. Ntshanga, *The Reactive*.
8. Wynter, "Unsettling," 288.
9. Mignolo, "Epistemic Disobedience," 160.
10. Quijano, "Coloniality of Power, Eurocentrism and Latin America," 533.
11. Wynter, "Unsettling," 267.
12. Moore, "The Rise of Cheap Nature," 89.
13. Moore, "Introduction," 4.
14. Moore, "Capitalocene and Planetary Justice," 54.
15. Moore, "Capitalocene and Planetary Justice," 54.
16. Moore, "Capitalocene and Planetary Justice," 54.
17. Lauro and Embry, "A Zombie Manifesto," 88.
18. Nayar, *Posthumanism*, 9.
19. Lauro and Embry, "Zombie Manifesto," 95.
20. Lauro and Embry, "Zombie Manifesto," 96.
21. Lauro and Embry, "Zombie Manifesto," 108, emphasis in original.
22. Lauro and Embry, "Zombie Manifesto," 95.
23. Wynter, "Unsettling," 260.
24. Nayar, *Posthumanism*, 11.
25. Mignolo and Walsh, *On Decoloniality*, 172.
26. Lauro and Embry, "Zombie Manifesto," 94.
27. Mignolo, "Geopolitics of Knowledge and the Colonial Difference," 58.
28. Mignolo, "Geopolitics of Sensing and Knowing," 133.
29. Mignolo, "Geopolitics of Sensing and Knowing," 132.
30. Oloff, "Greening the Zombie," 33.
31. Oloff, "Greening the Zombie," 34.
32. Ackermann and Gauthier, "The Ways and Nature of the Zombi," 490.
33. Garuba, "Explorations in Animist Materialism," 267.
34. Comaroff and Comaroff, "On Personhood," 273.
35. Comaroff and Comaroff, "On Personhood," 275.
36. Comaroff and Comaroff, "On Personhood," 275.

37 Comaroff and Comaroff, "Alien-Nation," 788.
38 McNally, *Monster of the Market*, 201.
39 Shapiro, "Transvaal/Transylvania," 31.
40 Oloff, "Greening the Zombie," 33–4.
41 Hecht, "Interscalar Vehicles for an African Anthropocene," 109.
42 McNally, *Monsters*, 204, emphasis in original.
43 Deckard et al., *Combined and Uneven Development*, 83.
44 Ntshanga, *The Reactive*, 165.
45 Buxbaum, "Risking Intimacy in Contemporary South African Fiction," 527.
46 Ntshanga, *The Reactive*, 94.
47 Ntshanga, *The Reactive*, 95.
48 Ntshanga, *The Reactive*, 177.
49 Ntshanga, *The Reactive*, 19.
50 Ntshanga, *The Reactive*, 21.
51 Ntshanga, *The Reactive*, 148–9.
52 Ntshanga, *The Reactive*, 10.
53 Ntshanga, *The Reactive*, 29.
54 Ntshanga, *The Reactive*, 132.
55 Fanon, *Black Skin, White Masks*, 83.
56 Fanon, *Black Skin, White Masks*, 82.
57 Fanon, *Black Skin, White Masks*, 85.
58 Frenkel, "Post-Liberation Temporalities," 75–6.
59 Ntshanga, *The Reactive*, 100.
60 Ntshanga, *The Reactive*, 160.
61 Christie and McKinney, "Decoloniality and 'Model C' Schools," 1–2.
62 Ntshanga, *The Reactive*, 161.
63 Buxbaum, "Risking Intimacy," 526.
64 Buxbaum, "Risking Intimacy," 525.
65 Buxbaum, "Risking Intimacy," 525.
66 Frenkel, "Post-Liberation Temporalities," 76.
67 Frenkel, "Post-Liberation Temporalities," 76.
68 Ntshanga, *The Reactive*, 183.
69 Ntshanga, *The Reactive*, 184.
70 Buxbaum, "Risking Intimacy," 526.
71 Ntshanga, *The Reactive*, 184.
72 Ntshanga, *The Reactive*, 113.
73 Frenkel, "Post-Liberation Temporalities," 77.
74 Ntshanga, *The Reactive*, 179.

Works Cited

Ackermann, Hans-W. and Jeanine Gauthier. "The Ways and Nature of the Zombi." *Journal of American Folklore* 104, no. 414 (1991): 466–94.

Buxbaum, Lara. "Risking Intimacy in Contemporary South African Fiction." *Textual Practice* 31, no. 3 (2017): 523–36.

Christie, Pam and Caroline McKinney. "Decoloniality and 'Model C' Schools: Ethos, Language and the Protests of 2016." *Education as Change* 21, no. 3 (2017): 1–21.

Comaroff, Jean and John L. Comaroff. "Alien-Nation: Zombies, Immigrants, and Millennial Capitalism." *South Atlantic Quarterly* 101, no. 4 (2002): 779–805.

Comaroff, John L. and Jean Comaroff. "On Personhood: An Anthropological Perspective from Africa." *Social Identities* 7, no. 2 (2001): 267–83.

Deckard, Sharae et al. *Combined and Uneven Development: Towards a New Theory of World-Literature*. Liverpool: Liverpool University Press, 2015.

Fanon, Frantz. *Black Skin, White Masks*. Translated by Charles Lam Markmann. London: Pluto, [1952] 2008.

Frenkel, Ronit. "Post-Liberation Temporalities, Utopian Afterlives and Three South African Novels by Masande Ntshanga, Mohale Mashigo and Niq Mhlongo." *English Studies in Africa* 62, no. 1 (2019): 70–80.

Garuba, Harry. "Explorations in Animist Materialism: Notes on Reading/Writing African, Literature, Culture and Society." *Public Culture* 15, no. 2 (2003): 261–85.

Hecht, Gabrielle. "Interscalar Vehicles for an African Anthropocene: On Waste, Temporality, and Violence." *Cultural Anthropology* 33, no. 1 (2018): 109–41.

Lauro Sarah Juliet and Karen Embry. "A Zombie Manifesto: The Nonhuman Condition in the Era Advanced Capitalism." *boundary 2* 35, no. 1 (2008): 85–108.

McNally, David. *Monsters of the Market: Zombies, Vampires and Global Capitalism*. Leiden and Boston: Brill, 2011.

Mignolo, Walter D. "Geopolitics of Knowledge and the Colonial Difference." *South Atlantic Quarterly* 103, no. 1 (2002): 57–96.

Mignolo, Walter D. "Epistemic Disobedience, Independent Thought and Decolonial Freedom." *Theory Culture & Society* 26, no. 7–8 (2009): 159–81.

Mignolo, Walter D. "Geopolitics of Sensing and Knowing: On (De)coloniality, Border Thinking, and Epistemic Disobedience." *Conferno* 1, no. 1 (2013): 129–50.

Mignolo, Walter D. and Catherine Walsh. *On Decoloniality: Concepts, Analytics, Praxis*. Durham: Duke University Press, 2018.

Moore, Jason W. "Introduction: Anthropocene or Capitalocene? Nature, History, and the Crisis of Capitalism." In *Anthropocene or Capitalocene?: Nature, History, and the Crisis of Capitalism*, edited by Jason W. Moore, 1–13. Oakland: PM Press, 2016.

Moore, Jason W. "The Rise of Cheap Nature." In *Anthropocene or Capitalocene?: Nature, History, and the Crisis of Capitalism*, edited by Jason W. Moore, 78–115. Oakland: PM Press, 2016.

Moore, Jason W. "Capitalocene and Planetary Justice." *Maize* 6 (2019): 49–54.

Nayar, Pramod K. *Posthumanism*. London: Polity, 2014.

Ndlovu-Gatsheni, Sabelo J. "Decoloniality as the Future of Africa." *History Compass* 13, no. 3 (2015): 485–96.

Ntshanga, Masande. *The Reactive*. London: Jacaranda, 2014.

Oloff, Kerstin. "'Greening' the Zombie: Caribbean Gothic, World Ecology, and Socio-Ecological Degradation." *Green Letters* 16, no. 1 (2012): 31–45.

Quijano, Anibal. "Coloniality of Power, Eurocentrism and Latin America." *Nepantla: Views from the South* 1, no. 3 (2000): 533–80.

Shapiro, Stephen. "Transvaal/Transylvania: Dracula's World-System and Gothic Periodicity." *Gothic Studies* 10, no. 1 (2008): 29–47.

Wynter, Sylvia. "Unsettling the Coloniality of Being/Power/Truth/Freedom: Towards the Human, after Man, Its Overrepresentation—an Argument." *The New Centennial Review* 3, no. 3 (2003): 157–337.

10

Zombies, Placelessness, and Transcultural Entanglement: Ahmed Saadawi's *Frankenstein in Baghdad*

Netty Mattar

The Whatsitsname (from the Iraqi Arabic word *shesma*) in Ahmed Saadawi's *Frankenstein in Baghdad* (2013) is a creature caught between life and death. Its rotting body emerges from the rubble and ruins of houses and buildings pummeled by the bombings that wreck Baghdad. A body emptied of its soul, the Whatsitsname is a figure of exile that lurks on the edges of the city, compelled by supernatural forces to kill its inhabitants. It is thus inherently tethered to Baghdad while simultaneously driven out of it. Saadawi's monster resembles the abject figure of the zombie, more specifically, the enslaved zombie of the American imaginary. The enslaved-style zombie is a soulless body under the control of another, a creature that must be contained and eradicated.[1] The Whatsitsname and the enslaved-style zombie share a crucial quality: they are radical figures of unbelonging, their attachments to place[2] severed, and yet they are bound to the lands they are no longer a part of. Theirs is a violent paradox of landlessness that constitutes their identity, and they wander the earth in a perpetual state of nonarrival.

The enslaved-style zombie we see in American popular culture is based on stories connected to Haitian vodou and folklore, but is essentially an American creation.[3] Popular depictions ignore the nuances of vodou belief,[4] appropriating Haitian folklore and turning the zombie into a "convenient boogeyman"[5] that has come to represent various cultural anxieties.[6] This enslaved-style zombie is greatly influenced by the writing of William Seabrook, an American journalist and explorer, who lived in Haiti and returned to the United States with detailed and sensationalistic accounts of the walking dead. His book, *The Magic Island* (1927), which became a primary source for early versions of the zombie in

America, offers stories of "soulless human corpse[s]… taken from the grave and endowed by sorcery with a mechanical semblance of life," transformed into mindless beings forced to labor on the fields or to commit crimes.[7] The subjective absence of the zombie evokes in the onlooker not only horror but "pit[y]."[8] Seabrook establishes in the American imagination the idea of the zombie as both a monster and a victim, which becomes deeply entwined with perceptions of Haiti. Seabrook's accounts, and the zombie narratives it has inspired such as "Zombie" (1932) and *White Zombie* (1932), thus erase the complex histories surrounding the Haitian conceptions. In the Haitian context, for example, the zombie is connected to the violent history of enslaved people forcibly sent by ship to the sugarcane plantations in the Caribbean from sub-Saharan Africa.[9] However, following the Haitian Revolution (1791–1804),[10] the zombie has also come to signify liberation from enslavement through rebellion and overcoming oppression. American appropriations typically detach the zombie figure from such subversive power.

The zombie did not enter Western popular culture by way of a well-known literary tradition[11] and so Western audiences do not have very rigid expectations of the monster. Writers and filmmakers are free to experiment with and modify the zombie.[12] In American narratives, the zombie has therefore been associated with a variety of fears including cannibalism (*Night of the Living Dead*, 1968), disease (*28 Days Later*, 2002), and rapid migration (*World War Z*, 2013). It is a shifting signifier, broadly signaling unbelonging and the loss of subjectivity, but also absorbing meanings that different artists impose upon it. This quality has enabled its use as a tool of American imperialism.

Zombies and Empire

The enslaved-style zombie arrives in America around the same time as the American occupation of Haiti from 1915 to 1934.[13] The United States had justified its invasion by pointing to Haiti's political instability and to the United States' role in restoring order. However, scholars argue that this was part of a strategy for expanding US imperial territory, an agenda established by the Monroe Doctrine of 1823, which essentially asserts America's dominance and its right to intervene anywhere in the world.[14] US military intervention into foreign lands expands the American empire through the establishment of a global network of military bases. According to Daniel Immerwahr (2019), these points "serve as staging grounds, launchpads, storage sites, beacons and laboratories," extensions of American territory that make up its "pointillist empire." The hundreds of points around the world that are the foundation of this empire reflect a radically different relationship to territory that has allowed the nation to hide its imperial expansion.[15] The US occupation of Haiti was connected to US control of Haiti's economy and of its territory as a strategic military location.[16] Jennifer Fay (2008) describes how the dispossession of the Haitian people as well as the revival of the colonial and slaver economy during the US occupation is connected to the enslaved-style zombie that had begun to circulate in American culture. The images of dehumanized monsters seen in films like *White Zombie* (1932) functioned as propaganda justifying the occupation.[17]

What is of interest to me is how the enslaved-style zombie trope has been redeployed in relation to the American invasion and occupation of Iraq (2003–11). The United States invaded Iraq in 2003 under the pretext of "liberating" it, a move widely recognized today as furthering the neocolonial project of securing Middle Eastern oil.[18] In the lead-up to the invasion, the US Secretary of State for Defense accused former Iraqi president Saddam Hussein of stockpiling "zombie gas," a chemical agent apparently capable of leaving victims disoriented and in a "zombie-like state." This accusation was meant to strengthen support for US military intervention in Iraq.[19] The film *28 Weeks Later* (2007) similarly likens Iraqis to zombies by imagining a zombie outbreak outside of a US-occupied Green Zone in London, a clear reference to the Green Zone in Iraq (also known as "Little America") captured by American forces in 2003. The implication is that the Iraqi people are monsters that will kill everyone if they are not contained and killed first. The zombie therefore recurs as a racist trope in essentializing narratives that serve to justify the invasion of Iraq and the subsequent reordering of its society.

The striking connection between these narratives of Haiti and Iraq is indicative of a binary paradigm of race that undergirds US history and its territorial expansion. This paradigm conflates all "others," assimilating differences in order to erase them. This conflation is clear in the memoir *Black Baghdad* (1933), which is about the US occupation of Haiti. The text deliberately frames Haiti through the same orientalist lens used to frame Iraq, describing it as a place from "the days of the Arabian Nights" where you can see "woolly-headed cannibals and silk-hatted savants side by side."[20] The connection of Haiti and Iraq through the figure of the zombie in later narratives highlights the continuing project of American imperial expansion: the enslaved-style zombie functions to strip away the humanity of a people, marking them as both monsters and victims, dispossessing them of their attendant rights to their property and land, which facilitates the takeover of territory, the main strategic motivation of the US empire. Grafted onto multiple others, the zombie is a flexible schematic that fixes the boundaries of Western ontology, reinforcing reductive self/other dualisms that determine the superiority of the Western self, positioning all "others" as inferior outsiders. This obscures the specific historical events surrounding each context and directs our attention away from the United States' role as perpetrator in the occupation of Haiti and Iraq.

The Whatsitsname, as I have suggested, evokes the enslaved-style zombie in that it is a menacing, undead creature with no soul or consciousness of its own in the Western sense. However, there are significant differences in Saadawi's iteration that interfere with these popular conceptions, particularly in the nature of its embodiment and its entanglements with inhabitants and with the city it moves through, as I will demonstrate. I argue that the Whatsitsname is a conscious attempt to express Iraqi solidarity with the Haitian oppressed, acknowledging a common experience of unbelonging, while at the same time introducing particular histories and memories that differentiate experiences and trouble assumptions about the other. In this way, Saadawi creates a transcultural figuration of the zombie that extends beyond facile and reductive conceptions. From a transcultural perspective, cultures and their symbolic systems "interfere" with other cultures in dynamic and multidirectional ways.[21] Cultures inhabit other cultures, enabling them to move beyond the presumed rigidity of cultural identities and the oppositional binaries these might entail. Differences are brought together, and there is a continuous negotiation of identity. These interactions of differences create new transcultural identities that exist at the border of, and beyond, any specific culture. Fixed identities are deconstructed and new creative possibilities enabled without losing specificities and without fusing identities into unified wholes.[22] This leads to the "proliferation of interpretive possibilities" and "unrestricted semantic play set free from any one signified," enabling "new *signifiables*" without "negating the 'signified.'"[23] Understanding the Whatsitsname as a creative possibility enabled by transcultural interference adds nuance to decolonial approaches. This perspective deconstructs European paradigms that divide, categorize, and segregate, paradigms that have long defined and confined the nations of the so-called Third World. By attending to the interactions and flows that bind the dispossessed of Haiti and Iraq, we can extend the study of Iraqi literature beyond national borders and attempt to place Iraqi history and culture in a global perspective that overturns cultural separatism, transcending the delineations of European enclosures.

Embodied Cartographies of Expulsion

Saadawi plays with the image of the zombie in order to destabilize its ontological boundaries. This is seen clearly in the Whatsitsname's body, which, unlike early Americanized zombies, is an "extraordinary composite—made up of disparate body parts"[24] from multiple corpses that are stitched together haphazardly. Throughout the novel, Saadawi draws our attention to the "fissures" where things are "coming apart,"[25] and to how the boundaries between parts rupture or "turn into liquid."[26] This results in pieces of flesh falling off, leaving "large holes,"[27] necessitating a constant replacement and restitching of parts. The focus on these fissures brings to mind the ongoing dividing up and stitching together of Iraq resulting from the long history of colonial intervention and violence, and the tenuousness of these boundaries. This connection is provoked by the frame narrative, which describes the administration of Iraqi territory by US military intelligence, which, in turn, echoes European colonialism in its attempt to control the territory and reconstruct its cultural system. The surveillance unit clamps down on "unusual" activity related to "astrologers and fortune-tellers" and suppresses "urban legends, and superstitious rumors,"[28] rationalizing events and then archiving and documenting these occurrences, activities that function, according to Foucault (1969), as the discursive means of Western political enforcement.

Iraq is a place defined, in modern times, by such colonial enforcement. For centuries, the land we now know as Iraq had been a "permeable cross-cultural passage" where people of different ethnicities and religions lived together in cities, maintaining trade and community connections.[29] Britain created the modern state of Iraq by carving up the land and cobbling together the Ottoman provinces of Basra, Mosul, and Baghdad, establishing borders that were not there. The ancient nomadic flows were replaced by exclusionary and hostile policies.[30] The abstract borders of Iraq constitute a forcible carving out of political space from the outside, which violently cut people off from communities they had long been part of. Communities were further reconfigured when the British reinvented the government, endorsing Sunni politicians and ignoring the other communities, giving rise to ethnic and religious tensions.[31] These tensions materialized into physical divisions when the United States invaded the nation. Under US policies, the land was carved up once again, resulting in a Sunni west, a Kurdish north, and a Shi'a south. Sectarian identities solidified as concrete walls and checkpoints were erected.[32] Kinship gave way to religious cleansing, and to a long and violent period of insurgency.[33] Military and sectarian violence progressively forced Iraqis out of their homes, destroying historic buildings and landmarks, creating in Iraq a state of imminent expulsion.

The Whatsitsname is born in the aftermath of this colonial division. Its body is a result of this constant state of expulsion and the annihilation of the city that comes with it. From the moment the story begins, we are confronted with a picture of the utter destruction of the city. The story begins with a "massive explosion" in Tayaran Square, a busy place of gathering in the center of Baghdad. Saadawi emphasizes that the destruction of place is also the destruction of the Iraqi people, and we witness the collapse of buildings alongside heaps of maimed bodies. This opening moment establishes a pattern of incessant violence in the novel: car bombs explode with alarming regularity in a "cycle of killing";[34] death is often gratuitous, transforming Baghdad into a "festival of death."[35] The novel conveys a picture of "place annihilation" that positions cities as not simply the backdrop for war but the very targets of violence. Here, the aim is to destroy not only buildings and infrastructure but also cultures and their expressions, and thus the civilian populations that reside within, such that the destruction of place and the eradication of its people cannot be seen as separate.[36] The weight of human loss is signaled by Saadawi through absence. Amid the chaos, characters remember the spaces of communal support and inter-religious harmony that have been destroyed, and the sons and daughters now "dispersed around the world." The absence of life is emphasized by grim traces of "blood and hair" smeared on electricity poles.[37] This absence creates a tension that brings into sharp relief the visceral picture of immanent dispossession.

The profound emotional toll of this violent instability is apparent in Hadi, the junk dealer, one of several central characters who must cope with imminent loss. Hadi is a troubled drunkard who is fixated on the traces of bloodshed on the streets of Baghdad. For Hadi, the explosion in Tayaran Square—the "smoke, the burning of plastic and seat cushions, the roasting of human flesh"[38]—triggers traumatic memories of his own loss, particularly the death of his closest friend, Nahem, who died in a similar explosion in Karrada months earlier. Hadi reacts to the destruction he witnesses through acts of reclamation. He collects body parts that remain at various bombing sites all over Baghdad, tearing them from the wreckage, just as he had tried to peel Nahem's flesh from the streets.[39] Hadi is prompted to assemble these parts into a "massive corpse" in hopes that these body parts are not forgotten or "treated as rubbish," and instead, "respected like other dead people and given a proper burial."[40] For Hadi, who sews these remnants together within the ruins of his half-demolished home, these remains are material testimonies of the horrors of unplacement. The corpse he assembles, which he calls the Whatsitsname, is thus born of destruction and division. The Whatsitsname unexpectedly awakens only to continue this cycle of violence, exacting revenge on "all those who did violence to those whose body parts [it is] made of."[41]

It becomes clear to the reader that, although sectarian violence rips through the city, Saadawi's zombie is a figure engendered in the US occupation of Iraq. Early in the novel, the 2003 US invasion of Baghdad is likened to "Death stalk[ing] the city, like a plague,"[42] a description that foreshadows the appearance of the Whatsitsname. The very first time the Whatsitsname is seen, watching the living from the shadows, we hear the "roar of American Apache helicopters flying overhead."[43] Later in the novel we are told that people believe that "it was the Americans who were behind this monster."[44] The insidious violence of the American military is felt throughout the novel. Saadawi reiterates that the citizens of Baghdad are "frightened by the Americans" who "operate[e] with considerable independence" and "no one could hold them to account for what they did."[45] The zombie is therefore historicized within these multiple contexts, ensuring that readers understand dispossession within the larger macrohistorical backdrop, thus making colonial violence visible. Saadawi's zombie is not simply the source of death and horror but rather also an embodiment of colonial repercussions. This interference serves to differentiate the Iraqi zombie from other versions, disrupting the reductive category of the non-Western other and unsettling colonial paradigms. In addition, its difference from the enslaved-style zombies connected to Haiti highlights the historical vacuum surrounding American appropriations of Haitian culture.

Significantly, Saadawi repositions the status of the zombie from radical outsider to being ontologically entangled with others around it. In other words, the meaning of the Whatsitsname is not fixed but continually redefined in its encounters with others. For example, in Sadr City it is "a Wahhabi," in Adamiya a "Shiite extremist," and to the Americans, it is a terrorist.[46] To Elishva, the old Assyrian Christian who is believed to have spiritual powers,[47] the Whatsitsname represents something hopeful. Elishva is the first to see the Whatsitsname hiding in the shadows. Believing that this might be her son, who had disappeared in the Iran-Iraq war, she invites it into her home and "[brings] him out of anonymity, with the name she [gives] him: Daniel."[48] This wretched creature becomes in her eyes an object of love, whom she clothes and feeds. Elishva shares with the monster the story of how her family had all left once the "demons had broken out of their dungeons" after the invasion. She tells the monster how she had "refused to leave her home" insisting that it "wasn't good that everyone should leave the country" and that things had been bad before but they "had stayed… and had survived."⁴⁹ The zombie here, while still a figure of malice, no longer evokes either pity or fear. Instead, its subjective lack allows Elishva to reconstruct the parameters of her experience, opening up a space for an alternative history, centered on resilience in the face of brutality, which problematizes univocal versions of Iraq's past and the victim status of its people, signaling again the insufficiency of colonizing logic. The Whatsitsname also becomes a figure of longing upon which Elishva projects a desire for a place and time that is no longer there. Given the name of Elishva's missing son, the Whatsitsname represents a transhistorical reconstruction of home and a return to the past. This return is also a refusal to submit to the fixed notions of progressive time and passive space that underpin deterministic, modern ideas of history rooted in the Enlightenment. It draws attention to a conception of space and time that is being erased. The zombie's lack is thus resignified as a site of active restoration of identity, a survival strategy in the face of expulsion. However, the fact that Elishva confuses the corpse for Daniel, and her unwillingness to see its face for what it is ("she would see only what she wanted to see"⁵⁰), seems to convey anxiety about the possibility that such acts of restoration and remembrance are mere nostalgia, and that the imagined home longed for was never truly real.

Unlike the enslaved-zombie of Seabrook's accounts, where the horror originates from the absence of subjectivity, here the horror lies in the Whatsitsname's body rotting and leaking. Gruesome descriptions of the corpse's body permeate the text. There are frequent descriptions of putrefaction, of "viscous liquids, light in colour, oozing" from cuts, and "piece[s] of flesh" that "won't stay in place… all runny" and "start[ing] to melt."⁵¹ Unable to look away, our attention is fixed on corporeality, particularly on where things are coming apart, and on the flesh and excretions beneath. These oozing edges are the sites of pain, sites of splitting. Saadawi shifts the source of horror to the abject. As Julia Kristeva (1982) explains, the abject is everything that reminds us of our own corporeal state. The corpse, open wounds, and excrement, for instance, are materials that are neither subject nor object, and that "distur[b] identity, system, order."⁵² The abject other causes disgust and provokes the desire to expel these materials as waste. The abject is linked to violence as the instinct to expel and purge waste is a violent energy the body directs upon itself.⁵³ Diverting from early depictions of the enslaved-style zombie in this way, Saadawi is able to suggest, on one level, how the Iraqi has been constructed as abject, to be kept out of the sphere of moral obligations and human and social rights, which thus maintains the boundary between Western "self" and Iraqi "other." As the zombie body is an alternative mapping of Iraqi space, as I have suggested, the attention to corporeal splitting also emphasizes that placelessness in Iraq is defined by the traumatic and painful tearing apart of the Iraqi people through the wounding of their land. The fact that the monstrous body's traumatic splitting involves the remains of multiple subjects sutured together suggests that Baghdad's wounding moves between bodies, and is both an individual experience and a collective one. As Cathy Caruth reminds us, "history like trauma is never simply one's own" but is "precisely the way we are implicated in each other's traumas."[54] What is significant here is the fact that the Whatsitsname is intent on continually replacing parts that rot and fall off with new parts, stitching them in, until they too fall out, in a continuing cycle of pain. This emphasizes how the experience of placelessness, of being tied to a place while being violently expelled from it, is a *desired* state, a willful returning to the moment of pain, a constant return to the traumatic past.

This willful return to the traumatic past is a kind of paralysis that has dangerous implications. It is not to a past comfort, as Elishva's yearning is. It is a return to a site of catastrophe and disorder, to trauma that is re-enacted through the cycle of killing and replacing parts. These re-enactments represent the continual, compulsive intrusion of the past into the present. Impelled by the grief and prayers of victims, the Whatsitsname enacts a version of justice by taking "revenge on all the criminals" so that the "poor" souls of Baghdad "no longer need to wait in agony for [it] to come."[55] Operating outside of the law, it kills mercenaries, extremists, and even beggars and security guards, as long as they are guilty of some harm.[56] It realizes that the desire to seek revenge through killing will never end: "Nothing in me lasts long, other than the desire to keep going. I kill in order to keep going" and this is its "only justification."[57] The Whatsitsname is therefore both victim and perpetrator, both master and enslaved, and this in-betweenness is something that Saadawi does not resolve. This constitutes an estrangement of the zombie figure, revealing that Iraqi identity cannot be confined within binary structures, and suggests that identities are more fluid than assumed and therefore can be changed.

The Whatsitsname represents the dark side of testifying to trauma, when the preoccupation with the pain of dispossession reifies both injury and injustice. And as we see with Whatsitsname's followers, different groups will use this trauma to advance different agendas. One group sees it as the "first true Iraq citizen" as its body is an "impossible mix" of diverse ethnic, racial, tribal groups "that was never achieved in the past"; the second believes it to be the apocalyptic "instrument of mass destruction" and instrument of divine justice; and the third group believes the Whatsitsname is "the savior" himself, and by following it, they will share in its "immortality."[58] Whatever the justification or cause, the mission for each disparate group is "essentially to kill, to kill new people every day."[59] Saadawi suggests that fixating on past trauma in this way only allows for unity on political grounds predicated on vengeance and killing.

The more the Whatsitsname kills, the less clarity it has about "who should be killed or why,"[60] because, it realizes, there are "no innocents who are completely innocent or criminals who are completely criminal."[61] In the end it recognizes that in killing, it is simply "ensuring his own survival."[62] This is the paradoxical nature of revenge, where the restoration of power comes with the intensification of violence and the diminution of meaning. The impulse to repeat harm can be connected to Sigmund Freud's notion of melancholia, which Freud distinguishes from mourning. According to Freud (1917), mourning is "regularly the reaction to the loss of a loved person, or to the loss of some abstraction which has taken the place of one, such as one's country, liberty, and ideal, and so on," and the mourner is eventually able to relinquish their attachment to the object, becoming free to attach itself to new objects. Mourning risks turning into melancholia, a pathological state where the person is not able to let go of the lost object, integrating the loss into the self, continuously returning to it, stuck in a cycle of self-loathing and unable to resolve their grief.[63] Fixated on pain, the Whatsitsname further fractures a broken city, so that the landscape resembles his patchwork body to an increasing extent. Just as this zombie repeatedly carves up people to replenish its butchered body in order to keep going, it re-creates Baghdad in its image in order to sustain itself. In the end, Baghdad becomes a city its people can "no longer recogniz[e]." It is as if the "city had abandoned [them], becoming a place of murder and gratuitous violence."[64]

Frankenstein in Baghdad is a novel that conveys the complexities of decolonization. Saadawi's zombie embodies both the possibilities of undoing colonial structures and the challenges Iraqis face being bound to the very violence that has destroyed the Iraqi people. The novel conveys how efforts to break free from colonial oppression have often led to the use of the same tools of colonial oppression to serve revolutionary action.[65] In the novel, these structures of mastery are turned inward and reflect how, in Iraq, acts of liberation constitute self-injury where fellow citizens are objectified and seen as parts to be used in a game of domination. The zombie here symbolizes the variety of ways in which the colonial past, in its various political and ideological forms, continues to inhabit the present, resulting in an agonizing self-imposed paralysis. At the end of the novel, a character, being slowly squeezed to death by the Whatsitsname, looks into its "dark face" and is "wholly convinced" now that this "composite face... was the face of his own personal past."[66]

Transcultural Interference: Difference and Diffraction

I have argued that Saadawi's zombie is an act of repossession, a cultural reclamation of a figure that has been used in popular culture to demonize and oppress Haitian/African and Arab "others." This repossession is not achieved through synthesis but through provocation, pushing the zombie figure beyond accepted or existing positions, allowing for the rewriting of a myth. These provocations are diffractive encounters in which Afro-Haitian and Iraqi identities and experiences interfere and overlap with one another, while differences between the cultures are maintained. The idea of diffraction comes initially from the field of physics to describe how phenomena are produced when waves encounter obstacles on their path. Put simply, waves curve and bend around obstacles, and overlap with other waves. New Materialist thinkers such as Donna Haraway (1992) and Karan Barad (2007) have adopted this idea to explore how entrenched dualisms inherited from the Enlightenment might be overcome. In the Western philosophical tradition, differences are defined and contained, in order to be assimilated and erased. Reading diffractively allows us to go beyond binary understandings of sameness and difference, to see how transcultural expressions interfere with one another, and co-establish each other's identities, while allowing for and encouraging the expression of cultural differences.

This idea of diffractive interference is clear when we consider how the title of the novel forces readers to pay attention to difference and offers the impulse to assimilate difference. From the beginning, readers are led to expect connections to Mary Shelley's Gothic novel. However, as critics have pointed out, the Whatsitsname bears little resemblance to the monster in *Frankenstein*.[67] The gothic predecessor, assembled from dead cadavers and brought to life by the scientist, is an abject figure that transgresses the boundaries between life and death, highlighting nineteenth-century anxieties about man's mastery of nature. Unlike Shelley's monster, however, the Whatsitsname comes into the world with language and purpose, and is never in awe of its creator. Importantly, it does not have a soul in the humanist sense, although it acknowledges that souls inhabit it and speak to it, without possessing it.[68] In fact, Saadawi's monster is never referred to as "Frankenstein's monster" and is instead given a number of other names: the

Criminal, Criminal X, the One Who Has No Name, the Savior, among others. The only time "Frankenstein" is mentioned in the text is in reference to how a magazine article about the Whatsitsname is retitled "Frankenstein in Baghdad," complete with a photo of Robert De Niro as the monster from the film *Mary Shelley's Frankenstein*.[69] This act of assimilation represents the appropriation of local mythologies by the global media; it disappoints the author of the article and Saadawi does not endorse this view in the rest of the novel. The title therefore raises expectations that are thwarted. We are instead given a monster that speaks to lost souls, and that consults with magicians who speak to the jinns, spirits that exist in Arab culture and Islamic belief. These elements suggest that the sources the Whatsitsname is based on are of non-European heritage and that the world it exists in is not the rational, enlightened world of Frankenstein's monster, which constitutes a shift in ideological valences.

In referencing *Frankenstein*, Saadawi forces us to see how our understanding of the Whatsitsname depends on its difference from Shelley's monster. We are confronted with the insufficiency of Shelley's monster as a symbol of otherness. Frankenstein's monster and the Whatsitsname are brought together in uneasy tension, and we are left with an ideological clash that is not the undoing of either monster, but rather a refusal to submit to a one-dimensional understanding of otherness, and a resistance to homogenizing forces of globalization. In relation to the Haitian zombie, however, as I have suggested, we become aware of how the interaction of differences can sometimes lead to spaces of entanglement where localized experiences overlap. The result of this entanglement, however, is a not a hybrid identity but rather an uncanny unfamiliarity that hinges on the fact that the zombie figure has been unsettled. Saadawi's zombie, in its placelessness, its lack of subjectivity, and its undead status, is recognizable. And yet the Whatsitsname is a strange kind of zombie at the same time. It is inhabited by different spirits without identifying with or being controlled by any of them. It has no soul and yet it is not mindless, nor without agency, suggesting a radically unfamiliar subjective state. It wanders the lands it is excluded from but its wandering is purposeful. We understand that Saadawi borrows the trope of another oppressed culture in order to express solidarity with it, but the estrangement of the figure emphasizes that there is diversity and difference within the experience of colonialism. Being attentive to such entanglements allows us to see how transcultural interference works at the edges of cultural boundaries, invalidating unitary understandings of culture. The new meanings that emerge from diffractive interactions emphasize the fundamental incompleteness of any one culture, and the need therefore for openness and exchange between cultures. Seeing cultures in this way offers possibilities for finding alternative spaces of meaning that dismantle Western colonial structures of antagonism and exclusion.

Notes

1. Kee, *Not Your Average Zombie*, 7–8, 13.
2. Yi-Fu, *Space and Place*, 6. Following Yi-Fu, "place" here refers to more than simply a location but rather one imbued with the meaning that people give to it. Place indicates security. This is different from "space," which is an abstract concept that indicates freedom.
3. Bishop, *American Zombie Gothic*, 12.
4. Ackermann and Gauthier, "The Ways and Nature of the Zombi," 473. According to Ackermann and Gauthier, there can be zombies of the body and zombies of the soul in vodou belief. Within this distinction, there are "many sub-types classified either according to their origin or to the mode of zombification."
5. McAlister, *Rara!*, 105. In Haitian accounts, it is not clear whether zombies are inherently malevolent.
6. Lauro and Embry, "A Zombie Manifesto," 87.
7. Seabrook, *The Magic Island*, 93.
8. Seabrook, *Voodoo Island*, 100–1.
9. Lauro, *The Transatlantic Zombie*, 8, 16.
10. Dayan, *Haiti, History, and the Gods*, 37. Dayan connects the zombie to Haitian revolutionary Jean Zombi, commenting that this gives those formerly enslaved power over the oppressors. This imbues the zombie figure with a revolutionary energy.
11. Dendle, *The Zombie Movie Encyclopedia*, 3.
12. Kee, *Not Your Average Zombie*, 8.
13. Dendle, "The Zombie as Barometer of Cultural Anxiety," 46.
14. Bellegarde-Smith et al., "Haiti and Its Occupation by the United States in 1915," 15.
15. Immerwahr, *How to Hide an Empire*, 35–6.
16. Laguerre, *The Military and Society in Haiti*, 65–6.
17. Fay, "Dead Subjectivity," 89, 93.
18. See Klare, "The New Geopolitics"; Chomsky, "It's Imperialism, Stupid," for example.
19. Brown and Burrel, "Iraqi 'zombie gas' Arsenal Revealed."
20. Craige, *Black Bagdad*, 1–2.
21. Berry and Epstein, *Transcultural Experiments*, 11.
22. Epstein, "Transculture," 333.

23 Berry and Epstein, *Transcultural Experiments*, 160–1.
24 Saadawi, *Frankenstein in Baghdad*, 51.
25 Saadawi, *Frankenstein in Baghdad*, 143.
26 Saadawi, *Frankenstein in Baghdad*, 136.
27 Saadawi, *Frankenstein in Baghdad*, 143–4.
28 Saadawi, *Frankenstein in Baghdad*, 1–2.
29 Simon and Tejirian, "Introduction: The Creation of Iraq."
30 Fletcher, "Running the Corridor," 187–8.
31 Simon and Tejirian, "Introduction: The Creation of Iraq."
32 Damaluji, "Securing Democracy in Iraq," xx.
33 Rubaii, "Tripartheid," 126.
34 Saadawi, *Frankenstein in Baghdad*, 118.
35 Saadawi, *Frankenstein in Baghdad*, 156.
36 Graham, "Cities as Strategic Sites," 32.
37 Saadawi, *Frankenstein in Baghdad*, 6–8.
38 Saadawi, *Frankenstein in Baghdad*, 19.
39 Saadawi, *Frankenstein in Baghdad*, 23.
40 Saadawi, *Frankenstein in Baghdad*, 25.
41 Saadawi, *Frankenstein in Baghdad*, 178.
42 Saadawi, *Frankenstein in Baghdad*, 6.
43 Saadawi, *Frankenstein in Baghdad*, 16.
44 Saadawi, *Frankenstein in Baghdad*, 259.
45 Saadawi, *Frankenstein in Baghdad*, 66, 68.
46 Saadawi, *Frankenstein in Baghdad*, 259.
47 Saadawi, *Frankenstein in Baghdad*, 5.
48 Saadawi, *Frankenstein in Baghdad*, 51.
49 Saadawi, *Frankenstein in Baghdad*, 62.
50 Saadawi, *Frankenstein in Baghdad*, 53.
51 Saadawi, *Frankenstein in Baghdad*, 24, 142.
52 Kristeva, *Powers of Horror*, 4.
53 Kristeva, *Powers of Horror*, 10.
54 Caruth, *Unclaimed Experience*, 24.
55 Saadawi, *Frankenstein in Baghdad*, 136–7.
56 Saadawi, *Frankenstein in Baghdad*, 146.
57 Saadawi, *Frankenstein in Baghdad*, 259.
58 Saadawi, *Frankenstein in Baghdad*, 140–1.
59 Saadawi, *Frankenstein in Baghdad*, 193.
60 Saadawi, *Frankenstein in Baghdad*, 193.
61 Saadawi, *Frankenstein in Baghdad*, 207.
62 Saadawi, *Frankenstein in Baghdad*, 194.

63 Freud, "Mourning and Melancholia," 243–4.
64 Saadawi, *Frankenstein in Baghdad*, 224.
65 Singh, *Unthinking Mastery*, Chap. 1.
66 Saadawi, *Frankenstein in Baghdad*, 250.
67 See Campbell, "Double Estrangement and Developments in Arabic Science Fiction," for example.
68 Saadawi, *Frankenstein in Baghdad*, 124.
69 Saadawi, *Frankenstein in Baghdad*, 133.

Works Cited

28 Days Later [Film] Dir. Danny Boyle, USA: 20th Century Fox Home Entertainment, 2003.

28 Weeks Later [Film] Dir. Juan Carlos Fresnadillo, USA: 20th Century Fox, 2007.

Ackermann, Hans-W. and Jeanine Gauthier. "The Ways and Nature of the Zombi." *Journal of American Folklore* 104, no. 414 (1991): 466–94.

Barad, Karen Michelle. *Meeting the Universe Halfway: Quantum Physics and the Entanglement of Matter and Meaning*. London: Duke University Press, 2007.

Bellegarde-Smith, Patrick, Alex Dupuy, Robert Fatton Jr., Mary Renda, Ermitte St. Jacques and Jeffrey Sommers. "Haiti and Its Occupation by the United States in 1915: Antecedents and Outcomes." *Journal of Haitian Studies* 21, no. 2 (2015): 10–43.

Bishop, Kyle. *American Zombie Gothic: The Rise and Fall (and Rise) of the Walking Dead in Popular Culture*. London: McFarland & Company, Inc., Publishers, 2010.

Brown, Colin and Ian Burrel. "Iraqi 'zombie gas' Arsenal Revealed," *Independent*, February 10, 1998. https://www.independent.co.uk/news/iraqi-zombie-gas-arsenal-revealed-1143947.html. Accessed July 30, 2021.

Burbank, Jane and Frederick Cooper. *Empires in World History: Power and the Politics of Difference*. New Jersey: Princeton University Press, 2010.

Campbell, Ian. "Double Estrangement and Developments in Arabic Science Fiction: Ahmed Sa'dāwi's *Frankenstein in Baghdad*." *Mashriq & Mahjar* 7, no. 2 (2020). https://lebanesestudies.ojs.chass.ncsu.edu/index.php/mashriq/article/view/255

Caruth, Cathy, ed. *Trauma: Explorations in Memory*. London: Johns Hopkins University, 1995.

Caruth, Cathy. *Unclaimed Experience: Trauma, Narrative, and History*. London: Johns Hopkins University Press, 1996.

Chomsky, Noam. "It's Imperialism, Stupid." *Khaleej Times*, July 10, 2005. www.khaleejtimes.com/DisplayArticle.asp?xfile=data/opinion/2005/July/opinion_july10.xml$ion=opinion&col=. Accessed February 2, 2021.

Craige, John. *Black Bagdad: The Arabian Nights Adventures of a Marine Captain in Haiti*. London: Stanley Paul & Co. Ltd., 1933.

Damaluji, Mona. "Securing Democracy in Iraq: Sectarian Politics and Segregation in Baghdad, 2003–2007." *Traditional Dwellings and Settlements Review* 21, no. 2 (2010): 71–87.

Dayan, Joan. *Haiti, History, and the Gods*. Berkeley: University of California Press, 1998.

Dendle, Peter. *The Zombie Movie Encyclopedia*. Jefferson: McFarland & Company, Inc. Publishers, 2001.

Dendle, Peter. "The Zombie as Barometer of Cultural Anxiety." In *Monsters and the Monstrous: Myths and Metaphors of Enduring Evil*, edited by Niall Scott, 45–60. New York: Rodopi, 2007.

Ellen E. Berry and Mikhail N. Epstein. *Transcultural Experiments: Russian and American Models of Creative Communication*. New York: St. Martin's Press, 1999.

Epstein, Mikhail. "Transculture: A Broad Way between Globalism and Multiculturalism." *American Journal of Economics and Sociology* 68, no. 1 (2009): 327–51.

Fay, Jennifer. "Dead Subjectivity: 'White Zombie,' Black Baghdad." *The New Centennial Review* 8, no. 1 (2008): 81–101.

Fletcher, Robert S. G. "Running the Corridor: Nomadic Societies and Imperial Rule in the Inter-War Syrian Desert." *Past & Present* 220, no. 1 (2013): 185–215.

Freud, Sigmund. "Mourning and Melancholia." In *The Stanford Edition of the Complete Psychological Works of Sigmund Freud*, vol. 14, edited by James Strachey, translated by James Strachey, 243–58. London: Hogarth Press, 1953.

Graham, Stephen. "Cities as Strategic Sites: Place Annihilation and Urban Geopolitics." In *Cities, War, and Terrorism: Towards an Urban Geopolitics*, edited by Stephen Graham, 31–53. New Jersey: Blackwell Publishing, 2004.

Haraway, Donna. *The Haraway Reader*, London: Routledge, 1992.

Immerwahr, Daniel. *How to Hide an Empire: A History of the Greater United States*. New York: Farrar, Straus and Giroux, 2019. EPUB e-book.

Kee, Chera. *Not Your Average Zombie: Rehumanizing the Undead from Voodoo to Zombie Walks*. Austin: University of Texas Press, 2017. Kindle edition.

Klare, Michael. "The New Geopolitics." *Monthly Review* 55, no. 3 (2003): 51–6.

Kristeva, Julia. *Powers of Horror: An Essay on Abjection*. Translated by Leon S. Roudiez. New York: Columbia University Press, 1982.

Laguerre, Michel S. *The Military and Society in Haiti*. Knoxville: University of Tennessee Press, 1993.

Lauro, Sarah Juliet. *The Transatlantic Zombie: Slavery, Rebellion, and Living Dead*. New Jersey: Rutgers University Press, 2015.

Lauro, Sarah Juliet and Karen Embry. "A Zombie Manifesto: The Nonhuman Condition in the Era of Advanced Capitalism." *Boundary 2* 35, no. 1 (2008): 85–108.

Luckhurst, Roger. *Zombies: A Cultural History*. London: Reaktion Books, 2015. Kindle edition.

Mary Shelley's Frankenstein [Film] Dir. Kenneth Branagh, USA: TriStar Pictures, 1994.

McAlister, Elizabeth. *Rara! Vodou, Power, and Performance in Haiti and Its Diaspora*. Berkeley: University of California Press, 2002.

Night of the Living Dead [Film] Dir. George A. Romero, USA: Continental Distributing, Inc., 1968.

Reeve Specter, Simon and Eleanor H. Tejirian. "Introduction: The Creation of Iraq: The Frontier as State." In *The Creation of Iraq, 1914–1921*, edited by Reeve Specter Simon and Eleanor H. Tejirian, chapter 1. New York: Columbia University Press, 2004. Kindle edition.

Rubaii, Kali J. "Tripartheid: How Sectarianism Became Internal to Being in Anbar, Iraq." *PoLAR: Political and Legal Anthropology Review* 42, no. 1 (2019): 125–41.

Saadawi, Ahmed. *Frankenstein in Baghdad*. New York: Simon and Schuster, 2018.

Seabrook, William. *The Magic Island*. New York: Harcourt Brace, 1929.

Seabrook, William. *Voodoo Island*. London: Four Square Books Ltd., 1966.

Shelley, Mary. *Frankenstein, or, the Modern Prometheus*. 1817. Reprinted with Notes and Introduction. London: Oxford University Press, 1998.

Singh, Julietta. *Unthinking Mastery: Dehumanism and Decolonial Entanglements*. London: Duke University Press, 2018.

Tuan Yi-Fu. *Space and Place: The Perspective of Experience*. London: University of Minnesota Press, 2001.

White Zombie. [Film] Dir. Victor Halperin, USA: United Artists, 1932.

World War Z. [Film] Dir. Marc Forster, USA: Plan B Entertainment, Apparatus Productions, 2013.

"Zombie". [Stage play] Dir. George Sherwood. Biltmore Theater, New York City, 1932.

11

"First They Bring the HIV, then the Zombie": Portrayal of the West in Contemporary Indian Zombie Literature and Cinema

Abhirup Mascharak

Nearly thirty minutes into Raj Nidimoru and Krishna D. K.'s *Go Goa Gone* (2013), billed as India's first zombie comedy, we see the protagonists—a trio of young men called Bunny, Hardik, and Luv—having a conversation. They had come the previous night to an island near the Indian state of Goa to attend a rave. The next day, they find that most of the other attendees have turned into lumbering, cannibalistic beings. Having run into the wilds to escape these creatures, the trio pause to catch their breaths and try to determine what, exactly, the attendees have morphed into. Hardik is the one who finally gets it: "They are zombies," he exclaims. "We have heard of ghosts in India," remark his friends, "but where did these zombies come from?" "Globalization," Hardik says. "These *firangis* [white foreigners] are a nuisance. First they brought the HIV, now the zombie."

It is easy to treat this remark as just a joke; the film is, after all, a zombie comedy. But this is not the only instance in *Go Goa Gone* where acrimonious thoughts on Westerners find expression, and given how the film, as a whole, portrays the West and Westernized Indians, it would be fair to say that there is more to this line than mere flippancy. But before we undertake an analysis of the film's stance on Westernization, it is essential to look at the earlier Indian narratives featuring zombies, since a contrast with those older tales alone can let us understand how *Go Goa Gone* marks a new phase in the portrayal of zombies in Indian popular culture, and study the factors which ushered in this phase.

Zombie films as we know them did not exist in Indian cinema before 2013, when, alongside *Go Goa Gone*, Luke Kenny and Devaki Singh's *Rise of the Zombie* had also released. The closest thing to a zombie film that Indian cinema had before 2013 is Shyam and Tulsi Ramsay's *Do Gaz Zameen Ke Neeche* (Two

Yards Below the Ground, 1972), which tells the story of Rajvansh, an aristocrat, who is seemingly murdered by his adulterous wife and her associates. Not long afterward, the killers find themselves pursued by what seems to be the reanimated corpse of Rajvansh. In the end, though, we learn that it was all an elaborate charade: Rajvansh is alive, and has been tormenting his enemies by masquerading as a zombie with the aid of his loyal servants. As per Kevin Boon's taxonomy of zombies, Rajvansh is a "zombie ruse,"[1] a phrase used to describe tales which seem to be about zombies but actually have little to do with them.

Indian literature, on the other hand, does have texts where actual zombies appear, such as the works of Hemendra Kumar Roy,[2] a pioneering figure in Bengali popular fiction. In *Manush-Pisach* (The Human Demon), for instance, Roy's detective heroes, Jayanta and Manik, battle a sorcerer who can infuse life into corpses, which are then sent to do his bidding. The murderer in *Maran Khelar Khelowar* (The Game of Death) likewise uses his sorcerous powers to revive corpses and sends them to murder his enemies. A zombie also appears in *Oloukik* (Paranormal), a short play by Roy, though it has no major role in the story. The antagonists in each of these stories—the Muslim cleric in *Manush-Pisach*, and the Hindu *tantriks* (the members of certain sects within Hinduism who, according to the lore that has developed around them, have mastered black magic) in *Manush-Pisach* and *Oloukik*—bring corpses to life by performing certain rituals and uttering incantations. Their zombies are what one may call the "zombie drone," which William Seabrook defines as a "soulless human corpse" that has been exhumed from the grave and "endowed by sorcery with a mechanical semblance of life"; this is done "occasionally for the commission of some crime, more often simply as the drudge around the habitation."[3] Roy writes exclusively of zombies belonging to this category, never envisioning any nonmagical means for creating zombies.

He also situates his zombies in a discernibly Indian milieu which betrays no influence of the Western books and films on zombies which were published or released during his lifetime. Shankar, the villain in *Oloukik*, worships a deity of the Santhals, a tribe that lives in eastern India. Shashanka, the villain in *Maran Khelar Khelowar*, creates his zombie killers by subjecting the corpses to rituals that involve worshipping them with flowers and sandalwood paste at the *shamshan* (Hindu cremation ground) on new moon nights—a process that is strikingly similar to *shava sadhana*, the *tantrik* ceremony which is believed to bring unspoiled corpses back to life. These details show that Roy, even within the handful of works of his that deal with zombies, was trying to create a zombie lore that is decidedly Indian and does not mimic the Western zombie stories.

One assumes this was part of Roy's agenda, expressed in the foreword of his novel *Abar Jaker Dhan* (Again a Treasure of the Yaksha), of leaving behind a literary oeuvre which will teach his young, Bengali readers to be themselves instead of succumbing to the myth of the superiority of the West. Till the onset of the new millennium, the zombie stories in Bengali popular literature, such as Manabendra Pal's *Oloukik Jallad* (The Paranormal Executioner, 1990), stuck to the traditions established by Roy: they feature the zombies of "zombie drone" variety (which have been created through sorcery) and employ an ethos that is dominantly Indian.

In contrast, contemporary Indian zombie novels, pertinent examples of which are Mainak Dhar's *Zombiestan* (2012) and *Chronicler of the Undead* (2015), are markedly influenced by Hollywood. They portray worlds beset with a zombie apocalypse, and the central characters are a ragtag group who must devise a way to end the apocalypse or rebuild their lives in a world that has changed beyond recognition. George Romero's *Night of the Living Dead* (1968), which has spawned many sequels, remakes, and imitations, and more recently Paul Anderson's *Resident Evil* (2001), which has also had multiple sequels, have popularized this particular zombie-story template, and Dhar's novels are evidence of that popularity. While the plots in these novels are not exact replicas of the storylines in the said films, reading them alongside Roy's zombie tales makes clear the comparatively Westernized nature of Dhar's works. Indian films have likewise chosen Hollywood as the model when it comes to producing zombie yarns. *Go Goa Gone* is evidently inspired by zombie comedies like Edgar Wright's *Shaun of the Dead* (2004) and Ruben Fleischer's *Zombieland* (2009), while the plot of *Rise of the Zombie*, which chronicles a man's gradual zombification, has similarities with Andrew Parkinson's *I, Zombie* (1998).

This emulation of Western zombie texts indicates that the target audience for such films is the young, urban, educated segment of the Indian population, who have seen the Hollywood films that Dhar's novels and the 2013 Hindi zombie films have emulated, and hence, are more likely to appreciate the tropes, conventions, and tenor employed in these new age Indian zombie stories. Liberalization of the Indian economy in 1991 and the subsequent globalization experienced by the country made it easier to access Hollywood cinema, whether in the multiplexes that began to spring up in the cities or via the DVDs which could be purchased or rented, or through the internet, from which films can be downloaded. The recent Indian zombie texts cater mainly to this generation that has grown up during the post-liberalization era, on a steady diet of Hollywood cinema. This is evident, also, in their choice of language—Dhar writes in English (unlike Roy, who wrote in Bengali), and the characters in *Rise of the Zombie* and *Go Goa Gone* mix a good deal of English into their conversations, which imparts to the films a "Western" veneer. Moreover, like the undead in most Hollywood zombie films, the zombies in these recent Indian novels and films combine in them the characteristics of the "bio zombie" (zombies which are created by chemical or biological agents) and the "zombie ghoul" (which eats humans).

The emulation of Western zombie cinema in these works exists, however, alongside a peculiar antipathy toward the West as a sociopolitical entity, a consistent "Other"-ing of the Westerners and the Westernized Indians. Each of them describes the zombie epidemic as having started in the West, and then engulfing the rest of the world. *Zombiestan* posits that a drone strike by the Americans on a cache of weapons belonging to terrorists in Afghanistan causes a chemical emission which converts the terrorists into zombies, who then bite others and turn them into the undead. The epidemic rapidly makes its way into India, and the novel shows the Indian characters not only battling zombies but also possessing the cure to the malaise. *Chronicler of the Undead* similarly mentions that the zombie epidemic which has ended the human civilization, as we know it, originated in the United States and shows Indians as heroically striving to sustain themselves amid the apocalypse. The impression conveyed in these novels, however subtly, is that the West creates troubles and leaves the rest of the world to clean up after it.

This idea is expressed more unambiguously, and with a more pronouncedly conservative bent, in the Hindi zombie films. The opening sequence of *Go Goa Gone* shows its main characters living a life which many Indians would deem antithetical to Indian values. They do not live, unlike "good" Indians, with their families, but by themselves in a rented apartment. With no adults supervising them, it is implied, their lives have degenerated into wanton excesses. Hardik and Luv's introductory scene shows them as so intoxicated with the marijuana that they have smoked that they cannot even pick up a remote and change the channel on the television. The developments in this scene, such as Hardik stating that the liquor and the pizza he has purchased were bought with the money he was supposed to have paid that month's electricity bills with, are obviously humorous, but the spectators are meant to laugh *at* the characters, not *with* them. They are portrayed as pathetic and ridiculous in their hedonistic way of life. What is more, the pot-induced glazed look in their eyes, their halting speech, and their inability to move their limbs indicate that the decadent life they lead has already zombified them metaphorically; what happens later, with actual zombies threatening to turn them into the undead, is but the outcome of the lifestyle they have chosen. This lifestyle is a decidedly Western one, its foreignness manifested not just in the characters' consumption of Western food items like pizza or their doping and drinking (which, in the popular Indian consciousness, are vices learned from the West) but also in their speech (which is replete with expressions like "STFU" and "WTF"), their clothes (which consist of shirts, trousers, and T-shirts), and their candid discussions on sex (which, as per the brand of conservatism endorsed by *Go Goa Gone*, is the worst of the vices Indians have imbibed from the West).

Indeed, it is with regard to sex that *Go Goa Gone*'s repudiation of the West is most visibly manifested. In this, it harks back to the slasher films of yore, like Sean Cunningham's *Friday the 13th* (1980) and John Carpenter's *Halloween* (1978), where having sex meant death. Since *Go Goa Gone* is a more lighthearted work, it avoids the ultra-violent death scenes which characterizes those films, but retains the sexphobia inherent in them, because this particular aspect of yesteryear slasher cinema is in tune with the unease over sex that is typical of the Indian mind-set. It is not an accident that Goa serves as the backdrop of the better part of the film. This Indian state's long stay under Portuguese colonial rule—while the rest of India was liberated from the British in 1947, Goa remained under Portugal's control till 1961—its large Christian population, the development of hippie settlements there during the 1960s, and its popularity as a tourist destination for Westerners have led the rest of the country to perceive it as a place more Western than Indian, a place where one can drink, dope, and have sex with a wantonness that the rest of India would not permit. That is the reason Hardik and Luv decide to go on a trip to Goa. Hardik's tryst with a female colleague has ended disastrously, while Luv discovers that his girlfriend has been cheating on him. Dejected, they decide that they need a headlong plunge into hedonism to recuperate, and the best place to indulge in such hedonism in India is, of course, Goa. The more straitlaced Bunny, who is set to attend a conference in Goa, does not want Hardik and Luv to accompany him. However, they insist on traveling with Bunny, and, upon reaching Goa, they even persuade him to come to the aforementioned rave, which is organized by the Russian mafia that, according to news reports in India, run a thriving drug business in Goa. It is during this rave that a new drug is served to the attendees, the consumption of which turns them into zombies. Bunny, Hardik, and Luv escape this zombification because they do not have the money to purchase drugs. However, they are still in mortal peril, because whomever these zombies bite also turn into zombies. Like Dhar's novels, then, *Go Goa Gone* portrays the zombie epidemic as having been started by Western/Westernized entities: the Russian mob, and their Indian agents. Consequently, every Westerner who had organized and attended this party is penalized with zombification, either through the drug or by the bites of those zombified by the drug. Not a single Westerner is allowed to escape the island.

Being Indian is not, however, a safeguard against zombification either; one must be the *right* sort of Indian. This is where the film's sexphobia comes in. The main characters—Bunny, Hardik, Luv, a drug-mafia leader who calls himself Boris, and a young woman, Luna, who had come to the party—manage to make it out of the island mainly because of their essential "goodness," the yardstick to measure which in *Go Goa Gone* is abstinence (whether voluntary or not) from sex. This subtext of sexphobia in the film, though well-concealed under a chic surface which references Hollywood zombie films and portrays sybaritic pleasures openly, does become evident once we look closely enough. Bunny, who is not uninterested in sex, yet lacks the confidence to approach women, is spared the zombification, despite some close shaves. Luv, who swears in an early scene to opt out of the hedonist life he has been living, is sucked back into it only because of his girlfriend's infidelity, and even then, he does not actually get to have sex, because Luna, who he pursues, turns him down. He had never slept with his girlfriend either, since he believed in "doing it" only after marriage. Hence, he escapes zombification, while his adulterous girlfriend, who, coincidentally, had also come to the rave, does not, and nor does her lover. Her consistent spurning of Hardik and Luv puts Luna in the "good" Indian category. Hardik constantly touts his "success" with the opposite sex, but since most women whom we see him flirt with ultimately spurn him, his claims of sleeping with a plethora of women are likely just tall tales. Indeed, he more or less acknowledges as much in the scene where he tearfully says that a woman he loved had jilted him, and that the louche persona he has subsequently adopted is just a shield for his broken heart. This means that Hardik, like his friends, is also, ultimately, a "good boy," and this is what spares him the zombification, despite his tryst with Ariana, a Russian woman he meets at the party.

As per the sexphobic paradigm of the film, this should have condemned him to zombiehood. Yet, since his rakishness is not innate, since he is not really a Casanova, he is spared that fate. Which is not to say that his liaison with Ariana goes completely unpunished: Boris, upon learning that Ariana had consumed the zombifying drug before sleeping with Hardik, almost kills the latter, since he thinks having sex with her will turn Hardik into a zombie. Hardik experiences that panic as well, even checking his genitals to see if they have been infected by the intercourse he had with Ariana. An earlier scene had informed the viewers that once zombified, a person loses all desires which sentient beings have, except that of hunger. In other words, *Go Goa Gone*, despite its comparative generosity toward Hardik, nonetheless threatens him, over his tryst with Ariana, with the loss of his capacity to have sex, not to mention the threat of losing his life to Boris and his aide, Nikolai. He is spared only because his Westernized exterior hides an inner "Indianness."

Such is also the case with Boris, an Indian masquerading as a Russian; the crisis of the zombie epidemic serves to bring out the Indian within him, which he has been trying, unsuccessfully, to conceal under his dyed hair and his ability to speak Russian fluently. This is symbolically portrayed in the scene where Bunny sees through Boris' "Russianness," and says that the latter looks "*desi*." With his masquerade thus punctured, Boris ceases to speak in Russian and the heavily accented English which he was conversing in till this point, and starts talking in Hindi, which marks the beginning of the recovery of his Indianhood. Though he is part of the mafia that had manufactured and sold the zombifying drug, his shepherding of Bunny, Hardik, Luv, and Luna to safety means that he has done his duty toward fellow Indians; his giving up of the large stash of cocaine in his possession to stop the zombies (who are stupefied when cocaine is sprinkled on them) signifies the severing of his ties with the drug trade run by Westerners; and he shows little interest in sex, which means his association with the Russians has not erased his Indian sense of "decency." That is why he can board the boat which takes the others out of the island, while Nikolai, who is truly Russian, cannot; like every other Westerner in the film, he turns into a zombie.

To sum up, living to tell the tale in *Go Goa Gone* is conditional on being ethnically Indian and repudiating Westernization, especially through the adoption of a puritanical view of sex. This puritanism, unsurprisingly, covers homosexuality, which is treated as a joke and associated with degeneration. Bunny, when he sees Hardik and Luv hugging, quips that he knew all along that they are gay, to which Hardik responds with an indignant "Fuck you"—a classic instance of gay panic "humor." Later, during the rave that leads to the zombie epidemic, two women are seen kissing. Placing a moment of lesbianism against a scenario of drug-induced revelry which culminates in something dreadful connects homosexuality to the Western decadence which the film deplores, and sex, of any and every sort (except maybe that which takes place within a monogamous heterosexual marriage), is, according to *Go Goa Gone*, the main characteristic of that decadence. The association it had drawn between zombiehood and HIV is thus part of this worldview. HIV is transmitted through sex, and in the diegetic universe of *Go Goa Gone*, the nontraditional, Westernized lifestyle where one can indulge in sex at will (as Luv's girlfriend and her lover did, and as, one can assume, the Westerners like Ariana, who have come to the rave, do) makes one a zombie.

Rise of the Zombie enunciates its stance against Westernization mainly through its casting. The central character, Neil Parker, is played by Luke Kenny, an actor of British and Italian descent. The part he plays—that of a man whom an insect bite turns into a zombie—does not require an actor of Kenny's ethnicity. Yet, not only does a white actor play Neil but his whiteness is underscored. As Neil slowly becomes a zombie, he ceases to maintain contact with humans, staying in the jungle where he had been camping. Vini, Neil's girlfriend, grows tense over his disappearance, and puts up missing persons' posters, where Neil is described as having "fair" skin, "hazel" eyes, and "light brown hair." Thus, despite having an Indian father (Neil's whiteness, one assumes, is something he has inherited from his deceased mother, though the film does not clarify this), an Indian best friend (called Aneesh), and an Indian girlfriend, not to mention a fluency in Hindi, Neil's white, Western identity is never in doubt, courtesy the casting of Kenny and the lifestyle Neil leads in the film. He attends bachelor parties, and travels with backpacks and his camera, his get-up resembling that of white tourists in India. As a wildlife photographer, he leads a bohemian life, spending months in the wilderness. Like the young men in *Go Goa Gone*, Neil does not have familial ties. He is estranged from his father, whose lament that he should have cared more for Neil after the death of the latter's mother indicates the film's ideological stance on what constitutes the "right" way of living: a single-parent household, it implies, is a deficient household, which can never teach a child to value relationships, and instead pushes him into a rudderless, wandering way of life. Neil does not spend much time with Vini either, which means that the possibility of him ever marrying and having children is slim. This shunning of a "normal" life to instead live an adventurous traveler's life which is glorified in Western literature and culture is what, the film suggests, imperils Neil, making him venture recklessly into jungles with deadly creatures, like the insect which bites him.

The sexphobia of *Go Goa Gone* is repeated here, in the scene where Neil, shortly after being bitten, meets a local girl and takes her to his tent. When he wakes up the next morning, she is nowhere to be seen, until Neil lifts his rug and discovers a severed human hand; his zombie tendencies have already started showing, causing Neil to devour the woman. The sort of no-strings-attached sex which Indians associate with Western lifestyles is shown here as something that is outright monstrous. The desire to not only link but underscore this monstrousness with the West is the reason, it can be plausibly assumed, that a white man like Kenny has been cast as Neil. That monstrousness leads to an epidemic when Neil starts biting the Indians living in the region, turning them into zombies. Much as the Russians start the zombie epidemic in *Go Goa Gone*, the white, Westernized Neil starts it in *Rise of the Zombie*, and as much as the Indian characters in Dhar's novels and *Go Goa Gone* must, to save their country, deal with the scourge unleashed by the West, so must Aneesh and Neil's father take up the task of killing the zombies Neil has created. The sudden, ambiguous ending of the film leaves it unclear whether they find Neil or what they will do if they locate him. What is clear, though, is the conservative repudiation of the West and all things Westernized as unhealthy and monstrous.

The roots of this mind-set which regards Indianness as incompatible with anything Western can be traced back to the days of British rule in India. The colonial enterprise of "civilizing" the denizens of the conquered lands involved not only indoctrinating them in the superiority of the West but also deploring indigenous cultures as outdated, superstitious, and lacking in philosophical, moral, and aesthetic value. Before long, Indians began retaliating against this blanket condemnation of their culture. An example of this can be seen in Bhubanchandra Mukhopadhyay's translation of G. W. M. Reynolds' *Joseph Wilmot* (1854), published under the title *Bilater Guptokotha* (The Secrets of England, 1889). Mukhopadhyay states that his purpose behind this translation is to undertake a comparative study of "civilization as it is manifested in the east and the west,"[4] and goes on to opine:

> Seeing that the English take a lot of interest in civilizing us and say that our culture must be cleansed with the touch of civilization as they define it, surely it is not wrong to inspect them in return and undertake an impartial observation of the decadence which characterizes the lives of the high and the mighty individuals among them... Those Indians that consider the Englishmen to be gods would certainly find in this story some English characters noble enough to merit the descriptor "godlike." However, they would see many others who are more akin to the devil.[5]

This is essentially Mukhopadhyay using the British's own work against them, using Reynolds' portrayal of the seamy underbelly of England's society and the debauchery of its aristocrats to demonstrate that the colonial rhetoric of a civilized West and a savage East is an untruthful one. The tendency among certain Indians, especially the upper classes, to ape British customs had also attracted the satirical opprobrium of Indian artists, as can be seen in Rabindranath Tagore's short story "Rajtika" (The Mark of a King, 1898) and the Bengali film *Bilat Pherot* (England-returned, 1921), directed by Dhiren Ganguly and N. C. Lahiri.

But while the crimes of the British in India were many, and the need to oppose their indoctrination program was genuine, it has had the unfortunate outcome of inculcating among a large segment of Indians a misguided belief that a truly Indian identity can only be forged through a *complete* repudiation of the West—especially its greater tolerance in the matters of love and marriage, and its general endorsement of individualism—and embracing, unquestioningly, traditional Indian values. Tagore's novel *Ghare-Baire* (The Home and the World, 1916), which unfolds against the anti-colonial Swadeshi movement in Bengal, portrays, critically, how jingoism and sociocultural orthodoxy can be legitimized under the guise of fighting colonialism. Postindependence Indian society, however, has largely ignored Tagore's warnings, instead valorizing "virtues" like obeying elders, not indulging in romantic and sexual relationships before marriage, marrying within one's own community, observing the social and religious customs of the milieu one is born into, living with and as per the rules and needs of the family (rather than pursuing one's own needs), and, most importantly, never emulating the ways of the West even if one must reside there to make a living (indeed, the concern over remaining true to one's culture and the worry that one's children will become Westernized are strongest among diasporic Indians).

This rigid definition of being a "true" Indian has sometimes been mocked in Hindi popular cinema, as in Hrishikesh Mukherjee's comedies *Golmaal* (Pandemonium, 1979) and *Kissise Naa Kehna* (Don't Tell Anyone, 1983). More often, though, this mind-set is uncritically celebrated. One egregious example of such celebration is Manoj Kumar's *Purab aur Paschim* (East and West, 1970), where the patriotic hero travels to London and educates the Indians living there (who have submerged themselves in the "decadence" of the West) on the glories of the traditional Indian lifestyle. Raj Kapoor's *Sangam* (Union, 1964) and Shakti Samanta's *An Evening in Paris* (1967) express similar ideas, portraying their Indian characters as maintaining their chastity even in the midst of whites who kiss each other openly. This strain of conservatism persisted in Indian cinema, in varying degrees, right up to the 1990s, when it received immense boost with releases like Aditya Chopra's *Dilwale Dulhaniya Le Jayenge* (Bravehearts Will Take Home the Brides, 1995) and Karan Johar's *Kuch Kuch Hota Hai* (Something Is Happening, 1998). In both, being well-versed in Indian socioreligious customs is celebrated, while *Dilwale Dulhaniya Le Jayenge* makes a fetish of deferring to parental approval when it comes to marriage.

In many ways, the 1990s had the ideal zeitgeist for making such films, whose definition of what constitutes Indianness is obdurate and inflexible. This was the era which saw the rise of the Bharatiya Janata Party (BJP), whose right-wing, quasi-theocratic principles entail conserving Indian culture (which, to them, is synonymous with Hindu culture) against Muslims (whom the BJP considers "outsiders" and "invaders" who pose a threat to Hinduism) and the Western civilization. Art, especially popular cinema, tends to reflect social, cultural, and political trends of the period it was made in, and films like *Kuch Kuch Hota Hai* and *Dilwale Dulhaniya Le Jayenge* served to assure the spectators of the 1990s, among whom the BJP's ideals were becoming increasingly popular, that the globalization which India was experiencing at the time need not lead to the erosion of "Indian culture" as defined by the BJP, that even if one grew up in the West, they could still be upholders of traditional values. The success of these films was evidence of the chord they had struck with the Indian audiences of the 1990s, and the conservative definition of Indianness contained in them has been repeated in many subsequent releases, such as Nikhil Advani's *Kal Ho Naa Ho* (Tomorrow May Not Come, 2003), Vipul Shah's *Namaste London* (Greetings, London, 2007), Shashank Khaitan's *Humpty Sharma ki Dulhaniya* (Humpty Sharma's Bride, 2014), Chopra's *Befikre* (Wild, 2015), and Nitin Kakkar's *Jawani Janeman* (My Darling Youth, 2020). The messages in these films—that cohabiting relationships are no substitutes for marriage, that refusing to settle down and start a family is the sign of moral deficiency, that homosexuality does not exist among Indians, that permission from the parents is a must in marriage—reek of the conservatism espoused by the BJP, their voters, and the 1990s hits which had vigorously popularized such ideas on the celluloid.

The films mentioned above are romantic melodramas, a genre that, at first glance, has nothing in common with the zombie films discussed in this chapter. Ideologically, however, *Rise of the Zombie* and *Go Goa Gone* traverse the same route as these romances in terms of their stance on the "evils" of Westernization. This is not surprising. With the right-wing on the rise in Indian politics, and their way of thinking gaining increasing traction in a society that was never liberal to begin with (as the hostile responses to the educational and social reforms of Henry Derozio, Ishwarchandra Vidyasagar, and Rammohun Roy in the nineteenth century demonstrate), popular cinema *would* cater to the zeitgeist in order to ensure commercial success. Though neither of the Hindi zombie films analyzed here were hits, and the sequels they were supposed to spawn never materialized, this was possibly owing to the dearth of zombie literature and cinema in India (unlike the West, where they have been a steady part of popular culture at least since Romero's films released), which meant that Indian viewers likely did not quite know what to make of them. The lack of stars (even Saif Ali Khan, who portrays Boris in *Go Goa Gone*, was no longer a top star in 2013) and, in the case of *Rise of the Zombie*, a lackluster, monotonously paced storyline had also contributed to their poor collections. It is hard to imagine that the conservative worldview in these films had, in any way, kept people away, given that other Hindi films with similarly orthodox worldviews have succeeded, and continue to succeed, commercially in India.

Nevertheless, some recent forays into zombie stories in Hindi cinema have moved beyond the India-versus-West binary that characterizes *Rise of the Zombie* and *Go Goa Gone*, or even, if only to a lesser extent, the novels of Dhar. In *Betaal* (2020), a web series helmed by Patrick Graham and Nikhil Mahajan, the zombies come in the shape of the reanimated corpses of the British soldiers of the East India Company. When these soldiers were trapped inside a tunnel by Indian rebels during the 1857 mutiny, their sorcery-practicing leader, Colonel Lynedoch, performed a ritual involving human sacrifice to immortalize himself as the living dead by worshipping Betaal, a lapsed god turned evil angel. He then bit and turned the others in his regiment into zombies as well. Upon their liberation 160 years later, they wreak havoc. This series could easily have become another story of Indian heroes battling a horde of Western zombies. Instead, Graham and Mahajan draw parallels between colonial savageries of Englishmen like Lynedoch and the atrocities committed by the Indians who rule the country now. The British zombies manage to escape from the tunnel only because an Indian military unit, operating under the orders of a greedy businessman called Mudhalvan (who has the backing of the ruling party), blasts open the tunnel to build a road, which requires the displacement of the tribals living nearby. The tribals, who know of the zombies living inside the tunnel, oppose Mudhalvan's venture. However, Mudhalvan and the commandos violently remove them, shooting some of the tribals dead.

Such violence is justified under the claim that the villagers are "Naxals." The term refers to an extremist leftist group that is active in parts of India, and claims to champion the country's impoverished tribal populations. The Naxals' aim of overthrowing parliamentary democracy through armed uprising and assassinations, the coercive methods they use to recruit new members, and their indulgence in drug trade and extortion to finance their activities deserve unsparing condemnation. However, the scenario in *Betaal*, where tribals with legitimate grievances are denounced as Naxals and get killed or imprisoned when they seek justice, is based on actual events as well. The displacing of tribals from the lands they have lived on for generations and giving those lands, which are rich in mineral resources, to large businesses that engage in rampant deforestation to mine those resources have also happened, with increasing frequency, under the BJP's rule. All of it is done under the guise of "development," of giving the tribals a more "civilized" life, just as the colonizers had justified their ventures through the reasoning that they wish to bring civilization to the unenlightened corners of the world. And much as the colonizers tolerated no dissent, anyone questioning or criticizing ventures like Mudhalvan's that have the backing of the ruling party are called traitors in today's India. If the colonizers needed regiments like Lynedoch's to consolidate their control over countries they conquered, the rulers in independent India likewise rely on military units of their own, like the one seen in *Betaal*, to ensure what they want is done. Hence, as the more sympathetic Indian characters fight the English zombies, they must, simultaneously, battle the indigenous oppressors who have replaced the British in independent India. The willingness on the part of *Betaal*'s makers to portray this continuum of oppression on Indian soil, from the days of the British to the twenty-first century, lends it more nuance and thematic richness than can be found in the earlier Hindi zombie films.

Even more daring is Dibakar Banerjee's short film *Monster*, which is a part of the anthology film *Ghost Stories* (2020), and which jettisons concerns over Western presence/influence in/on India altogether to focus, instead, on the ills plaguing the country from within. The protagonist of *Monster*, identified only as "Visitor" in the credits, is a government employee sent to a village, Beesgarah (or Smalltown), to assess the underperformance of its children in school. Upon reaching his destination, he discovers a village devoid of any denizens except two children, who inform him that the dwellers of Saugarah (Largetown) have eaten all those who lived in Beesgarah, and that the only way to remain alive is to either stay completely silent and out of the view of the Saugarah people or to become cannibalistic zombies like the latter, since they do not harm those who emulate them. The political subtext here is as obvious as it is resonant: the scenario where those belonging to the smaller community (Beesgarah) must either be "devoured" by the majority (Saugarah) or become invisible and silent, or mold themselves into replicas of that majority, has clear parallels with what non-Hindu communities, especially the Muslims, are told how they must live in BJP-ruled India. Three moments in *Monster* make the parallels with the situation in today's India disquietingly clear. When the boy with whom Visitor tries to escape Beesgarah is stopped by Saugarah's zombie leader, the child must eat the severed hand of the girl who lived with him to prove that he is like the zombies. The scene invokes such incidents as the beating of a Muslim man in Assam because he was selling beef; since cows are worshipped by Hindus, this was deemed a crime by the Hindu hardliners. Much as the boy has to eat human flesh to get past the zombies, this Muslim man had to eat pork, which is considered unholy among Muslims, in order to pacify the crowd that had gathered to "penalize" him. Then comes the scene where Visitor, chased by the Saugarah zombies, tries to run away, only to trip and fall into a ditch. As the head zombie hovers over him, Visitor silently folds his palms to beg mercy, asking the monsters not to kill him. The sight is eerily similar to the much-circulated photo of Qutubuddin Ansari, who, during the 2002 genocide in Gujarat, had similarly pleaded with Hindu extremists to spare his life.

In the end, Visitor wakes up in that ditch; it seems, initially, that all that he (and the viewers) had seen thus far is a dream. He walks into Beesgarah and finds that it is completely unpopulated and dilapidated. Just then, a car appears, and from it emerge the individuals whom he had seen as zombies in his "dream." They take him into the car, with the assurance that he is safe with them. They tell him not to think much of the children in Beesgarah, who, they state, are "useless" anyway. When Visitor says that it seems somebody has burned down Beesgarah, one of them replies, "If they upset others, of course they will burn," his words a direct echo of the statements which have been made in India in recent times to justify majoritarian violence against Muslims. Their leader then joins the conversation, telling Visitor that Saugarah was once a much renowned place. With him and his minions in charge, he remarks, "Those glory days will return." This line is obviously inspired by the slogan "*Achhe din aa gaye*" (Good days have come) that the BJP had adopted during the 2014 elections, which had brought them to power. Employing the zombie as a potent symbol of the discriminatory violence that the incumbent rulers in contemporary India has demonstrated on many occasions, this short film has opened up new avenues to explore in Indian zombie cinema, which, one hopes, would grow not just in size but also in quality in the years to come.

Notes

1 Boon, "And the Dead Shall Rise," 8.
2 The dates of publication of most of the works of Hemendra Kumar Roy have not been documented, so they have not been mentioned here either.
3 Seabrook, *The Magic Island*, 93.

4   Mukhopadhyay, *Bilati Guptokotha*, 5, translation mine.
5   Mukhopadhyay, *Bilati Guptokotha*, 5, translation mine.

Works Cited

Betaal. [Film] Dirs. Patrick Graham and Nikhil Mahajan, 2020.
Boon, Kevin. "And the Dead Shall Rise." In *Better Dead: The Evolution of the Zombie as Post-Human*, edited by Deborah Christie and Sarah Juliet Lauro, 5–8. New York: Fordham University Press, 2011.
Dhar, Mainak. *Chronicler of the Undead*. Chennai: Westland Publications, 2015.
Dhar, Mainak. *Zombiestan*. Chennai: Duckbill Publishers, 2012.
Do Gaz Zameen Ke Neeche. [Film] Dirs. Shyam Ramsay and Tulsi Ramsay, 1972.
Go Goa Gone. [Film] Dirs. Raj Nidimoru and Krishna D.K., 2013.
Monster, in *Ghost Stories*. [Film] Dir. Dibakar Banerjee, 2020.
Mukhopadhyay, Bhubanchandra. *Bilater Guptokotha*. Calcutta: Basumati Sahitya Mandir, Third Edition, N.D.
Rise of the Zombie. [Film] Dirs. Luke Kenny and Devaki Singh, 2013.
Roy, Hemendra Kumar. *Kishor Bhoutik Samagra*, Parts 1–3. Kolkata: Patra Bharati Publishers, 2005–6.
Seabrook, William. *The Magic Island*. New York: Dover Publications, 2016.

12

From the Mountain to the Shore: Migration, Water Crisis, and Revolutionary Zombies from Haiti to Peru

Giulia Champion

Introduction: The Zombie of the Capitalocene[1]

As we know it in popular culture, the zombie is a figure *of* the market and made *for* the market. It is governed by the market, not only because of its relation to fluctuating wealth and financial crises but also because it is effectively made, unmade, and remade by the marketplace. As many chapters in this collection discuss, while the zombie is primarily a filmic or literary trope, it is used for a variety of purposes, including advertisement: in 2019 Mexico City found its streets invaded by black and yellow posters, showing a yellow hand seemingly emerging from a tomb and accompanied by a message exclaiming, "*Lo zombies sí existen*" (Of course zombies exist), followed by a URL leading curious observers to an online webpage advertising Flanax® Nocto, an anti-inflammatory drug for the alleviation of light or moderate pains which might cause insomnia.[2] On the site, one can read about the supposed "*Efecto zombie*" (zombie effect), where someone might be "*un ZOMBIE DEL DOLOR*" (a PAIN ZOMBIE) if they are in too much pain to sleep. The zombie, driven by the market to sell anything from medicines to films, is a uniquely adaptable figure: the zombie is relevant when describing a drone-like lethargic state as well as a violent cataclysmic event—as embodied by the zombie apocalypse trope—and is even used to spice up romantic comedies, such as Isaac Marion's *Warm Bodies* (2010) and its subsequent 2013 film adaptation. As Kaiama L. Glover notes, "the zombie embodies the fluidity of the boundaries between living and dead, material and spiritual, natural and supernatural, etc."[3] The porous meaning of the zombie has only continued to grow, its role allocated to that which the market deems returns to be the highest.

Furthermore, in a time of accelerated anthropogenic climate crisis, the shaping and history of this figure of the marketplace are entangled with issues pertaining to natural resource extraction and exploitation as well as uneven wealth (re-)distribution, as is discussed in-depth by Kerstin Oloff in her groundbreaking article "From Sugar to Oil: The Ecology of George A. Romero's *Night of the Living Dead*" (2017):

> This simultaneity and multiplicity of zombie figures arises from a world-system that is profoundly uneven; one in which the spectacular benefits and liberties made possible by oil and other energy sources are only unevenly accessible. As a figure that has crossed from the world-systemic periphery to its new hegemonic core, the zombie is one that—perhaps like no other—is inscribed with local and global inequalities.[4]

Oloff's genealogical tree and nomenclature categorizing the "sugar-zombie" alongside the "petro-zombie" illuminates their connection, bringing forth the inextricable relation between plantation agriculture, enslaved labor, colonialism, and our current economic system. The legacy of excessive monocrop agricultural extractivism can be seen in current oil-extractive practices that abuse natural resources to produce more fossil fuel at the smallest possible cost. Whether these costs are economic, human, or environmental—all of which are deeply entangled—the zombie offers a way of reading how economic systems relate to the human and to the environment. Like petroleum, the zombie is fossilized, necrotic matter deeply sedimented in our modern epistemologies,[5] brought back to life and refined for contemporary entertainment. It can thus become an empty signifier made to represent and mean just what one wants it to; it sells easily and well. However, to have a full picture of the zombie, it is necessary to excavate and analyze the different uses and meanings of this figure. And such an archaeology of the zombie requires that we consider its origin: that is, the colonial and exploitative history that made the figure in the first place, and the same system which allows for its continued and multifaceted use—and misuse—as a trope and a character in popular culture.

This chapter aims to do this by analyzing the original zombie figure, unearthed in Haiti, and tracing its emancipatory character through to another revolutionary movement in Peru. Specifically, this chapter argues that the zombie in the Haitian context is not just a figure representing slavery and commodification—which, as noted above, is continued in some version of the contemporary popular culture zombie—but is also one deeply attached to the Haitian Revolution and its emancipatory impetus. Hence, this chapter aims to decolonize the zombie, first, by unearthing its emancipatory potential in the context of its creation in Haitian history and culture and, second, by comparatively considering how this potential can be identified in the Peruvian novel *Adiós, Ayacucho* (1986) (Goodbye, Ayacucho) authored by Julio Ortega. The history of Revolutions in Haiti and Peru shares similarities wherein undead characters such as the zombie highlight emancipation. I will therefore briefly focus on the Haitian context and how the zombie and vodou become core to the liberation of the island during the Revolution. I will then consider how the revolutionary potential of the zombie of the Haitian Revolution can be used to read the undead character in Ortega's novel by identifying similarities between both countries' revolutionary movements—the Túpac Amaru II Rebellion of 1780–2 and the Haitian Revolution of 1791–1804. Finally, I will discuss how, in my view, both revolutionary movements are paid insufficient scholarly attention regarding their role in both the advancement of human rights as well as their connection to other uprisings.

In its entirety, the above analysis lends a memorializing aspect to the project of decolonial zombie literature, as the epistemological and ontological significance of the zombie is reclaimed, and its revolutionary potential restored. The neglect and erasure of these features from academic discourse, alongside the socio-ecological impact of (neo-)imperialist extractivism in both countries, through plantation agriculture in Haiti and gold and silver mining in Peru, provide points of comparison between two very different nations. The undead character of Alfonso Cánepa in the novel is, for example, an emancipatory zombie figure that raises important issues about the Andean indigenous situation in a time of strife in Peru. Finally, my analysis will conclude on how the civil turmoil lasting from the early 1980s to 2000 continues to impact the indigenous population, exacerbated by accelerated climate change in a space where mining and export agriculture are further worsening the water crisis.

Recognizing and Rehabilitating the Emancipatory Zombie

As Joan Dayan explains, "born out of the experience of slavery, the sea passage from Africa to the New World, and revolution on the soil of Saint-Domingue, the *zombi* tells the story of colonization."[6] She goes on to explain that the term "*zombie*" is a "Creole word that means spirit, revenant," which became associated with Jean Zombi, a formerly enslaved revolutionary, whereby it

> thus became a terrible composite power: slave turned rebel ancestor turned lwa, an incongruous, demonic spirit recognized through dreams, divination, or possession.... "While the Haitian does not welcome any encounter with a zombie, his real dread is that of being made into one himself." This incarnation of negation or vacancy is as much a part of history as the man Jean Zombi.[7]

Here Dayan notes the original dichotomy of the zombie, both a curse that brings resting Haitians back to a never-ending life of forced labor and a mythologized historical figure who played a crucial role in the Haitian Revolution. However, the Revolution and its symbols, including vodou, its main actors, zombies, and the island itself, were debased and degraded in Western rhetoric and politics as Europe saw Haiti setting an undesirable example for their other colonies. From then began an economic and trade embargo to which the island was subjected for several decades. Haiti could only attempt to extirpate itself from this boycott by paying an independence debt demanded by Charles X in 1825 to compensate French planters for the loss of their lands and their enslaved people. The extortionate amount demanded by France meant Haiti had to borrow money, beginning a vicious cycle of indebtedness:

> The denial of political existence was accompanied by other attacks on sovereignty. In 1825 the Haitian government agreed to pay an indemnity to France in return for diplomatic and economic relations. Exiled planters had been clamoring for such a payment for years: it was meant to repay them for what they had lost in Saint-Domingue, including the money invested in their slaves, and amounted to a fine for revolution. Unable to pay, the Haitian government took loans from French banks, entering a cycle of debt that would last into the twentieth century.[8]

This cycle was accompanied by substantial negative propaganda about the island. Consequently, the zombie figure became an exotic bogeyman along with vodou, which was characterized as barbaric black magic. Renewed accusations of savagery and cannibalism were made, part of a broader discourse of "otherness" finding its roots in European history, as Kate Ramsey argues:

> many of the historically most feared forms of supernatural aggression in Haiti—including anthropophagy and the transformation of humans into animals—strongly resemble the supernatural crimes attributed to "sorcerers" in Europe in the late Middle Ages, and later to African and African-descended ritual specialists in the context of the slave trade and colonization.... Haiti's

nineteenth-century European detractors seized upon such rumors as proof of the regression of civilization in the "Black Republic."[9]

Additionally, the rise of the United States as a superpower, since its independence and its expansion to the south of its borders, led to the American occupation and a second colonization of Haiti. With the excuse of "civilizing" their southern neighbors, the United States occupied Cuba twice, for instance, where American investment in sugar plantation had enormously increased.[10] The occupation of Haiti recalls colonization due to the military and financial control exerted over the island by the United States. To further exploit the island, the United States went so far as to forcibly change Jean-Jacques Dessalines' 1804 independence law-forbidding foreigners to own land in Haiti by drafting a new constitution lifting this ban. When Haiti's parliament refused to approve this change, the US Marines dissolved this legislative body "under the nominal authority of the client government. This charter was later 'passed' by an extraconstitutional plebiscite, in which it is estimated that less than 5 percent of the Haitian population participated, under an armed guard of marines."[11] This first legal change was the first in a long line that allowed the United States to appropriate most of Haiti's natural resources.

It is within this "surreal" situation dominated by corporate interests and racism that the contemporary version of the zombie was produced. In 1929, William Seabrook published a fictional, first-person-narrated pseudo-anthropological work on Haiti entitled *The Magic Island*, accompanied by highly racist and stereotypical engravings that further contributed to the perception of Haiti as an exotic and dangerous island. In a chapter entitled "... Dead Men Working in the Cane Fields," he presents the following dialogue between himself and his friend Polynice:

> "At this very moment, in the moonlight, there are *zombies* working in this island, less than two hours' ride from my own habitation. We know about them, but we do not dare to interfere so long as our own dead are left unmolested. If you will ride with me tomorrow night, yes, I will show you dead men working in the cane field. Close even to the cities, there are sometimes *zombies*. Perhaps you have already heard of those that were at Hasco..." "What about Hasco?" I interrupted him, for in the whole of Haiti, Hasco is perhaps the last name anybody would think of connecting with either sorcery or superstition.[12]

Seabrook's incredulity, based on the fact that it cannot be possible for the Haitian-American Sugar Company (HASCO) to be involved with any "voodoo nonsense," shows the racist and patronizing attitude that the American occupation promoted.[13] It also speaks to a fear of miscegenation that will continually feature in other instances of the zombie figure in American popular culture.

This is similar to anxieties surrounding cannibalism, exemplified by explorers' and colonizers' fears of being consumed by "mysterious" and "savage" people met during the US occupation of Haiti. The contact with the island and its "natives"—the descendants of forcibly displaced and enslaved peoples—generated new tropes to translate American anxieties. Seabrook's novel inspired the 1932 film *White Zombie*, in which a young white American woman, Madeleine, is zombified by a "voodoo master" who has fallen in love with her. Overnight, as a zombie, she leaves her husband, Neil, to follow the call of her "new master." Her husband begins to look for her everywhere; when he loses any hope of finding her, his companion encourages him to keep searching, to which Neil replies: "Well, surely you don't think she's alive, in the hands of natives? Oh no, better dead than that!"[14] Neil's hope that Madeleine be dead rather than alive and "in the hands of the natives" reveals how Haiti became a space for the United States to negotiate "the politics of race, gender, sexuality, and national identity.... Since the long occupation, Haiti has continued to serve, in more and less veiled ways, as a reflection of U.S. American fears and desires, and thus as a salable commodity."[15] In Seabrook's novel and the first movies of the 1930s and 1940s it was the character of the "voodoo master" which was feared, since they had the power to take over and control any corpse, and thus reminded spectators of Haiti's "barbarity" and supposed black magic. Since George Romero's 1968 *Night of the Living Dead*, the dread of the racialized, colonized "other" is displaced onto the creature of the zombie itself. The figure has continually evolved in contemporary cinema, sometimes appearing as a quick and violent cannibalistic drone, and other times being humanized.

Thus, from its origins as a Haitian, black magic, undead worker on the plantation controlled by an evil master to profit from their labor, the zombie evolved into a cannibalistic ghoul starring in Hollywood's biggest blockbusters. In this way, though its characterization changed, its employment did not: it continued to remain a creature of the market and for the market, to generate profit for those who control it. It is not a stretch to say that the figure of the zombie has, in fact, lived the same fate as Haitian sugar, being extracted from the island in order to be refined and sold on the US marketplace and generating profit there, far from its original context and meaning. Little is left of the original, emancipatory figure of the Haitian revolution (1791–1804) in most of the Western contemporary productions in which zombies appear. This is because the Haitian Revolution itself has been erased from Western historiography in a neocolonial gesture, with the emancipatory zombie disappearing alongside it and facilitating the creation of the westernized zombie. Gurminder K. Bhambra notes how the Haitian Revolution's long intellectual embargo has endured, as it is seldom considered alongside those of the United States (1765–91) and France (1789–99), despite the fact that it embodied global ideals of equality to a greater extent:

> So, what might we learn about the birth of the modern world and its transformation (and the politics of knowledge production, more generally) if we took the Haitian revolution seriously? First, in terms of Haiti itself, we would learn about the ways in which those who had been enslaved, on achieving their freedom and independence, honoured the people who preceded them on the land.... The Haitian constitution was itself predicated on an understanding of citizenship that had greater universal applicability than similar notions developed in the French Revolution. According to Fischer (2004: 266), by making freedom from enslavement and racial discrimination the bedrock of political understandings and unlinking citizenship from race, the Haitian constitution radicalized and universalized the idea of equality.... The Haitian revolution was the most radical of its age and silenced, precisely, for its radical nature.[16]

Indeed, this "radical nature" did not permit first France and then the United States to continue to exploit Haiti's natural resources, so it needed to be silenced and erased. This is why authors like Gina Athena Ulysse remind us that "Haiti needs new narratives."[17] Further, the world not only needs new narratives about the Haitian Revolution but also needs them from a non-Eurocentric perspective, to conceptually allow us to grasp the central role this insurrection had in the development of the "modern" world. Modernity continues to be a term that is challenging to define, though scholars have been attempting to do so for years. In his 1995 article entitled "The End of What Modernity?" Immanuel Wallerstein considers our need to "trace the history of [the] confusing symbiosis of the two modernities—the modernity of technology and the modernity of liberation" when attempting to articulate this concept.[18] Crucially, he later notes:

> It was the French Revolution that forced the issue, not merely for France but for the modern world-system as a whole. The French Revolution was not an isolated event. It might rather be thought of as the eye of a hurricane. It was bounded (preceded and succeeded) by the decolonization of the Americas—the settler decolonizations of British North America, Hispanic America, and Brazil; the slave revolution of Haiti; and the abortive Native American uprisings such as Túpac Amaru in Peru.[19]

Wallerstein begins to shape his definition of what he calls the "Age of the Revolutions," which he further develops in his chapter entitled "The French Revolution as World-Historical Event" in 2001.[20] His association of decolonial movements with the Haitian Revolution and the Peruvian Túpac Amaru II rebellion asks whether issues of memorialization and rewriting of history are not also crucial in the context of this South American country. If one needs to learn more from the Haitian revolution, could one also aim to learn from the Peruvian one? Indeed, their similarities and differences make them both global phenomena in and of the Americas. Moreover, these issues of memory and rewriting are crucial to the figure of the zombie, as I have argued until now, as well as for Ortega's novel, which I will shortly discuss. The next section, though, briefly contextualizes the role of the Túpac Amaru rebellion in relation to the short story which itself is focused on an internal strife that took place in the country about 200 years later.

Indigenous Resistance and Fragmented Corporeality in Peruvian Hi/Story from Túpac Amaru II to Alfonso Cánepa

The Túpac Amaru II rebellion was the culmination of a wave of insurrections that took place across the Andes in what is now contemporary Peru and Bolivia between 1720 and 1790.[21] Though this rebellion was the most significant and largest organized of all these events, it was understood differently by people living across the Andes at the time, hence, as Alberto Flores Galindo notes, there "was not just one,... but many faces to the rebellion":

> while in Cuzco, his [Túpac Amaru II] proclamations were interpreted to call for respect for the property and lives of mixed-bloods (*mestizos*) and creoles (*criollos*); in La Paz it was believed that the Inca [as he was called by everyone] wanted all non-Indians put to death in a kind of ethnic cleansing.... In Arequipa in 1789 and in Oruro in 1781, by contrast, rebel leaders were actually creoles with urban followers composed of a mix of Indian and mixed-bloods.[22]

The Inca's real name was José Gabriel Condorcanqui. He was an indigenous nobleman who was also a prosperous trader and who claimed direct descent from the last Inca King, Túpac Amaru, executed in 1572 during the Spanish *Conquista*—hence asserting a direct connection between himself and pre-Hispanic populations. However, as Flores Galindo notes, "Túpac Amaru [II]'s army replicated the hierarchy of colonial society. In fact, this restoration of the 'authentic' Inca monarchy demonstrated the influence of European concepts on the indigenous aristocracy."[23] This influence translates the fact that the violence of the *Conquista* was not just physical and material but also epistemological, as Inca practices became alienated even as the revolution sought to identify with the culture. Amaru's death did not bring forth the end of this insurrection as the "city of La Paz was taken twice by Julián Apasa Túpac Katari... and in June 1781, Felipe Velasco Túpac Inca... tried to organize a rebellion in the mountains of Huarochirí... Only the execution of Diego Cristóbal in August 1783 ended this convulsive period of Andean rebellion which lasted more than three years."[24] Amaru's and Cristóbal's executions were powerful events insofar as the violence and will to destroy their bodies fragmented Andean identities:

> For those who viewed Túpac Amaru as an Inca, however, the body was not that of a prisoner. Rather, it stood for the Indian nation. To quarter and burn Túpac Amaru's body was to destroy symbolically the Inca empire. Years later, when Diego Cristóbal made peace with the Spaniards, Cristóbal assembled the supposed remains of Túpac Amaru and with great pomp buried them in Cuzco's San Francisco church. Shortly thereafter, however, the Spanish judge Mata Linares had Cristóbal arrested and condemned him to be hanged. After the execution, his body was also quartered and his houses sacked and destroyed.[25]

This violence on Andean bodies has continued, and is registered and represented by Ortega's character's broken corporeality. Moreover, the marginalization and demonization of Andean groups, languages, practices, and customs that followed these deaths, in order to curb further rebellions, resembles the economic, diplomatic, and cultural embargo of Haiti: "On Túpac Amaru's death, the colonial authorities prohibited Inca nobility from using titles, ordered the destruction of paintings of the Incas, and forced the Indians to dress in Western clothes."[26] This included a rewriting "of history in terms of European superiority," as Flores Galindo notes, which, in the Peruvian context, echoes the academic erasure of the Haitian revolution discussed by Bhambra above.[27]

Forgetting and occluding these revolutions and their contexts engages with how the historical archive is shaped by colonial practices. Saidiya Hartman in her work on the Atlantic trade argues that

> the archive dictates what can be said about the past and the kinds of stories that can be told about the persons catalogued, embalmed, and sealed away in box files and folios. To read the archive is to enter a mortuary; it permits one final viewing and allows for a last glimpse of persons about to disappear into the slave hold.[28]

Furthermore, these "dead" images in the "mortuary" of the archives are akin to revenant figures, undead zombies, and ghosts. These are signifiers of how *monstrous* relations and developments under colonialism were and continue to be. My emphasis on the adjective monstrous is crucial to the understanding of the zombie as a monster. As I have argued elsewhere,

> Scholars have, in general, focused solely on [the] connection of *monstrum* to *monere*: interestingly, none seem to have considered the close etymological relation that the term "monster" bears with "monument." Indeed, *monere* also means "to remind, bring to one's recollection," which is the root for the term monument, to which the adverbial suffix—*mentum* is added ("Monster"). The myriad of terms associated with memory and commemoration implied in the word is crucial in understanding monstrosity and monstrous figures as monuments of colonialism. Crucially, monuments play a critical role in relation to colonisation, being physical reminders of western hegemony. Hence, monstrous figures… can be understood as literary monuments of colonial relations, signifiers that represent a vestige of this history, and they can be read as depicting the monumental ruins, or material traces, of colonial pasts and monstrosity as representing the corporeal embodiment of empire's violence.[29]

The zombie embodies this description, and its position at the nexus of the monstrous and memorializing is emphasized in Ortega's novel. Julio Ortega's *Adiós, Ayacucho* (1986) traces the journey Alfonso Cánepa undertakes from Ayacucho to Lima to retrieve some of his missing bones in order to give himself a proper burial after he is violently mutilated and murdered by the military police. Once he reaches Lima, Cánepa effectively rewrites the archive embodied by Francisco Pizzaro's tomb by fusing his incomplete corpse with the conquistador's relics. In this gesture, Cánepa can be seen as setting the historical record straight on what the archive should contain: a full recounting of events that does not silence violence but rather recognizes these realities and their structural, material, and systemic legacies. Cánepa's character is a revenant that has been mostly described as a specter; Talía Dajes, for instance, rejects the view that Cánepa could be interpreted as a zombie, arguing that "while Cánepa's representation encompasses some of the elements present in zombie mythology, it lacks one of its defining components, that is, the total annulment of the self."[30] Her analysis of Cánepa through different layers of Peruvian history and Andean folklore is crucial; however, reading this character as a zombie permits us to articulate him as an emancipatory figure. Indeed, as Glover concludes, in respect to the zombie's potentiality in the Haitian context and her readings of Depestre's, Franketienne's, and Alexis' works, "the zombie functions as a catalyzing metaphor for considering questions of community-building and alienation in an economically, politically, and even psychically fractured society"[31] and she also notes that "for the most part... [these] are tales of zombies reborn."[32] These zombies and Cánepa are not simply specters haunting their narratives but are instilled with agency, taking action to redress injustices and putting themselves to rest in peace, rather than requiring an exorcism. These are thus zombies reborn and reburied.

"I came to Lima to recover my corpse": Memorializing and Re-Burying the Undead

Ortega's novel begins by unsettling linear temporality, as the first sentence is Cánepa's past tense statement: "*Vine a Lima a recobrar mi cadaver*" (I came to Lima to recover my corpse), followed by an explanation noting: "*Así comenzaría mi discurso cuando llegase a Lima*" (This is how I would begin my speech when I would reach Lima).[33] As Cánepa emerges from the "pit" where he has been thrown, after having been mutilated and killed, he prepares the reader for what he plans to do by the end of the novel: recompose his broken body and bury himself again to rest in peace. Cánepa's story thus can only be told by his undead corpse as he travels across Peru, from the city of Ayacucho in the Andes to the littoral urban space of Lima, or from the mountains to the shore. By inverting linear storytelling temporality, Cánepa's narrative voice begins by what is closer to his reader's present, his future, and thus by signaling the incomplete history we might receive unless he is allowed to tell his story.

Ortega's novel is inspired by a journal article he read about the gruesome and violent torture and mutilation of Jesús Oropeza in 1984, "a peasant activist from Ayacucho."[34] The novel also engages with the investigative commission prompted by President Fernando Belaúnde the year before, in February 1983 headed by Mario Vargas Llosa following the murder of eight journalists in January 1983 in the village of Uchuraccay. As Víctor Vich and Alexandra Hibbett argue, the attempt to objectively reconstruct the events leading to the death of the journalists in Uchuraccay was thwarted by stereotypes and preconceived ideas about Andean indigenous peoples. They argue that despite these attempts, the commission's report is "alimented by a very traditional rhetoric, which led it to judge the events from preestablished ideas about Andean culture and the complex process of modernity in Perú."[35]

These events, along with the death of 135 community members of Uchuraccay, principally Quechua indigenous people, are part of a wider period known as the *Manchay tiempo*, a hybrid denomination including *Manchay*, the Quechua word for fear, followed by the Spanish term for time. This period, which is considered as lasting from the early 1980s to 2000, was the theater to many violent struggles between the Marxist-Maoist Guerrilla group *Sendero Luminoso* (Shining Path) and the military government. Quechua *campesinos* (peasant farmers) were often caught in the crossfire, resulting in several violent deaths of indigenous communities. For this reason, by "the start of the 1990s, the Quechua had started to establish themselves in defense patrols known as *rondas campesinas*."[36] In Ortega's novel, Cánepa is identified as the leader of one of these patrols, thus identifying the violence committed against him as an attempt to curb and neutralize indigenous resistance. Hence, reading his revived corpse as an emancipatory zombie aims to suggest a de-objectification and de-demonization of Andean groups.

Throughout Ortega's novel, the irony and humor used to describe Cánepa's fragmented body urge the reader to consider the importance of each life and what happens when marginalized communities are the ones "allowed" to die. This can only be done, as Victor Quiroz argues, by tackling and challenging the types of discourse that have been objectifying indigenous people and their culture: "a carnivalization of the journalistic, *indigenista* and anthropological discourse is constructed in *Adiós, Ayacucho*, which are rhetoric that objectify the Andean other."[37] By confronting institutionalized discourse that reifies otherness—that employs techniques and dynamics analogous with those used during colonial times—Ortega's novel aims to, first, consider how history is written and, second, rewrite this archive and, in so doing, decolonizing the writing of history itself. This is continued when Cánepa decides to complete his skeleton by taking Pizarro's bones, which, as Quiroz contends, functions as a deposit and archive of colonial history and power, noting that because only his bones remain, "it is a symbol of the decline of the colonial system continued by the modern *criollo* Peruvian state."[38] In Hartman's words, quoted above, the archive can be considered a mortuary; this idea is materialized in the novel through Pizarro's tomb being read as an archive. Both the colonial and the authoritarian powers leave their victims anonymous and objectified in communal graves and in sealed files. Cánepa attempts to challenge this history of depersonalization and objectification by contesting modes of knowledge production through challenging the characters of the journalist and the anthropologist that appear in the novel, and also by envisaging a Peruvian body politics and social body that unifies its origins in Cánepa's reassembled body.

Cánepa's fragmented corporeality is a signifier of the violence endured by indigenous population caught in the crossfire during the *Manchay Tiempo*—despite their constitution of defense patrol, Quechua communities remained the principal victims of this period—and the fragmented social body of Peru. Furthermore, as Mónica Cárdenas Moreno notes, Cánepa represents indigenous migrants displaced to Lima due to this violence and who bring with them the deep traumas accompanying this violence.[39] Robin Kirk notes that "until the 1940s, more than half of Peru's population lived in the Andes.... By 1981 the proportion of Peruvian living in the Andes had fallen to 36 percent."[40] Cánepa's travel from Ayacucho to Lima can also be seen as referring back to the journey undertaken by Felipe Guamán Poma de Ayala, a Quechua nobleman, who wrote *El primer nueva corónica y buen gobierno* between 1600 to 1615, addressed to King Philip III, critiquing Spanish colonial rule and its impact on the indigenous populations.[41] Here rewriting history becomes crucial, as Cárdenas Moreno notes, given that his mission came to be symbolic over the centuries, though it was not fruitful in his own time, and "Cánepa's pilgrimage also seeks a symbolic transformation, the resignification of history: attacking the center of power and its history, which is to say, Lima and the bones of conquistador Francisco Pizarro."[42] The novel challenges both the colonial historical archive and the official national one established by the government. In one of his speeches, Cánepa considers how rapidly one dies in "this country":

> *La verdadera historia nacional sería este cuento de las variaciones en la matanza en los mataderos de turno. Cada estilo de matar señalaría una época, cada muerto ilustre (Atahualpa, Túpac Amaru, José Olaya, Alfonso Ugarte, Atusparia, y tantos otros), pero también cada muerto anónimo, da cuenta de su cuerpo condenado y torturado, y, en esto tiempos de guerra sucia, desaparecido después de despedazado. Este cementerio nacional es un velar sin término, un luto del alma.*[43]

> [The true national history should be a recounting of slaughtering variations and of slaughterers on shift. Each style of killing would signify an epoch, each famous dead (Atahualpa, Túpac Amaru, José Olaya, Alfonso Ugarte, Atusparia, and many others), but also each anonymous dead, would relate their condemned and tortured body, and, in these times of dirty war, each disappeared would come after each broken body. This national cemetery is an endless wake, a mourning of the soul.]

Here Cánepa considers a genealogy of death which connects the Peruvian colonial past with the violent present of the *Manchay tiempo*. In a gesture redolent of the necropolitics theorized by Achille Mbembe, he also rhetorically aligns anonymous deaths with those of famous people, reminding readers that each death, and life, is important and hence re-sensitizing them to mass killings. Cánepa, representing the broken body of Peru, also represents its scarred history and in trying to reassemble his skeleton seeks reparations.[44] Cánepa thus finally creates a space in which what Judith Butler has called "ungrievable lives" are finally mourned in their death, including his own.[45]

The novel rewrites the historical archive seeking to repair the psychological and socioeconomic *and* environmental scars of colonialism, which never truly disappear, in the novel's attempt to offer a political ecology through Cánepa's claim that Peruvian economists "*han saldado el país al extranjero, y lo han hecho sin remordimientos, con una convicción absoluta*" (have sold the country to foreigners, and they have done so without remorse and with absolute conviction).[46] This statement and Cánepa's broken corporeality in the novel echo Eduardo Galeano's seminal work *Las venas abierta de América Latina* (*The Open Veins of Latin America*) and its understanding of Latin America as a body fragmented by colonial and (neo-)imperial endeavors. Moreover, when Cánepa cannot find his own bones, he decides to complete his body by taking the colonizer's bones in Fernando Pizarro's tomb, or, as described in Spanish, the "monument."[47] Here the narrative explicitly situates the broken corporeality of Cánepa in relation to the colonial past and its consequences. Cánepa's claim feels even more real given the current environmental situation in Peru. In particular, given the water crisis the country is encountering, which is exacerbated by export monocrop asparagus agriculture and by (illegal) gold mining, as both industries "require significant amounts of increasingly scarce water."[48] In the Peruvian Andes, illegal alluvial gold mining impacts not only the environment but also indigenous communities, predominantly Quechua and Aymara, as the bulk of this activity takes place "within a nature reserve that is home to indigenous peoples and huge biodiversity," causing it to be classified as illegal, but it also contributes to increased number of forced sexual and labor exploitation.[49] In the case of the Madre de Dios mines, for instance, "majority of those trafficked or exploited hail from the Cusco region."[50]

Conclusion: Why the Andes, and Zombies, Need New Narratives

It is more crucial than ever then to decolonize narratives surrounding indigenous groups in order to avoid situations in which they continue to be most vulnerable to exploitative industries and the environmental impacts these have. Andean cultures and spaces need to be de-objectified to conceive them as more than a space from which to extract resources. Similarly, by decolonizing the zombie and providing new narratives for this figure, one can attempt to return it its emancipatory power and recognize its role in a crucial Revolution that makes Haiti more than a space of victimhood, exploitation, or monstrosity, as noted by Ulysse in *Why Haiti Needs New Narratives*.

Notes

1. I am grateful to those whose precious input and feedback have greatly improved this chapter, in particular Roxanne Douglas and Matthew Chennells.
2. All translations are mine unless specified otherwise.
3. Glover, *Haiti Unbound*, 60.
4. Oloff, "From Sugar to Oil," 326.
5. I'd like to thank Harry Pitt Scott, who helped me formulate this thought in a PhD chapter on extractivism and I now realize it fits this work better.
6. Dayan, *Haiti, History, and the Gods*, 36–7.
7. Dayan, *Haiti, History, and the Gods*, 37.
8. Dubois, *Avengers of the New World*, 303–4.
9. Ramsey, *The Spirits and the Law*, 79.
10. Ramsey, *The Spirits and the Law*, 118.
11. Ramsey, *The Spirits and the Law*, 119.
12. Seabrook, *The Magic Island*, 94–5, emphasis in original.
13. In this instance specifically, as in other below, I use the Americanized spelling of vaudou to distinguish this negative view of the syncretic religion as black magic from its reality.
14. "*White Zombie*," n.p.
15. Renda, *Taking Haiti*, 215.
16. Bhambra, "Undoing the Epistemic Disavowal of the Haitian Revolution," 7.
17. Ulysse, *Why Haiti Needs New Narratives*.
18. Wallerstein, "The End of What Modernity?," 472.
19. Wallerstein, "The End of What Modernity?," 474.
20. Wallerstein, "The French Revolution as World-Historical Event."
21. Flores Galindo, "The Rebellion of Túpac Amaru," 159.
22. Flores Galindo, "The Rebellion of Túpac Amaru," 160–1.
23. Flores Galindo, "The Rebellion of Túpac Amaru," 164.
24. Flores Galindo, "The Rebellion of Túpac Amaru," 160.
25. Flores Galindo, "The Rebellion of Túpac Amaru," 166.
26. Flores Galindo, "The Rebellion of Túpac Amaru," 166.
27. Flores Galindo, "The Rebellion of Túpac Amaru," 167.

28 Hartman, *Lose Your Mother*, 17.
29 Champion, "Imperialism Is a Plague too: Transatlantic Pandemic Imaginaries in César Mba Abogo's 'El sueño de Dayo' (2007) and Junot Díaz's 'Monstro' (2012)," 170.
30 Dajes, "Peru's Living Dead," 6.
31 Glover, "Exploiting the Undead," 121.
32 Glover, "Exploiting the Undead," 108.
33 Ortega, *Adiós, Ayacucho*, 9.
34 Cala Buendía, "Truth in the Time of Fear: *Adiós, Ayacucho*'s Poetics of Memory and the Peruvian Transitional Justice Process," 348.
35 Vich and Hibbett, "La risa irónica de un cuerpo roto," 176–7.
36 Williams, *Indigenous Peoples*, 899, emphasis in original.
37 Quiroz, "La carnavalización del archivo en *Adiós, Ayacucho* de Julio Ortega," 41.
38 Quiroz, "La carnavalización del archivo en *Adiós, Ayacucho* de Julio Ortega," 57.
39 Cárdenas Moreno, "Ruptura del cuerpo y ruptura del lenguaje en la novela de la memoria histórica en el Perú," 25.
40 Kirk, "Chaqwa," 370–1.
41 See Beardsell, *Europe and Latin America*, 56–8.
42 Cárdenas Moreno, "Ruptura del cuerpo y ruptura del lenguaje en la novela de la memoria histórica en el Perú," 22.
43 Ortega, *Adiós, Ayacucho*, 15–16.
44 Mbembe, *Critique de la raison nègre*, 262.
45 See Butler, *Frames of War*.
46 Ortega, *Adiós, Ayacucho*, 33.
47 Ortega, *Adiós, Ayacucho*, 64.
48 O'Connell, *From a Vicious to a Virtuous Circle*, 7.
49 O'Connell, *From a Vicious to a Virtuous Circle*, 19.
50 O'Connell, *From a Vicious to a Virtuous Circle*, 20.

Works Cited

Beardsell, Peter. *Europe and Latin America: Returning the Gaze*. Manchester: Manchester University Press, 2000.

Bhambra, Gurminder K. "Undoing the Epistemic Disavowal of the Haitian Revolution: A Contribution to Global Social Thought." *Journal of Intercultural Studies* 37, no. 1 (2016): 1–16.

Butler, Judith. *Frames of War: When Is Life Grievable?* London: Verso Books, 2016.

Cala Buendía, Felipe. "Truth in the Time of Fear: *Adiós, Ayacucho*'s Poetics of Memory and the Peruvian Transitional Justice Process." *The International Journal of Transitional Justice* 6 (2012): 344–54.

Cárdenas Moreno, Mónica. "Ruptura del cuerpo y ruptura del lenguaje en la novela de la memoria histórica en el Perú. Estudio comparativo de *Adiós, Ayacucho* de Julio Ortega y *La sangre de la aurora* de Claudia Salazar." *Revista del Instituto Riva Agüero* 1, no. 2 (2016): 11–46.

Champion, Giulia. "Imperialism Is a Plague Too: Transatlantic Pandemic Imaginaries in César Mba Abogo's 'El Sueño de Dayo' (2007) and Junot Díaz's 'Monstro' (2012)." *Science Fiction Research Association Review* 51, no. 2 (2021): 167–74.

Dajes, Talía. "Peru's Living Dead: Spectrality, Untimeliness, and The Internal Armed Conflict." *Romance Quarterly* 67, no. 4 (2020): 181–95.

Dayan, Joan. *Haiti, History, and the Gods*. Berkeley: University of California Press, 1995.

Dubois, Laurent. *Avengers of the New World: The Story of the Haitian Revolution*. Cambridge: Harvard University Press, 2004.

Flores Galindo, Alberto. "The Rebellion of Túpac Amaru." In *The Peru Reader: History, Culture, Politics*, 159–68. Durham: Duke University Press, 2005.

Glover, Kaiama. "Exploiting the Undead: The Usefulness of the Zombie in Haitian Literature." *The Journal of Haitian Studies* 11, no. 2 (2005): 105–21.

Glover, Kaiama. *Haiti Unbound: A Spiralist Challenge to the Postcolonial Canon*. Liverpool: Liverpool University Press, 2010.

Hartman, Saidiya. *Lose Your Mother: A Journey along the Atlantic Slave Route*. New York: Farrar, Straus & Giroux, 2008.

Kirk, Robin. "Chaqwa." In *The Peru Reader: History, Culture, Politics*, 370–83. Durham: Duke University Press, 2005.

Mbembe, Achille. *Critique de La Raison Nègre*. Paris: Découverte, 2013.

O'Connell, Chris. "From a Vicious to a Virtuous Circle: Addressing Climate Change, Environmental Destruction and Contemporary Slavery." Report Web. Anti-Slavery International, 2020. https://www.antislavery.org/wp-content/uploads/2021/04/ASI_ViciousCycle_Report_web2.pdf.

Oloff, Kerstin. "From Sugar to Oil: The Ecology of George A. Romero's Night of the Living Dead." *Journal of Postcolonial Writing* 53, no. 3 (2017): 316–28.

Ortega, Julio. *Adiós, Ayacucho seguido de El oro de Moscú y otros peligros que acechan a los adolescentes en sus primeros pasos hacia la vida adulta*. Philadephia and Lima: Ishi Publications/Mosca Azul Editores, 1986.

Quiroz, Victor. "La carnavalización del archivo en *Adiós, Ayacucho* de Julio Ortega." *Mester* 43, no. 1 (2014): 41–64.

Ramsey, Kate. *The Spirits and the Law: Vodou and Power in Haiti*. Chicago: University of Chicago Press, 2011.

Renda, Mary A. *Taking Haiti: Military Occupation and the Culture of U.S. Imperialism, 1915–1940*. Chapel Hill: The University of North Carolina Press, 2001.

Seabrook, William B. *The Magic Island*. New York: Harcourt, Brace and Company, 1929.

Ulysse, Gina Athena. *Why Haiti Needs New Narratives: A Post-Quake Chronicle*. Middletown: Wesleyan University Press, 2015.

Vich, Víctor and Alexandra Hibbett. "La risa irónica de un cuerpo roto: *Adiós, Ayacucho* de Julio Ortega." In *Contra el sueño de los justos: La literatura peruana ante la violencia política*, edited by Juan Carlo Ubilluz, Víctor Vich and Alexandra Hibbett, 175–89. Lima: Institudo de Estudios Peruanos, 2009.

Wallerstein, Immanuel. "The End of What Modernity?" *Theory and Society* 24, no. 4 (1995): 471–88.

Wallerstein, Immanuel. "The French Revolution as World-Historical Event." In *Unthinking Social Science: The Limits of Nineteenth-Century Paradigms*, edited by Immanuel Wallerstein, 7–23. Philadelphia: Temple University Press, 2001.

"White Zombie (1932) Movie Script." https://www.springfieldspringfield.co.uk/movie_script.php?movie=white-zombie. Accessed March 6, 2020.

Williams, Victoria R. *Indigenous Peoples: An Encyclopedia of Culture, History, and Threats to Survival*. Santa Barbara: ABC-CLIO, 2020.

Decolonizing Zombie Cultural Practice: An Afterword

Stephen Shapiro

An afterword to a collection of essays seems like a metonymic equivalent to a zombie. Caught indeterminately between the vibrant stuff of the prior arguments and delaying a final release for the reader, the afterword often feels like its main function is to remind readers of that cinematic rule about dealing with the undead, never forget the double-tap. In the spirit of self-determination and *tacheles* (the Yiddish word for straight talk or no bullshit), I don't wish here to offer a prophylactic summary or condensation of the preceding arguments, preferring to let our authors speak for themselves, but instead wish to speak firstly about the *politics* driving the call to decolonize the undead through cultural commentary. In one of its most basic forms, the call to decolonize the arts and humanities seeks to move beyond the idea of democratic enlargement, the notion that if we offer a more diverse reading list, then all will be well and the scars of the past can be forgotten. Instead, any effort to decolonize culture means forcing ourselves to examine how we came to make differentiating evaluations in the first place. In this way, even the most Eurocentric syllabus needs to be as carefully probed for its sins of omission as for its sins of commission, the structure of its silences and erasures as much for its casual bigotries.

Christina Sharpe's *In the Wake: On Blackness and Being* (2016) offers one way forward through its complex use of the term "wake."[1] Sharpe suggests an entanglement with the traumatic legacy of Atlantic slavery, the wake of the ship carrying those in the Middle Passage of the flesh trade; a funeral wake, where a community gives testimony and tribute to the passed, while also taking care to nurture each other in a moment of sharp pain and sense of injustice; and a sense of heightened political consciousness, an awakening through cognitive transformation resulting in what today we call being "woke."

Previous studies of the material often placed in the categories of Gothic, Horror, and the Weird (GoHoW) could be thought of as a sort of cultural entomology, where we squashed the bug of bourgeois narrative to see what oozed out. Today, a new mood has arisen as the genres that often seemed dedicated to "othering" have become taken up by those groups of readers and writers previously marginalized by these narratives (women, non-whites, nonheterosexuals, and trans) as a means for the kind of remembering, restoration, and redistribution in the way that Sharpe suggests. Is there a way that this new cultural movement can decolonize even those on the previously dominant side of the equation? What if, though, Sharpe's study had to mean something even for those who do not consider themselves to be the implied readers or inheritors of this tragic penumbra? What if the decolonial impulse was as fundamentally necessary, as basically constitutive, as a prior dedication to universal human rights? I want to argue, unsurprisingly perhaps, that the answer is yes, and that there's much ground to till here.

In *Men, Women, and Chainsaws: Gender in the Modern Horror Film*, Carol Clover introduced the now widespread concept of the "final girl," the "boyish," female-identified sole survivor, and deliverer of vengeful justice against pursuing and torturing figure(s).[2] While many readers today use this term to convey the staging of feminist empowerment, this was not Clover's main interest in the monograph. Instead, through a series of contemporaneous field observation of cinema audiences for 1980s slasher films, Clover noticed that the primary fanbase seemed to be men. Clover then suggested that the attraction of these films was not mainly to provide a voyeuristic and misogynist opportunity to relish in the denuded female body in pain but to create a new kind of audience affiliation. The study's hypothesis was that a male audience identified with the final girl because they saw themselves in her tribulations. This was a viewer who might have easily himself been bullied having failed to achieve dominant ideals of muscular, heterosexual masculinity. And for male Americans in a time of renewed Reaganesque Rambo-ism, the final girl was their representational device to express their own, perhaps not entirely politicized, discontent.

In our own neoliberal times, the zombie seems to often function similarly as a paradoxical figure of release. In a phase where authorities tell us to celebrate the anxiety of risk, amid their destruction of state welfare schemes of protection in times of unemployment and health crisis, becoming a zombie seems like a good option. For zombies no longer need to worry about bodily crisis, wage precarity, or bullying over not having the right dress style or physical shape. Zombies, after all, seem to be the only ones nowadays who have the opportunity to hang out with each other, free from the pressures of either waged work or social media's narcissistic transactionalism. The challenge, however, is to find a way to articulate this desire for escape from contemporary capitalism by white Euro-Americans with the wake-work of historical awareness about imperialism, colonialism, and domestic racial privilege. Can the undead also decolonize *us*?

One example here might seem counterintuitive to this collection's project: George Romero's *Night of the Living Dead* (1968). Romero's film remains canonized as a threshold event for zombie curation, not least as it transforms zombies from being figures of coerced production under the will of a despotic master into (neoliberal) ones driven by insatiable consumption without any state-like control whatsoever. And while Romero claims to have been unaware of the film's transgression of cinematic segregation, by using a Black male lead (Duane Jones) whose character insists on being acknowledged as the leader on top, consigning white bullies to the basement, *Night of the Living Dead*, nonetheless, captures the spirit of late 1960s racial tensions.

Romero's film also registers and helps constitute a break from the industrial legacy of liberal media regulation. For the two main institutional forces driving American cinema in the twentieth century were the onset of the Hays Code, which morally policed the classic Hollywood studio system, and the 1948 Supreme Court case *United States v. Paramount Pictures*, which broke the studios' monopolistic control by forcing them to sell their cinemas, thus ending control of the entire chain of filmic production and distribution.

The Motion Picture Production Code, usually called the Hays code after its primary author Will H. Hays, was a self-imposed mechanism wherein the studios voluntarily censored their narrative content and filmic form. The Code contains both a theoretical section and a prescriptive list of prohibited narrative elements. The theoretical section interestingly hews closely to many of the cultural industry arguments later associated with the Frankfurt School. Film is considered necessary to have guidelines because the form is dangerous to social regulation and hierarchies. Hays argued that while prior art forms were class segregated, cinema dangerously brings all together, wherein intermingling might dissolve the prior class separations on which American society depends, despite its rhetoric of democratic universalism. Moreover, film distribution allows rural audiences to hear and see the modernizing social transformations that urban coastal (and international) communities were experiencing, in ways that even radio, with its tightly controlled broadcast reach limits, was not capable of accomplishing. The Hays Code felt that farming regions, still necessary for a United States before agro-capitalism began massifying farms and internationalizing food circulation, had to be protected against a disturbing awareness of social changes to life expectations and interaction happening elsewhere. In this spirit of paternalism, the Hays Code then provided an explicit checklist of what studios were not allowed to do. Its power stands as an example of how conservative coalitions emerge, as the old joke goes that Jewish studio heads hired Catholic Hays to tell them what could be shown to Protestant audiences. In any case, it is conventional to note the difference between pre-code and classic Hollywood studio films, not least for their bringing to an end to the spate of horror films that arose during the 1930s.

United States v. Paramount, however, helped begin the end of Hays, since it meant that the studios could no longer entirely control what was being shown onscreen. The anti-monopoly law eventually provided the foundation for independent and art-house cinemas that could now show nonstudio films without retribution. Consequently, European and international films began to be more easily seen by American audiences, provided they were in the handful of cities with an art-house cinema. Given that European artists were more willing to violate the Hays Code, which exemplified American puritanism, *United States v. Paramount* let the cat out of the bag as it facilitated the importation of films that did not play by Hays' rules. The decreasing power of the Code meant that the Motion Picture Association of America (MPAA) introduced a film rating system in 1968 that sought to discourage, but no longer disallow, content that Hays had forbidden.

It is thus no accident that *Night of the Living Dead* appears in the same year as the end of Hays. The Code's list of what films should not do provides a neat checklist of what happens in Romero's film, as if one of the main motivations was to persistently violate everything named in the Code. No nudity? Then let's have a brief, mid-length shot of a naked female ghoul. Nothing that challenges the final harmony of the nuclear family? Then let's have mommy and daddy eaten by their monster-child, and so on. In this way, Romero's film changed up the rules of mid-century zombies to break the structure of what was considered "normal" for a film in order to prod viewers to consider what they had not previously—the force of cultural policing by a nonstate structure. But if Romero's zombie was culturally dissident, can we claim it as likewise politically radical, as helping to engineer anti-capitalist revolution? In other words, is it decolonial?

In *Noise Uprising: The Audiopolitics of a World Musical Revolution*, Michael Denning suggests that throughout the 1920s, before the Great Depression, a material convergence of new sound technologies and a large-scale investment in shipping yards throughout the world brought hinterland peoples into harbor cities where their traditional music encountered modernizing urban conditions to produce new kinds of popular music.[3] This act of revivifying folk tunes in new scorings exemplifies what I have called a curation, rather than a tradition, of culture. Denning then argues that this sonic transformation was not simply contained within a particular nation but was internationalizing, as portable records and playing devices were carried from one port to another, so that previously regionalized ethnic groups could hear each other's cultural expressions of their analogous experiences in historically new ways. Denning suggests that these new records provided the soundtrack and back tempo to the emergence of independence movements that may have often been nationalistic but were often aware of a shared non-Eurocentric lifeworld, a decolonial one.

I want to suggest that something similar might be happening today with zombie figurations. On the one hand, we are experiencing something akin to the old studio system as the streaming services, like Netflix and Amazon, are recapturing control of production and distribution in ways similar to the conditions of pre-*United States v. Paramount*. And like the classic studios' need for a constant stream of content for their cinemas, which resulted in the normalization of the swiftly made and lightly financed "B-films," the category for most horror films, the streaming services require much larger amounts of content creation. On the other hand, unlike the studio system that protected American audiences from seeing international content, the streaming services have vastly eased access to foreign material. Indeed, without the rise of digital, internet resources, from the ease of piracy to the streaming services, many of this collection's authors would not have had access to the sources they consider. And zombie films, with their speechless characters, are a genre that is easily internationalized, since subtitles are not as necessary. Indeed, one could possibly enjoy a non-English zombie film even without any translation at all.

If the new networks of cultural consumption are replicating the conditions of musical exchange that Denning suggests were the prelude to anti-colonial and anti-imperialist politics, then the question we might want to ask is, if the same is true for the zombie today?

Notes

1   Sharpe, *In the Wake*.
2   Clover, *Men, Women, and Chainsaws*.
3   Denning, *Noise Uprising*.

Works Cited

Clover, Carol. *Men, Women, and Chainsaws: Gender in the Modern Horror Film.* Princeton: Princeton University Press, 1992.

Denning, Michael. *Noise Uprising: The Audiopolitics of a World Musical Revolution.* London: Verso, 2015.

Sharpe, Christina. *In the Wake: On Blackness and Being.* Durham: Duke University Press, 2016.

Contributors

Cécile Accilien is Chair of the Interdisciplinary Studies Department at Kennesaw State University in Georgia. She specializes in Caribbean Literature and Cultures. Her publication includes *Rethinking Marriage in Francophone African and Caribbean Literatures* (2008), coeditor of *Revolutionary Freedoms: A History of Survival, Strength and Imagination in Haiti* (2006), *Just Below South: Intercultural Performance in the Caribbean and the U.S. South* (2007), and *Teaching Haiti: Strategies for Creating New Narratives* (2021). She is coauthor of *English-Haitian Creole Phrasebook* (2010) and *Francophone Cultures through Film* (2013). Her work is also in the *Journal of Haitian Studies* and *Women, Gender and Families of Color*.

Giulia Champion is Lecturer in the Interdisciplinary Studies Centre at the University of Essex and Research Assistant at the Centre for Interdisciplinary Methodologies at the University of Warwick. Her research investigates decolonial theory, Latin American studies, extractivism, and the blue humanities. She is the coeditor of *Ethical Futures and Global Science Fiction* (2020) and editor of *Interdisciplinary Essays on Cannibalism: Bites Here and There* (2021). She has also coedited two journal special issues forthcoming in 2022 on "Animal Futurity" with *Green Letters: Studies in Ecocriticism* and on "Intersections of Activism and Academia" with the *Bulletin of Latin American Research*.

Roxanne Douglas is Teaching Fellow at the University of Warwick in the English and Comparative Literary Studies Department. She specializes in feminist approaches to the Gothic, aiming to decolonize our contemporary understanding of the genre using world literary studies. She has recently published a paper "Situating Arab women's writing in a feminist 'global gothic': madness, mothers and ghosts" (2021). Roxanne also regularly gives public lectures on her research as part of the "Romancing the Gothic" project.

Rebecca Duncan is Research Fellow at the Linnaeus University Centre for Concurrences in Colonial and Postcolonial Studies (Sweden), where she coordinates the "Aesthetics of Empire" Research Cluster. Her first monograph,

South African Gothic (2018), was shortlisted for the 2019 Allan Lloyd Smith prize, and her recent work appears in the journals *ARIEL* and *Science Fiction Film and Television*, and in collections for University of Minnesota Press, Routledge and Palgrave. She is the coeditor of *Patrick McGrath and His Worlds* (2020) and the *Edinburgh Companion to Globalgothic* (2023), and also of "The Body Now" (2020), a special issue of *Interventions*. Her guest-edited special issue of *Gothic Studies*—"Decolonizing Gothic"—is forthcoming in 2022. Rebecca is recipient of a Riksbankens Jubileumsfond Project Grant (2021–4).

Fiona Farnsworth is Early Career Researcher and Associate Fellow based at the University of Warwick between the Department of English and Comparative Literary Studies and the Institute of Advanced Study. Her doctoral research focused on foodways in contemporary women's literatures of migration between sub-Saharan Africa and the United States, reading food as a site which shapes—and is shaped by—struggles surrounding identity and power within the modern world-system. She is working currently at the intersection of food studies, world-literature, and environmental humanities, exploring issues of food justice and food sovereignty in literary and cultural production.

Frank Jacob is Professor of Global History at Nord Universitet, Norway. He received his PhD in Japanese studies from Erlangen University, Germany, in 2012. Before joining Nord Universitet, he held positions at Würzburg University, Germany, and the City University of New York (QCC). Jacob is author or editor of more than eighty books and his research foci include Japanese Film, revolution theory, and transatlantic radicalism.

Elizabeth Kelly is currently a faculty member at Florida Polytechnic University. Her work on literary connections across boundaries of language, geography, and culture and the formations of identity in nineteenth-century Caribbean works was recently published in *Caribbean Literature in Transition: 1800–1920*. Her research considers the multidirectional influence of early American and Caribbean texts and focuses primarily on the roles of embodiment and disembodiment in literatures that resist, reimagine, and reassert notions of sovereignty in these settings.

Abhirup Mascharak is currently pursuing his PhD at Jadavpur University, Kolkata, India. His areas of interest include adaptation studies, popular literature, and queer studies. His recent publications include the essays "Humorous Afterlives of a Keatsian Epiphany" in *Middle Flight* 5 no. 1 (2016), "Architects of Their Own Peripherality: Joseph Conrad's *Lord Jim* and Its Hindi Film Adaptations" in *Middle Flight* 6 no. 1 (2017), and (in coauthorship with Prodosh Bhattacharya) "'Wilde desire' across Cultures: *Dracula* and Its Bengali Adaptations" in *Imperial Maladies: Literatures on Healthcare and Psychoanalysis in India* (2018).

Netty Mattar currently teaches English literature at the International Islamic University of Malaysia (IIUM). She has also taught at the National University of Singapore, where she completed her PhD. Her current research interests include contemporary and global speculative fiction, posthumanism, decolonization, and literary representations of trauma.

Stephen Shapiro teaches in the Department of English and comparative literary studies at the University of Warwick. Author or editor of seventeen books, his most recent publications include *Pentecostal Modernism: Lovecraft, Los Angeles, and World-Systems Culture* (2017), with Philip Barnard, and *Cambridge Companion to American Horror* (2022), edited with Mark Storey.

Josephine Taylor has just recently completed her PhD in comparative literature and culture at Royal Holloway, University of London, where she also teaches philosophy and politics. Her research focuses on the intersection of petrocultures and animal studies, exploring the nonhuman's place in histories of extraction and energy. She is member of the Beyond Gender Research collective and has published collectively with them on queer theory and science fiction. She is a guest editor for a special issue on "Transdisciplinary Approaches to Climate Justice" for *Sociální studia/Social Studies*.

Thomas Waller teaches at the University of Nottingham in the Department of Modern Languages and Cultures. His interests include world-systems analysis, materialist theories of world literature, the environmental humanities, and Marxist critical theory. His research has appeared in journals such as *Modern Fiction Studies*, *Textual Practice*, *African Identities*, and *Critique*.

Index

anthropocene 78, 85, 88, 147, 156, 157
anthropology 4, 5, 12, 43, 44, 49, 51, 157, 175, 195, 202
apocalypse 6, 30, 37, 38, 65, 72, 74, 80, 83, 150, 167, 178, 179, 191

body 3, 4, 5, 8, 9, 15, 16, 17, 18, 20, 21, 23, 25, 26, 27, 34, 35, 49, 50, 65, 66, 76, 78, 79, 82, 88, 91, 97, 107, 121, 123, 124, 125, 127, 129, 130, 131, 132, 133, 135, 137, 145, 146, 150, 151, 152, 153, 154, 159, 163, 164, 165, 166, 167, 168, 171, 189, 195, 199, 201, 202, 203, 204, 210, 216

Cameroon 8, 90, 92, 93, 94, 95, 98, 99, 101, 102, 104, 114, 183
Cape Verde 110, 111, 112, 113, 114, 115, 116, 117, 119
capitalism 4, 8, 11, 12, 32, 40, 41, 55, 56, 70, 75, 82, 83, 87, 91, 92, 96, 97, 104, 107, 118, 119, 120, 121, 122, 124, 136, 137, 157, 174, 211
Caribbean 2, 6, 7, 34, 36, 49, 50, 52, 53, 54, 55, 87, 107, 108, 112, 120, 142, 146, 158, 160, 215, 216
  see also Haiti
  see also Martinique
CDC (Center for Disease Control) 30
cinema 9, 10, 39, 48, 52, 53, 55, 61, 69, 70, 71, 72, 97, 108, 109, 111, 112, 113, 114, 116, 117, 118, 119, 120, 124, 128, 176, 178, 179, 180, 185, 186, 187, 189, 196, 209, 210, 211, 212, 213
  see also film
  see also Netflix
  see also TV
climate change 96, 99, 100, 101, 141, 193, 207
colonialism 1, 4, 5, 6, 7, 30, 32, 34, 36, 37, 40, 41, 66, 67, 68, 73, 78, 83, 84, 110, 111, 120, 124, 126, 134, 163, 170, 185, 192, 200, 204, 211
  see also imperialism
contagion 10, 12, 75, 77, 78, 79, 97
control 6, 8, 9, 21, 25, 30, 32, 42, 43, 44, 48, 61, 64, 76, 78, 81, 82, 92, 101, 107, 122, 123, 127, 131, 132, 133, 147, 159, 161, 163, 170, 180, 188, 195, 196, 211, 212, 213
Costa, Pedro 9, 106, 108, 109, 110, 111, 113, 114, 115, 116, 117, 118, 119, 120, 217
Couldry, Nick 4, 11, 12, 40, 41, 55, 56, 71, 124, 125, 126, 134, 135, 136
crisis 4, 8, 9, 10, 26, 44, 47, 75, 82, 89, 90, 91, 92, 93, 95, 96, 97, 99, 100, 101, 102, 103, 104, 105, 116, 117, 129, 130, 150, 157, 182, 191, 192, 193, 204, 210

Dayan, Joan 1, 11, 12, 15, 22, 23, 25, 27, 28, 29, 171, 174, 193, 194, 205, 207
Deckard, Sharae 75, 87, 106, 110, 118, 156, 157
decolonial 3, 5, 6, 8, 9, 10, 40, 41, 45, 52, 53, 55, 74, 76, 80, 141, 142, 145, 148, 162, 193, 198, 210, 212, 213
decoloniality 41, 45, 142
decolonization 2, 9, 45, 67, 75, 76, 77, 79, 142, 145, 147, 153, 154, 168, 197
decolonize 1, 10, 11, 40, 41, 45, 55, 68, 193, 204, 209, 210
decolonizing 1, 4, 6, 8, 10, 40, 45, 52, 145, 152, 202, 205, 209, 216
  see also colonialism
  see also empire
  see also imperialism
  see also indigenous
  see also postcolonial
Dessalines, Jean Jacques 8, 15, 16, 17, 18, 20, 21, 22, 23, 24, 27, 47, 195
Dunham, Katherine 3, 4, 5, 11, 12, 49, 50, 51, 56

empire 4, 28, 29, 43, 62, 67, 69, 71, 73, 76, 160, 161, 162, 171, 173, 174, 199, 200, 215
Europe 2, 3, 4, 5, 31, 36, 43, 44, 45, 50, 53, 76, 80, 89, 107, 111, 113, 116, 120, 127, 147, 162, 163, 170, 194, 195, 199, 206, 212
extractivism 4, 8, 74, 75, 76, 77, 70, 80, 81, 82, 83, 85, 87, 99, 147, 150, 192, 193, 205, 215, 217

Fanon, Frantz 151, 156, 157
fascism 63
feminism 48, 121, 123, 126, 133, 134, 135, 137, 138
film 6, 7, 8, 9, 10, 12, 31, 32, 35, 37, 47, 48, 49, 51, 52, 53, 54, 55, 61, 62, 63, 65, 66, 68, 69, 70, 71, 73, 88, 90, 97, 99, 107, 108, 109, 110, 111, 112, 113, 114, 115, 116, 117, 118, 119, 122, 127, 128, 132, 160, 161, 170, 176, 177, 178, 179, 180, 181, 182, 183, 184, 185, 186, 187, 188, 189, 191, 196, 210, 211, 212, 213, 214, 215, 216, 217
  see also cinema
  see also Netflix
  see also TV
flesh 74, 78, 79, 80, 98, 122, 129, 130, 131, 150, 163, 164, 166, 189, 209
folklore 3, 5, 6, 7, 9, 34, 46, 49, 50, 63, 71, 90, 92, 95, 126, 127, 141, 157, 159, 173, 200
food 33, 127, 129, 180, 212, 216
France 16, 19, 28, 43, 44, 45, 46, 112, 117, 119, 194, 197

gender 6, 26, 39, 48, 49, 106, 122, 124, 130, 133, 134, 141, 143, 165, 196, 210, 214, 215, 217
global 4, 6, 10, 29, 30, 40, 41, 44, 45, 52, 57, 64, 84, 85, 90, 92, 93, 95, 96, 97, 99, 100, 119, 120, 125, 137, 141, 143, 147, 157, 160, 162, 170, 174, 192, 197, 198, 206, 215, 216, 217
  globalization 4, 8, 9, 10, 73, 170, 176, 178, 186

Gómez-Barris, Macarena 74, 75, 85, 87
  see also extractivism

Haiti 1, 3, 5, 7, 8, 10, 11, 12, 15, 16, 17, 19, 20, 21, 22, 23, 24, 26, 27, 28, 29, 30, 31, 32, 34, 35, 36, 37, 38, 41, 46, 47, 48, 49, 50, 51, 52, 54, 56, 64, 70, 73, 76, 77, 78, 80, 81, 83, 85, 93, 107, 125, 126, 127, 129, 133, 146, 147, 159, 160, 161, 162, 165, 169, 170, 171, 173, 174, 191, 192, 193, 194, 195, 197, 198, 199, 200, 205, 206, 207, 215
Halperin, Victor 6, 31, 37, 38, 108, 137, 175

I Walked With a Zombie 8, 31, 32, 40, 47, 48, 52, 53, 55, 108, 111, 112, 113, 114, 117, 128
India 6, 9, 36, 43, 108, 120, 176, 177, 178, 179, 180, 181, 182, 183, 184, 185, 186, 187, 188, 189, 198, 199, 216, 217
imperialism 1, 31, 36, 37, 40, 44, 48, 52, 62, 67, 71, 75, 77, 80, 85, 108, 160, 161, 171, 173, 193, 204, 206, 207, 211, 213, 217
  see also colonialism
  see also empire
indigenous 2, 5, 24, 32, 41, 52, 84, 91, 93, 107, 124, 145, 148, 184, 188, 193, 198, 199, 202, 204, 206, 208

Japan 6, 8, 61, 62, 63, 64, 65, 66, 67, 68, 69, 70, 71, 72, 73, 216

labor 5, 6, 7, 8, 9, 18, 34, 35, 36, 41, 47, 76, 83, 106, 107, 108, 110, 111, 112, 116, 117, 126, 127, 127, 133, 143, 147, 148, 149, 160, 192, 194, 196, 204
Lauro, Sarah Juliet 4, 5, 7, 11, 12, 27, 29, 38, 39, 56, 64, 70, 79, 81, 82, 83, 85, 86, 87, 88, 97, 99, 102, 103, 104, 122, 130, 132, 134, 135, 136, 137, 144, 145, 154, 155, 157, 171, 174, 190
liberalism 8, 9, 40, 41, 42, 43, 44, 45, 46, 47, 50, 52, 53, 55, 56, 57, 79, 80, 81, 84, 87, 106, 109, 111, 116, 117, 118,

119, 121, 123, 124, 127, 128, 129, 133, 138, 147, 148, 149, 150, 151, 178, 186, 210, 211
  see also neoliberalism
Louverture, Toussaint 15, 17, 18, 19, 20, 21, 22, 27, 28, 29

Magic Island, The 7, 8, 31, 48, 107, 159, 195
  see also William B. Seabrook
Martinique 4
Marx, Karl 42, 57, 91, 202, 217
Mejias, Ulises A. 4, 11, 12, 56, 71, 124, 125, 126, 134, 135, 136
menopause 121, 124, 130, 133, 134, 135, 136, 137
Miéville, China 8, 75, 77, 78, 82, 83, 84, 86, 87
Moore, Jason W. 91, 102, 104, 143, 144, 147, 155, 157, 158

nationalism 44, 62, 66, 70, 71, 72, 116, 212, 213
Negarestani, Reza 8, 75, 77, 78, 79, 80, 81, 84, 86, 87
neoliberalism 9, 40, 44, 87, 106, 109, 111, 116, 117, 118, 119, 121, 123, 124, 127, 128, 129, 133, 138, 147, 148, 149, 150, 151, 210, 211
Netflix 6, 9, 10, 67, 121, 122, 123, 124, 125, 130, 132, 133, 134, 135, 135, 136, 137, 213
  see also cinema
  see also film
  see also TV
Niblett, Michael 102, 104
Nkweti, Nana 8, 89, 90, 91, 92, 94, 96, 97, 98, 101, 102, 103, 104
Ntshanga, Masande 9, 142, 146, 148, 149, 150, 152, 153, 154, 155, 157, 158

oil 8, 74, 75, 76, 77, 78, 79, 80, 81, 82, 83, 84, 85, 87, 96, 99, 100, 101, 102, 103, 104, 105, 130, 161, 192, 205, 207
  see also extractivism
  see also petrol
Oloff, Kerstin 75, 85, 87, 91, 102, 105, 107, 118, 120, 146 147, 155, 156, 158, 192, 205, 207

Ortega, Julio 10, 193, 198, 199, 200, 201, 202, 206, 207, 208
otherness 1, 34, 170, 194, 202

Peru 10, 191, 192, 193, 197, 198, 199, 200, 201, 202, 203, 204, 206, 207, 208
petrol 75, 77, 79, 83, 104, 192
  see also extractivism
  see also oil
Pick, Anat 75, 78, 80, 82, 85, 86, 88
postcolonial 6, 8, 9, 40, 41, 45, 55, 57, 87, 89, 104, 105, 110, 111, 112, 113, 115, 119, 120, 142, 147, 207, 215
posthumanism 9, 86, 87, 88, 122, 141, 144, 145, 154, 155, 158, 217

race 4, 8, 9, 12, 21, 22, 30, 32, 34, 36, 39, 42, 47, 51, 72, 106, 107, 116, 129, 135, 136, 141, 143, 152, 161, 196, 197
Romero, George 4, 32, 37, 39, 51, 63, 87, 88, 97, 105, 121, 137, 174, 178, 187, 192, 196, 207, 211, 212

Saadawi, Ahmad 9, 159, 162, 163, 164, 165, 166, 167, 168, 169, 170, 172, 173, 175
samurai 8, 61, 62, 63, 64, 65, 66, 67, 68, 69, 70, 71, 73
Santa Clarita Diet 9, 121, 122, 123, 124, 126, 127, 129, 130, 131, 132, 133, 134, 135, 137
Seabrook, William B. 6, 7, 8, 31, 37, 39, 48, 107, 159, 160, 166, 171, 175, 177, 189, 190, 195, 196, 196, 205, 207
Sharpe, Christina 2, 11, 12, 209, 210, 213, 214
slavery 1, 2, 7, 17, 29, 30, 31, 32, 34, 36, 38, 46, 47, 53, 54, 55, 57, 64, 72, 78, 80, 83, 86, 87, 97, 107, 126, 174, 192, 193, 207, 209
sexuality 9, 182, 186, 196
South Africa 9, 52, 93, 104, 141, 142, 146, 148, 149, 150, 152, 153, 156, 157, 158, 215, 216

Tourneur, Jacques 37, 39, 52, 53, 54, 108, 111, 112, 113, 114, 116, 119, 137
Tuck, Eve 4, 11, 12, 67, 71, 73, 168, 178
TV 37, 64, 131, 137

utopia 85, 87, 122, 157

vampire 1, 94, 137, 157
virus 10, 86, 88, 93, 100, 152, 154
   Covid-19 10, 12
Voodoo 6, 7, 31, 32
   see also Vodou
Vodou 3, 7, 16, 20, 26, 30, 31, 35, 46, 47, 48, 49, 50, 51, 54, 107, 108, 112, 113, 128, 159, 193, 194
   see also Voodoo

Wallerstein, Immanuel 41, 42, 55, 56, 57, 109, 118, 120, 197, 198, 205, 208
west 1, 3, 4, 6, 8, 9, 15, 20, 22, 23, 24, 29, 30, 32, 33, 37, 38, 39, 41, 43, 45, 46, 47, 49, 54, 55, 57, 61, 62, 63, 66, 68, 70, 76, 77, 80, 81, 82, 89, 92, 93, 102, 104, 107, 108, 110, 111, 146, 160, 162, 163, 165, 166, 169, 171, 176, 177, 178, 179, 180, 181, 182, 183, 184, 185, 186, 187, 188, 190, 194, 196, 197, 199, 200
White Zombie 6, 8, 31, 32, 35, 36, 46, 48, 63, 108, 128, 160, 161, 196
world-ecology 87, 91, 92, 93, 101, 102, 104, 105
Wynter, Sylvia 76, 80, 85, 88, 141, 142, 143, 144, 148, 152, 153, 155, 158

Yang, K. Wayne 4, 11, 12, 67, 71, 73
Yusoff, Kathryn 76, 77, 78, 79, 85, 88

Zombi 1, 3, 4, 6, 7, 17, 93, 193
   see also Jean Zombi
Zombi, Jean 22, 194

www.ingramcontent.com/pod-product-compliance
Lightning Source LLC
Chambersburg PA
CBHW062221300426
44115CB00012BA/2169